T0355572

Journalism in the Movies

THE HISTORY OF COMMUNICATION

Robert W. McChesney and John C. Nerone, editors

A list of books in the series
appears at the end of this book.

JOURNALISM IN THE MOVIES

Matthew C. Ehrlich

University of Illinois Press

Urbana and Chicago

First Illinois paperback, 2006
© 2004 by the Board of Trustees
of the University of Illinois
All rights reserved

Printed and bound in Great Britain by

Marston Book Services Ltd, Oxfordshire

∞ This book is printed on acid-free paper.

The Library of Congress cataloged the cloth edition as follows:
Ehrlich, Matthew C., 1962–
Journalism in the movies / Matthew C. Ehrlich.
p.   cm. — (The history of communication)
Includes bibliographical references and index.
ISBN 0-252-02934-8 (alk. paper)
1. Journalists in motion pictures. I. Title. II. Series.
PN1995.9.J6E38   2004
791.43'60704—dc22   2003026963

PAPERBACK ISBN 978-0-252-07432-5

For my family

CONTENTS

❧ ACKNOWLEDGMENTS

"People are going to know who's responsible." So said Charles Foster Kane, although as usual he was thinking only of himself. In my case, I am happy to acknowledge shared responsibility for all that is good in the coming pages. (Anything not so good is my responsibility alone.)

For research assistance, thanks to the staffs of the Rare Book and Special Collections Library, University of Illinois at Urbana-Champaign; the Chicago Historical Society Research Center; the New York Public Library for the Performing Arts, New York City; the Motion Picture and Television Reading Room, Library of Congress, Washington, D.C.; the Wisconsin Center for Film and Theater Research, Wisconsin Historical Society, Madison; the Cinema-Television Library, University of Southern California, Los Angeles; the Arts Library Special Collections, University of California at Los Angeles; and, above all, the Margaret Herrick Library, Academy of Motion Picture Arts and Sciences, Beverly Hills, California.

For in various ways helping to nudge this book a little closer to what I originally envisioned it as being, thanks to D. Charles Whitney, Howard Good, John J. Pauly, Barbie Zelizer, and Joe Saltzman—the last being the proud director of the Image of the Journalist in Popular Culture project at the University of Southern California.

For helping launch this project many years ago, thanks to Norman K. Denzin and James W. Carey, who co-supervised an independent study while I was a communication doctoral student at the University of Illinois. Given that background, I am especially pleased to see this book appear in the History of Communication series of the University of Illinois Press. The late Kim Rotzoll, a devoted movie fan, suggested that I submit this manuscript to the press. Thanks to the press's Richard Martin for first expressing interest in the project and to Kerry Callahan for helping bring it to fruition. Series co-editor John Nerone provided helpful, detailed feedback.

Finally, for consistently providing an intellectually vital place to investigate and think, I thank the students, faculty, and staff of the Department of Journalism and the College of Communications at the University of Illinois.

Journalism in the Movies

Studying Journalism through Movies

This is a story of how movies have depicted American journalism from the start of the sound era to the present. It examines such films as *The Front Page, His Girl Friday, Mr. Smith Goes to Washington, Citizen Kane, Ace in the Hole, Deadline, USA, All the President's Men, Network, Absence of Malice, The Killing Fields, Broadcast News,* and *The Insider.* The movies have portrayed journalists both as upstanding citizens and heroes and as scruffy outsiders and villains. Either way, Hollywood has reproduced myths in which the press is always at the heart of things and always makes a difference. The films regularly have suggested that the journalist can see through lies and hypocrisy, stick up for the little guy, uncover the truth, and serve democracy—or that if those things are no longer true because the journalist and the press have lost their way, they were true once upon a time and someday could be true again.

Such an argument is both consistent and at odds with the perceptions of many journalists and media critics. They wholeheartedly agree that the press is important. Bill Kovach and Tom Rosenstiel declare that its duty is to provide "independent, reliable, accurate, and comprehensive information that citizens require to be free." That makes journalism every bit as vital as law and medicine, if not more so. In theory, if law is the pursuit of justice and medicine is the pursuit of healing, journalism is the pursuit of truth; seeking and reporting it is the press's most important obligation.[1]

However, just as many believe that the current practices of law and medicine fall well short of meeting their social responsibilities, so is contemporary journalism found lacking. It is said to be more concerned with profit than with truth, too timid and beholden to the powers that be.[2] It is thought to be corrosively cynical to the point of undermining participation in the democratic process.[3] It is seen as running roughshod over the individuals who are fodder for its headlines and as pandering to the basest instincts in a desperate quest for ratings and circulation.[4] It is declared to be facing an identity crisis or even extinction. "Modern journalism began around 1890 with the advent of a national system of communication and has had a pretty long run," James Carey has written. "Its time now seems to be about up." Others put it more bluntly: "Organized journalism is dead." Or if it is not actually in the grave, it is "pooped, confused, and broke," irrelevant in the face of "a hybrid New News— dazzling, adolescent, irresponsible, fearless, frightening, and powerful," encompassing infotainment in its many forms and the interactivity of the Internet.[5]

Symptomatic of the press's travails is its lowly status in the public eye, with polls showing journalists deemed little more trustworthy than used car salesmen or lawyers. Some in the news media suggest that the press itself is not the primary culprit. Instead, as one trade magazine has written only half in jest, Hollywood is to blame for "those loathsome misconceptions that journalists are hard-drinking, foul-mouthed, dim-witted social misfits concerned only with twisting the truth into scandal and otherwise devoid of conscience, respect for basic human dignity or a healthy fear of God." The same has been said of movies about lawyers, doctors, scientists, and others: With too few exceptions, they present distorted portrayals and negative stereotypes that are at best an irritant and at worst dangerous in how they undermine professional authority and institutions.[6]

Yet that is precisely why such movies deserve serious scholarly attention. They "can be read as a culture thinking out loud about itself."[7] That includes the roles that professionals play in that culture and the precise meaning of such lofty concepts as truth and justice. Inevitably, movies "think" about those things differently from the way professional groups do; they speak a different language. And yes, sometimes they present unflattering depictions that contradict the way professionals see themselves, even if the depictions sometimes have validity. The *Columbia Journalism Review* has written that "much of the most enduring contemporary criticism of the press comes from those outside journalism," with movies being a key example.[8]

However, the movies do not simply sneer at the press in response to contemporary crises. They have addressed tensions and conflicts that long have been part of journalism's cultural and institutional fabric. And more often than not, they have resolved those conflicts in a manner stressing that journalism can and should be performed well and that the press is essential to American life and democracy.

THE JOURNALISM MOVIE GENRE

This book analyzes journalism movies in just that way: as a distinct genre that embodies myths colored by nostalgia and that addresses contradictions at the heart of both journalism and American culture. Thus, the book goes beyond the criticisms many journalists have offered regarding cinematic depictions of the news media, and it also differs from previous scholarly studies of such films.

From the silent era onward, journalists have taken note of movies about the press. Their notion that popular culture is to blame for the public's dim view of their occupation is nothing new. As far back as 1928, a *New York Times* editorial writer charged that the original stage production of *The Front Page* presented a grossly distorted view of newspapers. After the 1931 film version was released along with other early journalism talkies, *American Press* editorialized that they could encourage press censorship. Not long after, newspaper editor Stanley Walker warned prospective young journalists to disregard the movies' depiction of the reporter who "writes best on twelve Scotch highballs" and "insults everybody in earshot." So it has continued over the decades, with organizations including the American Newspaper Publishers Association, the American Society of Newspaper Editors, and the Society of Professional Journalists lobbying Hollywood for more positive portrayals.[9]

Some journalists have taken a slightly different tack: The movies used to treat us well, they say, but that is no longer the case. "In movies of the 1930s, reporters were gritty characters, instinctively siding with the Common Man," writes James Fallows. He notes that in the 1970s, Woodward and Bernstein took on Nixon in *All the President's Men.* But starting in "the early 1980s, the journalists who have shown up in movies have been portrayed, on average, as more loathsome than the lawyers, politicians, or business moguls who are the traditional bad guys in films about the white-collar world." To Fallows, that is symptomatic of how journalism's current failings have diminished its public credibility. Another critic has said there "is a lag between when an institution develops the symptoms of an illness and when the movies respond, by which point the disease is often far advanced." In journalism's case, "sensationalism and a profits-above-all philosophy metastasized through our news organs, weakening their standards and enfeebling their public spirit." The movies' increasingly negative portrayal of the press merely reflected the cancer's spread.[10]

Such arguments echo those who say journalism is, if not dead, at least in serious trouble. Still, no one can suggest that *The Front Page* is a completely upbeat portrayal of the press as champion of the people, much less 1931's *Five Star Final,* in which a tabloid drives a wife and husband to suicide. The journalists and press organizations that were criticizing the movies in the 1930s had a point: Hollywood was hardly painting an idealized portrait of their profession.

It is equally misleading to suggest that more recent movies about journalism have been completely negative. In *The Paper* (1994), a tabloid editor successfully fights to publish a story that can free two African American youths wrongly accused of murder. *Up Close and Personal* (1996), ostensibly based on the life of television anchor Jessica Savitch, could have been a savage and largely fact-based exposé of broadcast news; instead it presented a glossy romance between two noble television reporters. Thus a fundamental ambivalence has always been at work in the movies' portrayals.[11]

When scholars have examined those portrayals, some have focused on the more negative depictions of the journalist as "a cynical observer of the human scene who seeks to fill his column at some victim's expense." Howard Good has penned studies of reporters as alcoholics and social outcasts as well as both propagators and victims of sexism.[12]

Others have asserted that, if anything, the movies have been too accommodating toward the media. One says although films occasionally have depicted broadcast news critically, they have assumed a largely "subservient position" to television. Norman Denzin argues that movies such as *All the President's Men* glorify journalism's self-serving claims to be able to discover objective truth and its position as an institution dedicated to surveillance. At the same time, though, he says movies such as *Citizen Kane* help deconstruct those claims to truth, serving as "a counter-body of subversive texts which suggests that things aren't the way they appear to be."[13]

That points to what Joe Saltzman calls a "dichotomy" in the movies' depictions both reflecting and contributing to "the public's confusion about the media in American society." Loren Ghiglione notes that although fictional portrayals of the press can foster "dangerous illusions that distort Americans' understanding not only of the journalist but also of themselves," they also can "entertainingly capture an element of the journalist's character." Many such elements have appeared on screen, as the chapter titles of Alex Barris's 1976 book on journalism movies indicated: "The Reporter as Scandalmonger," "The Reporter as Villain," "The Reporter as Crime Buster," and "The Reporter as Crusader."[14]

Even with the occasional negative portrayal, some have argued that the relationship between journalism and films has been symbiotic. Newspapers have promoted the movies while movies have given newspapers advertising revenue and many favorable depictions. Thomas Zynda has gone so far as to say the two media perform similar watchdog functions: "As the press serves as a watchdog on government, so Hollywood, likewise on behalf of the public and with a like commercial basis, keeps an eye on the press."[15]

The present study builds on such work while staking out new territory. It does not try to provide a comprehensive list of journalism movies, a task others have ably undertaken. Nor does it concentrate on a single filmmaker, work, or era, or on specific subgenres, archetypes, or ethical concerns as they have appeared on screen.[16] Instead it analyzes key texts from the 1920s to the present while drawing on scholarship on the relationships between movies, myths, and culture.

MYTH AND MOVIE GENRES

It is important to stress that *myth* in this context does not imply falsehood. In Jack Lule's words, a myth is "a sacred, societal story that draws from arche-typical figures and forms to offer exemplary models for human life." Myth presents a commonsensical, taken-for-granted view of the world serving to "represent shared values, confirm core beliefs, deny other beliefs, and help people engage with, appreciate, and understand the complex joys and sorrows" of our existence.[17]

In confirming core beliefs, mass-mediated myth plays a important ritual-istic role.[18] One example is movie genres such as Westerns or musicals that show "familiar characters performing familiar actions which celebrate famil-iar values." They ritualistically reaffirm what a culture holds most dear, as when the romantic couple unites in a musical and preserves the sanctity of love and marriage or when the hero vanquishes the villain in a Western and upholds law and order. Scholars such as Richard Slotkin have argued that Americans need myths "capable of organizing the thought and feeling of a genuine and usable national consensus" and allowing them to "recover a true (or truer) understanding of our history."[19]

However, Slotkin also notes that "powerful corporate and political institu-tions" can exploit myth in "manipulating and directing public opinion." He asserts that movie Westerns have perpetuated a frontier myth that regularly has been used to justify violence in the national interest and "reify our nos-talgia for a falsely idealized past." That is to say, myth also plays an ideologi-cal role: It maintains the existing distribution of power while distorting his-torical understanding of power's uses and abuses. "If a society is founded upon inequality, that society's dominant myths 'explain' and support such inequal-ity," writes Jack Lule.[20]

Besides Westerns, other movie genres have tended to reflect and reinforce such inequities. Film scholar Robert Ray argues that Hollywood has consis-tently fostered the myth that Americans can avoid making difficult choices except when absolutely necessary. (*Casablanca,* in which Humphrey Bogart's character refuses to stick his neck out until the very end, is just one example.) That in turn has "fostered an ideology of improvisation, individualism, and ad hoc solutions for problems depicted as crises."[21] Such an ideology masks or ignores social divisions and discourages a collective, systemic response to society's ills.

Still, myth is not invariably a means of keeping things the way they are; it also can critique or even change the status quo. Once more, genre films are an example. Thomas Schatz declares that "what is so fascinating and confound-ing" about them is "their capacity to 'play it both ways,' to both criticize and reinforce the values, beliefs, and ideals of our culture within the same narrative context."[22]

That is reflected in Hollywood's treatment of the professions. Movies about lawyers, for example, "raise questions about the proper and possible role of law in society." On one hand, they show attorneys acting spectacularly badly; on the other, they bolster "ideas that courts work as institutions and that law in general can be trusted both in its articulation and application." Popular films and TV shows can make doctors seem arrogant and incompetent while also lionizing them at the expense of a more searching examination of institutionalized medicine.[23] And movies about journalism present myths that journalists themselves may find offensive but also ennobling or seductive.[24] The films underscore journalism's preeminence in American life even as they highlight tensions at the profession's core.

JOURNALISM AS PROFESSION AND POP CULTURE

To begin with, some question whether journalism is a profession at all. The constant imperative in many newsrooms to grind out copy on deadline and amass profits for the parent company conflicts with notions of professional autonomy and public service. There are no universally applied standards or means of disbarment. The specialized education and license that one must obtain to practice law or medicine are not required in journalism.[25] Anyone can do it, regardless of training or scruples.

The result has been that journalism has hosted a wide range of characters: everyone from dedicated pursuers of truth to venal tycoons and confidence men.[26] Just as the barriers of entry have been low, so have the barriers to exit. One rarely dabbles in law or medicine before moving on to something else. In contrast, one can move into and out of journalism easily, and many have applied the skills they learned in newsrooms to politics, public relations, novels, and films.

Those who have turned their journalistic experiences into fiction or screenplays have expressed a dialectic of sorts. On one side, they have extolled the importance of a free press, celebrated its triumphs, and condemned its miscreants. On the other, they have reveled in the press's seediness, its infatuation with juicy scoops, and its wanderings on the dark side. They have exalted professional virtue by telling tales of "ethical practitioners versus amoral hacks";[27] at the same time, they have broadly hinted at how much fun amoral hacks can have and be. The image that has emerged is a press that has had its failings and black eyes and yet is powerfully exciting and important, an image not far removed from journalism's fondest self-conceptions.

A prime example is the multi–million-dollar "Newseum" that opened in suburban Washington, D.C., in 1997. It announced its arrival by billing itself "the world's only interactive museum of news," designed "to help the public and the news media understand one another better."[28] Toward that end, it offered displays on the responsibilities of the First Amendment. It invited visitors to partake of computer simulations in which they faced tough ethical dilemmas or tried to cover a story properly. It also featured a twenty-four-foot-high memorial listing the names of more than 1,000 journalists killed in the line of duty. As if to emphasize the press's status as a national institution, the Newseum by 2002 was preparing to move to a much larger facility on Pennsylvania Avenue between the Capitol and the White House.

Not everything was sober and serious at the Newseum, however. It displayed artifacts such as the hidden camera a tabloid newsman used in 1928 to photograph murderer Ruth Snyder at the moment of her electrocution. It published a book with stories not just of the profession's heroes but its rogues—"the Newseum's Most Intriguing Newspeople."[29] And it continually showed a short film titled "Fact or Fiction: Hollywood Looks at the News."

That film begins with director Ron Howard declaring that movies have portrayed the journalist as both "a hero and a scoundrel, a lover and a fighter, a gossip and a sage" and the press as both the "defender of the common man and the corrupt instrument of power-hungry machines." He adds that the movies have found journalism a continual source of fascination because it is marked by "rich, dramatic tensions" and an "overwhelming sense of urgency."

Then comes a montage of silver screen journalists in their full glory and shame: fighting journalists, sassy journalists, crooked journalists, drunken journalists. There are journalists on deadline, under fire, and in love, embodied by the biggest Hollywood stars of their day: Humphrey Bogart insolently greeting a gangster on the phone with "Hello, baby!" Paul Newman telling Sally Field that she probably is "a hell of a reporter," and Field sadly replying: "Not yet." Pat O'Brien, embracing his long-suffering fiancée: "I'll cut out drinking and swearing and everything else connected with the crazy newspaper business!" Peter Finch in soaking overcoat with arms outstretched: "I'm as mad as hell!" And finally, Orson Welles in his guise as the young Charles Foster Kane, sternly informing his ex-guardian, "I am the publisher of the *Inquirer*. As such, it is my duty—I'll let you in on a secret—it is also my pleasure—to see to it that the decent, hard-working people of this community aren't robbed blind by a pack of money-mad pirates just because they haven't anybody to look after their interests!"

The Newseum film concludes without showing what eventually happens to Kane: how he abandons his principles, scorns his public, and dies with only the memory of Rosebud to keep him company. However, the point has been made: Movies (many of them written or directed by ex-journalists) present an entertaining, long-running commentary on the press that has incorporated the spirit of both the Newseum's high-minded exhibits and its more down-and-dirty ones. The movies address "rich, dramatic tensions" not only in journalism but in our culture. The task is to see more precisely what those tensions are and how films have confronted them.

OFFICIAL AND OUTLAW HEROES AND VILLAINS

In performing mythic and ideological roles, myth seeks to resolve cultural contradictions—to reconcile the irreconcilable.[30] As purveyors of myth, movies try to do the same.

Robert Ray says Hollywood films historically have centered around a "pair of competing myths: the outlaw hero and the official hero." The outlaw hero, as commonly represented by "the adventurer, explorer, gunfighter, wanderer, and loner," reflects "that part of the American imagination valuing self-determination and freedom from entanglements." The official hero, as typically represented by "a teacher, lawyer, politician, farmer, or family man," reflects "the American belief in collective action, and the objective legal process that supercede[s] private notions of right and wrong." The movies' "ideology of improvisation, individualism, and ad hoc solutions" stems from the characteristically American desire to reconcile the outlaw and official visions, or at least avoid making a permanent choice between the two.[31]

In this book I argue that journalism movies similarly have featured those competing myths from the earliest days of the genre. In film director Roland Joffé's apt summary, they show "the journalist as renegade, the journalist as outsider, the journalist who in his anger comments on the fakeries, the falsities of society; and the journalist as kind of philosopher [and] Greek citizen who works to make society better."[32] The renegade outsider or "outlaw" journalist is akin to the wanderers and loners of American popular culture. He (or she, but most often he) holds no particular hope for society's betterment. He views the world and especially the institutions of government and big business as inherently corrupt. Resolutely independent, he shuns convention and obligation and scorns officially sanctioned truth and morality.

In contrast, the "Greek citizen" or "official" journalist is a dedicated public servant comparable to the dedicated teachers and lawyers in other popular texts. He (or she—but again, this applies more to men) believes that journalism can facilitate constructive change through careful investigation and reporting of the truth. He is a respectable, upright member of society who works for the common good.

The outlaw and official journalists both represent mythic virtues. On one hand, the outlaw journalist stands for individualism and freedom. No others are his superior, no matter how much power or wealth they hold. He is invulnerable to being snookered or co-opted. On the other hand, the official journalist stands for community and progress. He is a pillar who helps ensure democracy's proper functioning while embodying white-collar ideals of public service and social mobility. His dedicated hard work betters society even as it furthers his career.[33]

Along with the outlaw and official heroes in journalism movies are outlaw and official villains. As an outsider opposed to conventional morality, the outlaw villain poses a threat. He is in it only for himself, exploiting innocent others just to get a scoop or make a buck. He mocks the sacred bonds of marriage and family. The official villain represents official immorality and subjugation. He works for "The Media," a technologically invasive force in league with other powerful forces opposed to individual autonomy and liberty.

It is through such conflicting myths that movies have depicted the journalist as both "a hero and a scoundrel" and the press as both the "defender of the common man and the corrupt instrument of power-hungry machines." The heroic version in both its outlaw and official versions sees journalism as the path to something desirable: finding excitement or serving the public. Alongside that is another version: journalism as shallow, oppressive, and compromised. Hence the films present their dialectic: the press as promoting individual and social interests versus undermining individual and social interests, something a culture's myths celebrate or that they denigrate, something that preserves democratic values and social order or that threatens values and order.

However, I argue that even when movies portray the journalist as a scoundrel and the press as corrupt, they still tend not to challenge seriously the idea that the press can and should play a central role in society. By presenting morality tales in which wayward reporters are duly punished for their sins, the films also highlight rules of proper professional and personal conduct; a common function of myth is to use a deviant or scapegoat figure to reassert and enforce social norms.[34] And even if the movies show present journalistic practice to be lacking, they often look nostalgically to an idealized past for examples of what the present could be. This too is typical of myth; in Michael Schudson's words, its role is "not to tell us in empirical detail who we are but what we may have been once, what we might again become, what we would be like 'if.'"[35]

In such ways, movies simultaneously embrace two highly attractive if contradictory visions: the journalist as cool professional and as cheeky upstart. At the same time, the films dramatize journalistic failings while drawing lessons from them in a way that typically maintains the status quo and journalism's place in it.

GENRE AND DUALISMS

Journalism movies are similar to other genre films in that they generate meaning through oppositions, or dualisms. The official-outlaw dichotomy is one; there are others familiar to any movie fan. For example, musicals and romantic comedies commonly focus on a male-female couple who represent conflicting values. Their eventual union symbolizes a rapprochement between those opposites and the smoothing away of cultural rifts. The Western is similarly built around good guys and bad guys, dance hall women and schoolmarms, civilization and the frontier.[36]

Rick Altman outlines a "semantic-syntactic" approach to genre films that takes such oppositions into account. A genre's "semantics" are its stock settings, characters, and so forth, and its "syntax" is the enduring patterns in which those stock elements are woven into the films' plots. Altman argues that journalism movies never developed a stable syntax and hence never solidified into a formal genre comparable to the musical or Western.[37] Still, certain semantic elements persist in the films and tend to interact in predictable ways, or in what can be called a basic syntax.

The most important elements are the reporter and the story. The films typically feature a reporter character (or a pair of reporters, or a reporter with a sidekick) pursuing a story that is usually embodied by one or more other characters. Other stock elements are the editor and the love interest. The editor is most often an older man who interacts with the reporter in a professional setting such as a newsroom and prods or restrains the reporter. The love interest most often appears in a domestic setting, providing a contrast to the journalistic environment, and either helps the reporter or protests that the pursuit of the story is going too far. Often the story and love interest combine into one, as do the editor and love interest. Not every movie features each of these four elements—*All the President's Men,* for example, does not have a love interest—and some movies feature additional elements such as a media owner or publisher.[38] Nevertheless, the reporter, story, editor, and love interest appear most often.

The plots of the movies typically revolve around the obstacles the reporter faces in chasing the story and the consequences of that chase. As in other genre movies, the conflicts and tensions that develop between the characters represent broader conflicts and tensions. They include ones that particularly concern those who argue that journalism has strayed from its proper course or that its day may have passed altogether.

For example, there is the tension between cynicism and idealism. "Critics are beginning to fear that cynical press coverage is helping to create a nation of cynics," one commentator has said.[39] The difficulty is in how journalists

10

maintain skepticism toward authority while also maintaining a belief in democratic institutions and a functioning public. In the movies, reporters stand up to the powerful and pursue stories out of a selfless interest in the truth. They also pander to the powerful and chase stories through a selfish interest in furthering their careers and confirming their worst instincts about humankind.

Movies also address the tension between home and work in journalism. That is felt especially acutely by women journalists, who one such journalist says "have performed ably—often brilliantly—but at a personal cost that has often been unnecessarily and unforgivably high."[40] The movies have depicted female reporters from the beginning of the genre. When the films show women forced to choose between their jobs and their prospective mates, or when they show the toll on men's domestic tranquility that single-minded devotion to a story can exert, they raise questions about whether journalists can reconcile their personal and private lives.

Conflicts between public interest and private interest and between public interest and institutional interest are of particular concern. The first arises when the journalist encounters vulnerable people in the pursuit of news, which at worst can become what has been acidly characterized as "gaining their trust and betraying them without remorse" in the name of "'the public's right to know.'"[41] The second arises when journalism's public service responsibilities are subordinated to market considerations and dominant political and economic concerns, as critics have charged is increasingly the case. In the movies, reporters may report vitally important information or pander to salacious curiosity; they may stop abuses of power or find the powerful stopping them.

Finally, there is what can be described as the conflict between objectivity and subjectivity, the tension that arises when journalists try to remain neutral in covering the news and use systematic, scientific methods to uncover the truth. Some have argued that the press's code of objectivity evolved to serve commercial more than moral ends and that the press cannot claim the ability to discover value-free truth. Journalists themselves acknowledge that total objectivity is impossible, but they still stress the paramount importance of verifying what they report and giving the citizenry the information it needs for self-governance.[42]

Just as the nature of truth is at the heart of journalism itself, so is it at the heart of journalism movies. Richard Ness writes that "the basic pattern of the films is developed in terms of what truth is being sought or suppressed in the film and how and by whom it is controlled"; conflict is "generated by who knows the truth and who is trying to find out about it."[43] On screen, reporters may triumphantly discover the true facts or be thwarted in their quest via their own arrogance or obsession.

Again, the tensions the movies address are hardly unique to contemporary journalism; they have persisted for generations. Moreover, they are central to American culture and myth, including the outlaw-official dichotomy Robert Ray describes. The movies use the journalist as a symbolic figure to grapple with those tensions.[44]

Thus the conflict between home and work symbolizes a broader struggle over "traditional thought [that] prescribes that women are suited for the private, personal realm, and men for the public, professional one"—that is, the notion that men can more properly aspire to the status of official or outlaw hero than women can. It also represents a clash between iconoclasm and conformity, between living outside conventional social roles (an outlaw ideal) and being integrated into them (an official ideal). Cynicism versus idealism pits the desire to see through pretense and phoniness (as the outlaw does) against the desire to believe in the American dream (as the official does). Public versus private and institutional interests expresses tensions between the individual and society. Powerful institutions including the media may be depicted as the individual's protector or oppressor; public interest may be defined as serving the common good or as sating the voyeuristic, sheeplike masses. Objectivity versus subjectivity pits a scientific and impartial approach to life against a more intuitive and less detached approach. It also symbolizes a contest over professional privilege and over who gets to define truth and reality in a mass-mediated world.[45]

The movies speak to both sides of that contest. One scholar has noted that "the same democratic culture that makes professional status so alluring also remains deeply suspicious of the claims and pretensions of professionals," particularly "the extent to which such claims serve as masks for financial greed." Similarly, Daniel Czitrom has argued that from the earliest days of the telegraph, Americans have seen communication technologies in terms of both their "progressive or utopian possibilities" and "their disposition as instruments of domination and exploitation."[46]

On balance, though, movies tend to resolve such dilemmas in endorsing treasured myths: that personal and professional roles can be reconciled, that public service and profit-making can go hand in hand, that objective, scientific methods can discover truth, that democracy can work. The coming chapters discuss how the movies do this and what its implications are.

PLAN OF PROCEDURE

A journalism filmography lists more than 2,000 entries including silents, foreign films, made-for-TV movies, and countless B pictures.[47] However, in many if not most of those, journalists play peripheral roles. The focus here is on a handful of movies in which journalists are protagonists and their occupation is key to the plot. Some are considered to be among the greatest of all American films. Others include those particularly loved or reviled by journalists themselves or those that ex-journalists were instrumental in creating.[48]

Chapter 2 focuses on *The Front Page,* "the best known critique and cliché of American journalism" that journalists have been "trying to live down or up to" since it first was staged on Broadway in 1928 and turned into a movie three years later.[49] The chapter shows how the play was shaped by the development of modern journalism in Chicago and by early novels and plays. *The Front Page* crystallized the outlaw vision of the press while expressing ambivalence toward it. It also established stock characters and relationships that have persisted to this day in journalism movies.

From there the book proceeds roughly chronologically. Chapter 3, "Screwball Comedy and Frank Capra," contrasts the press's depictions in the romantic comedies of the 1930s and 1940s with those in Frank Capra's "social problem" trilogy of *Mr. Deeds Goes to Town, Mr. Smith Goes to Washington,* and *Meet John Doe.* Whereas screwball romances revel in journalistic cynicism and invest their female characters with power and autonomy, the Capra films are far more skeptical toward the existing press and the wiseacre women who work for it. Still, they express abiding faith in democracy and the people. Chapter 4 looks at *Citizen Kane,* which has been described as "the biggest newspaper picture of them all."[50] The movie presents a biting critique of journalistic hubris while in many ways painting an attractive, intriguing portrait of Kane.

Citizen Kane also serves as a bridge from the screwball era to the postwar film noir era that is the focus of chapter 5, "News in a Noir World." Films such as *Gentleman's Agreement, Call Northside 777,* and *Deadline, USA* show professional journalists seeking justice in a corrupt milieu. *Ace in the Hole* (a.k.a. *The Big Carnival*) and *Sweet Smell of Success* portray journalists falling prey to corruption and alienation themselves and paying the price for it. Chapter 6, "News and Conspiracy," compares two classic 1970s films in which government, big business, and other institutions join in conspiracies to hide secrets. In *All the President's Men,* two newspaper reporters defy the odds to uncover the truth; in *Network,* evil forces including the TV network itself threaten to destroy journalistic voices of conscience.

Chapter 7, "Myth and Antimyth in Contemporary Film," looks at portrayals of the news media in the post-Watergate era. That was when many say journalism developed a crisis of confidence against a landscape increasingly dominated by TV, infotainment, and celebrity obsession. The chapter focuses on such films as *Absence of Malice, The Killing Fields, The Insider, The Paper, Broadcast News,* and *To Die For.* The movies both reinforce and challenge the mythic notion of journalism as a force for democratic good; again, though, they all place the journalist and the media front and center. Chapter 8, "An Unseen

Power," returns to *The Front Page* and examines how the movies that have followed in its wake have perpetuated powerful myths about the press and how those myths in turn relate to popular impressions of the press's power in society.

In progressing from screwball comedy to film noir and conspiracy movies, the book in many ways follows a conventional rendering of film history that some critics have questioned.[51] Certainly the cinematic depiction of journalists has not been limited to those specific kinds of films appearing in those specific periods. For example, the screwball era also saw journalists as prominent characters in horror and gangster movies, and the film noir era saw them as the protagonists of musicals. And journalists continued to appear in romantic comedies long after screwball's heyday ended.

Even in such cases, however, the journalist characters tended to echo their counterparts in other films. For example, the reporters in 1930s horror movies demonstrated the same wisecracking skepticism they showed in the contemporaneous screwball films. Indeed, the movies were sometimes explicit remakes of earlier films: The musicals *Living It Up* (1954) and *High Society* (1956) copied the screwball-era comedies *Nothing Sacred* and *The Philadelphia Story.* Furthermore, the eras of screwball comedy, film noir, and the 1970s conspiracy film were marked not only by exceptional creativity in Hollywood but also by a distinctly ambiguous stance toward truth and morality.[52] Thus, movies from those periods offer especially provocative portraits of journalism.

Hollywood's assessments of what will attract audiences have changed over the years in response to dramatic transformations in its production and distribution system. Journalism also has changed with television's ascendancy, the media's increasingly visible role in public affairs, and the journalist's increasing claims to professional authority and expertise.[53] In this book I examine how the movies' portrayal of the press has evolved to reflect those changes. I relate the pictures to their historical, social, and political contexts and to each other, taking into account such factors as the artistic sensibilities and journalistic backgrounds of the films' creators, the historical events the films depict, and the institutional relationships between Hollywood studios, movie censors, and professional journalism organizations. That context is drawn from everything from studio archives and scholarly analyses of journalism and cinema to movie reviews and biographies of reporters, editors, directors, and stars.

At the same time, I focus on that which has endured in the films' depictions. James Carey notes that changes in popular texts represent "transformations on a given cultural tradition, a tradition that insists on reasserting itself."[54] The book seeks to uncover that tradition by highlighting how Hollywood has presented recurring characters, relationships, and tensions that represent an ongoing clash between opposing cultural values.

There is no claim on ultimate truth here. This is *a* story of journalism in the movies, not necessarily *the* story. It also should be understood that reading about a film is no substitute for viewing it. One test of the worth of a book about popular culture is whether it provokes readers to watch, read, or listen to the book's subject matter, even if some only want to satisfy themselves that the author is wrong. I hope that this book is worthy enough to achieve that goal.

Above all, the book is designed to enhance our understanding of how movies help make journalism matter in the popular consciousness. As Kevin Barnhurst and John Nerone argue, popular culture has regularly endorsed the press's "power to expose and enlighten."[55] To study how movies have accomplished that is to gain a better perspective on both our journalism and ourselves.

NOTES

1. Bill Kovach and Tom Rosenstiel, *The Elements of Journalism* (New York: Crown, 2001), pp. 11, 36–49; Leonard Downie Jr. and Robert G. Kaiser, *The News about the News: American Journalism in Peril* (New York: Knopf, 2002); Jay Black, Bob Steele, and Ralph Barney, *Doing Ethics in Journalism*, 3rd ed. (Boston: Allyn and Bacon, 1999).

2. Ben Bagdikian, *The Media Monopoly*, 6th ed. (Boston: Beacon, 2000); W. Lance Bennett, *News: The Politics of Illusion*, 3rd ed. (White Plains, N.Y.: Longman, 1996); Edward S. Herman and Noam Chomsky, *Manufacturing Consent: The Political Economy of the Mass Media* (New York: Pantheon, 1988); Robert W. McChesney, *Rich Media, Poor Democracy* (Urbana: University of Illinois Press, 1999); John H. McManus, *Market-Driven Journalism* (Newbury Park, Calif.: Sage, 1994); Doug Underwood, *When MBAs Rule the Newsroom* (New York: Columbia University Press, 1993).

3. Joseph N. Cappella and Kathleen Hall Jamieson, *Spiral of Cynicism: The Press and the Public Good* (New York: Oxford University Press, 1997); James S. Ettema and Theodore L. Glasser, "The Irony in—and of—Journalism: A Case Study in the Moral Language of Liberal Democracy," *Journal of Communication* 44:2 (1994): 5–28; James Fallows, *Breaking the News: How the Media Undermine American Democracy* (New York: Vintage, 1997); Todd Gitlin, "Bites and Blips: Chunk News, Savvy Talk and the Bifurcation of American Politics," in *Communication and Citizenship: Journalism and the Public Sphere*, ed. Peter Dahlgren and Colin Sparks (London: Routledge, 1991), pp. 119–36; Roderick P. Hart, *Seducing America: How Television Charms the Modern American Voter* (New York: Oxford University Press, 1994); Howard Kurtz, *Media Circus: The Trouble with America's Newspapers* (New York: Times Books, 1993); Davis Merritt, *Public Journalism and Public Life: Why Telling the News Is Not Enough* (Hillsdale, N.J.: Erlbaum, 1995); Jay Rosen, *What Are Journalists For?* (New Haven, Conn.: Yale University Press, 1999).

4. George Garneau, "Trash Journalism," *Editor & Publisher,* October 29, 1994, p. 8; Janet Malcolm, *The Journalist and the Murderer* (New York: Alfred A. Knopf, 1990).

5. James W. Carey, "The Mass Media and Democracy: Between the Modern and the Postmodern," *Journal of International Affairs* 47:1 (1993): 3–4; David L. Altheide and Robert P. Snow, *Media Worlds in the Postjournalism Era* (New York: Aldine de Gruyter, 1991), p. 51; Jon Katz, "Rock, Rap, and Movies Bring You the News," *Rolling Stone*, March 5, 1992, p. 33. See also Jon Katz, *Virtuous Reality* (New York: Random House, 1997).

6. Chip Rowe, "Hacks on Film," *Washington Journalism Review,* November 1992, p. 27. See also Jennifer Harper, "Poll Finds Reporters Obnoxious," *Washington Times,* December 18, 1996, p. A4; Michael Asimow, "Bad Lawyers in the Movies," *Nova Law Review* 24:2 (2000): 531–81; Richard K. Sherwin, *When Law Goes Pop* (Chicago: University of Chicago Press, 2000); Krin Gabbard and Glen O. Gabbard, *Psychiatry and the Cinema* (Chicago: University of Chicago Press, 1987); M. Z. Ribalow, "Script Doctors," *The Sciences* 38:6 (1998): 26.

7. Chandra Mukerji and Michael Schudson, "Introduction: Rethinking Popular Culture," in *Rethinking Popular Culture,* ed. Chandra Mukerji and Michael Schudson (Berkeley: University of California Press, 1991), p. 23. Television, radio, and comic books also have offered popular depictions of journalism, as have plays and novels (as discussed in chapter 2). See Loren Ghiglione and Joe Saltzman, "Fact or Fiction: Hollywood Looks at the News," *IJPC Journal,* online at <http://www.ijpc.org/journal.html> (2002); Loren Ghiglione, *The American Journalist: Paradox of the Press* (Washington, D.C.: Library of Congress, 1990).

8. Tom Goldstein, "Wanted: More Outspoken Views," *Columbia Journalism Review,* November–December, 2001, p. 145. See also Anthony Chase, *Movies on Trial* (New York: New Press, 2002); Bonnie Brennen, "Sweat Not Melodrama: Reading the Structure of Feeling in *All the President's Men,*" *Journalism: Theory, Practice, Criticism* 4:1 (2003): 113–31.

9. Joe Saltzman, *Frank Capra and the Image of the Journalist in American Film* (Los Angeles: Image of the Journalist in Popular Culture, 2002), p. 6; George Gordon Battle, "Stage Profanity Again under Fire," *New York Times,* September 9, 1928, sec. 10, p. 2; Frank Parker Stockbridge, "Public Gets False Picture of Journalism," *American Press,* November 1931, pp. 1–2; Stanley Walker, *City Editor* (New York: Frederick A. Stokes, 1934), p. 37; Stephen Vaughn and Bruce Evensen, "Democracy's Guardians: Hollywood's Portrait of Reporters, 1930–1945," *Journalism Quarterly* 68 (1991): 829–38; Jon Anderson, "We Scribes Are Mad as Hell, See?" *Chicago Tribune,* August 13, 1986, p. C1.

10. Fallows, *Breaking the News,* p. 44; Christopher Hanson, "Where Have All the Heroes Gone?" *Columbia Journalism Review,* March–April 1996, p. 46; Glenn Garelik, "Stop the Presses! Movies Blast Media. Viewers Cheer," *New York Times,* January 31, 1993, sec. 2, pp. 11, 18.

11. Bernard Weinraub, "Bad Guys, Good Guys: Journalists in the Movies," *New York Times,* October 13, 1997, pp. B1, B7.

12. Roger Manvell, "Media Ethics: How Movies Portray the Press and Broadcasters," in *Questioning Media Ethics,* ed. Bernard Rubin (New York: Praeger, 1978), p. 230; Howard Good, *Outcasts: The Image of Journalists in Contemporary Film* (Metuchen, N.J.: Scarecrow, 1989); Howard Good, *Girl Reporter* (Lanham, Md.: Scarecrow, 1998);

Howard Good, *The Drunken Journalist: The Biography of a Film Stereotype* (Lanham, Md.: Scarecrow, 2000).

13. Todd Gitlin, "Down the Tubes," in *Seeing through Movies,* ed. Mark Crispin Miller (New York: Pantheon, 1990), p. 40; Norman K. Denzin, *The Cinematic Society* (Thousand Oaks, Calif.: Sage, 1995); Norman K. Denzin, *Images of Postmodern Society: Social Theory and Contemporary Cinema* (London: Sage, 1991), p. 145.

14. Saltzman, *Frank Capra and the Image of the Journalist in American Film,* pp. 147–48; Ghiglione, *The American Journalist,* p. 99; Alex Barris, *Stop the Presses!* (South Brunswick, N.J.: A.S. Barnes, 1976).

15. Deac Rossell, "The Fourth Estate and the Seventh Art," in *Questioning Media Ethics,* ed. Bernard Rubin (New York: Praeger, 1978), pp. 232–82; Vaughn and Evensen, "Democracy's Guardians"; Thomas H. Zynda, "The Hollywood Version: Movie Portrayals of the Press," *Journalism History* 6:1 (1979): 32.

16. See especially Richard R. Ness's monumental *From Headline Hunter to Superman: A Journalism Filmography* (Lanham, Md.: Scarecrow, 1997). See also Larry Langman, *The Media in the Movies: A Catalog of American Journalism Films,* 1900–1996 (Jefferson, N.C.: McFarland, 1998); Norma Fay Green, *"The Front Page" on Film as a Case Study of American Journalism Mythology in Motion* (Unpublished Ph.D. dissertation, Michigan State University, 1993); Thomas C. Leonard, *News for All: America's Coming-of-Age with the Press* (New York: Oxford University Press, 1995); Howard Good and Michael J. Dillon, *Media Ethics Goes to the Movies* (Westport, Conn.: Praeger, 2002).

17. Jack Lule, *Daily News, Eternal Stories: The Mythological Role of Journalism* (New York: Guilford, 2001), pp. 15, 21–25.

18. See for example Eric W. Rothenbuhler, "The Living Room Celebration of the Olympic Games," *Journal of Communication* 38:4 (1988): 61–81; Daniel Dayan and Elihu Katz, *Media Events: The Live Broadcasting of History* (Cambridge, Mass.: Harvard University Press, 1992); Jack Lule, "Myth and Terror on the Editorial Page: The *New York Times* Responds to September 11, 2001," *Journalism & Mass Communication Quarterly* 79 (Summer 2002): 275–93.

19. Thomas Schatz, *Hollywood Genres* (New York: McGraw-Hill, 1981), p. 22; Richard Slotkin, *Gunfighter Nation: The Myth of the Frontier in Twentieth-Century America* (Norman: University of Oklahoma Press, 1998), pp. 653, 656.

20. Slotkin, *Gunfighter Nation,* pp. 659–60; Lule, *Daily News, Eternal Stories,* p. 145. See also Roland Barthes, *Mythologies,* trans. Annette Lavers (London: Jonathan Cape, 1972).

21. Robert B. Ray, *A Certain Tendency of the American Cinema* (Princeton, N.J.: Princeton University Press, 1985), p. 63. See also Judith Hess Wright, "Genre Films and the Status Quo," in *Film Genre Reader,* ed. Barry Keith Grant (Austin: University of Texas Press, 1986), pp. 41–49.

22. Schatz, *Hollywood Genres,* p. 35; Lule, *Daily News, Eternal Stories,* pp. 192–93.

23. Nancy Hauserman, review of *Legal Reelism: Movies as Legal Texts* by John Denvir, *Journal of Legal Studies Education* 16 (Summer/Fall 1998): 358; David Ray Papke, "Conventional Wisdom: The Courtroom Trial in American Popular Culture," *Mar-*

quette Law Review 82 (Spring 1999): 488; Peter E. Dans, *Doctors in the Movies* (Bloomington, Ill.: Medi-Ed, 2000); Joseph Turow, *Playing Doctor: Television, Storytelling, and Medical Power* (New York: Oxford University Press, 1989).

24. See for example Don Hewitt, *Tell Me a Story* (New York: Public Affairs, 2001), on how pictures such as *The Front Page* and *Foreign Correspondent* attracted him to the profession and Pete Hamill, *News Is a Verb* (New York: Ballantine, 1998), on how *Deadline, USA* reminds him of why he became a journalist. See also Ghiglione, *The American Journalist,* pp. 8–9.

25. Pamela J. Shoemaker and Stephen D. Reese, *Mediating the Message: Theories of Influences on Mass Media Content,* 2nd ed. (White Plains, N.Y.: Longman, 1996), pp. 92–95.

26. Eric Newton, ed., *Crusaders, Scoundrels, Journalists: The Newseum's Most Intriguing Newspeople* (New York: Times Books, 1999).

27. James W. Carey, "A Plea for the University Tradition," *Journalism Quarterly* 55 (Winter 1978): 849.

28. *Newseum: The Official Guide* (Arlington, Va.: The Freedom Forum, 1999), p. 48.

29. Newton, *Crusaders, Scoundrels, Journalists.*

30. Lule, *Daily News, Eternal Stories,* pp. 144–45.

31. Ray, *A Certain Tendency of the American Cinema,* pp. 58–63.

32. Roland Joffé, Director's Commentary, *The Killing Fields* DVD, Warner Brothers, 2001.

33. Burton J. Bledstein, *The Culture of Professionalism: The Middle Class and the Development of Higher Education in America* (New York: W.W. Norton, 1976).

34. Lule, *Daily News, Eternal Stories,* pp. 22–23, 60–80; Shoemaker and Reese, *Mediating the Message,* pp. 46–48, 225–27.

35. Michael Schudson, *Watergate in American Memory* (New York: Basic Books, 1992), p. 124.

36. Rick Altman, *The American Film Musical* (Bloomington: Indiana University Press, 1987); Stuart M. Kaminsky, *American Film Genres,* 2nd ed. (Chicago: Nelson-Hall, 1985); Schatz, *Hollywood Genres.*

37. Altman, *The American Film Musical,* p. 101.

38. Joe Saltzman provides a more detailed list of the stock characters in journalism movies in *Frank Capra and the Image of the Journalist in American Film.*

39. Paul Starobin, "A Generation of Vipers: Journalists and the New Cynicism," *Columbia Journalism Review,* March–April 1995, p. 26.

40. Jo Thomas, "Sagas of Women Journalists," *Journal of Communication* 44:1 (1994): 130.

41. Malcolm, *The Journalist and the Murderer,* p. 3.

42. Bagdikian, *The Media Monopoly;* Michael Schudson, *Discovering the News* (New York: Basic, 1978); Denzin, *The Cinematic Society;* Kovach and Rosenstiel, *The Elements of Journalism,* pp. 70–93.

43. Richard R. Ness, *From Headline Hunter to Superman: A Journalism Filmography* (Lanham, Md.: Scarecrow, 1997), pp. 6, 5. See also Zynda, "The Hollywood Version."

44. John J. Pauly, "The Professional Communicator as a Symbolic Figure," *American Journalism* 2:1 (1985): 79–92.

45. Bonnie J. Dow, "Hegemony, Feminist Criticism and *The Mary Tyler Moore Show,*" *Critical Studies in Mass Communication* 7 (1990): 268; Jeffrey C. Goldfarb, *The Cynical Society* (Chicago: University of Chicago Press, 1991); Barbie Zelizer, *Covering the Body: The Kennedy Assassination, the Media, and the Shaping of Collective Memory* (Chicago: University of Chicago Press, 1992).

46. Nathan O. Hatch, "Introduction: The Professions in a Democratic Culture," in *The Professions in American History,* ed. Nathan O. Hatch (Notre Dame, Ind.: Notre Dame University Press, 1988), pp. 2–3; Daniel J. Czitrom, *Media and the American Mind: From Morse to McLuhan* (Chapel Hill: University of North Carolina Press, 1982), p. 184.

47. Ness, *From Headline Hunter to Superman.*

48. See for example Barris, *Stop the Presses!;* Good, *Outcasts;* Jerry Roberts, "Newspaper Videos," *Editor & Publisher,* April 22, 1989, pp. 80–81, 112–13; Rowe, "Hacks on Film"; Zynda, "The Hollywood Version."

49. Doug Fetherling, *The Five Lives of Ben Hecht* (Toronto: Lester and Orphen, 1977), pp. 67–68.

50. Pauline Kael, "Raising Kane," in *The Citizen Kane Book,* by Pauline Kael, Herman J. Mankiewicz, and Orson Welles (New York: Limelight, 1984), p. 20.

51. See for example Lary May, *The Big Tomorrow* (Chicago: University of Chicago Press, 2000).

52. See James Harvey, *Romantic Comedy* (New York: Alfred A. Knopf, 1987); Foster Hirsch, *The Dark Side of the Screen: Film Noir* (New York: Da Capo, 1981); Schatz, *Hollywood Genres;* Ed Sikov, *Screwball* (New York: Crown, 1989); Alain Silver and Elizabeth Ward, eds., *Film Noir,* 3rd ed. (Woodstock, N.Y.: Overlook, 1992); Ray Pratt, *Projecting Paranoia: Conspiratorial Visions in American Film* (Lawrence: University Press of Kansas, 2001).

53. Kevin G. Barnhurst and John Nerone, *The Form of News: A History* (New York: Guilford, 2001).

54. James W. Carey, "Taking Culture Seriously," in *Media, Myths, and Narratives,* ed. James W. Carey (Newbury Park, Calif.: Sage, 1988), p. 16.

55. Barnhurst and Nerone, *The Form of News,* p. 1.

✤ 2

The Front Page

The Front Page is the prototype of the journalism movie genre.[1] It was not popular culture's first depiction of the press; many novels, plays, and silent films preceded its 1928 Broadway premiere. However, Ben Hecht and Charles MacArthur's tale of a reporter who tries to escape journalism for marriage and an advertising career firmly established such familiar characters as the callous and cynical press corps, the conniving editor who stops at nothing for a story, and the feckless newshound wildly unsuitable for matrimony or any other conventional relationship. As such, it might be seen as an act of revenge perpetrated by two bitter ex-journalists on their former trade.

However, the authors' epilogue to the published play suggests a different story:

> When we applied ourselves to write a newspaper play we had in mind a piece of work which would reflect our intellectual disdain of and superiority to the Newspaper.
>
> What we finally turned out, as the reader may verify if he will, is a romantic and rather doting tale of our old friends—the reporters of Chicago. . . .
>
> As a result *The Front Page,* despite its oaths and realisms is a Valentine thrown to the past, a Ballad (to us) full of Heim Weh and Love.
>
> So it remains for more stern and uncompromising intellects than ours to write of the true Significance of the Press. Therefore our apology to such bombinators, radicals, Utopians and Schoengeisten who might read this work expecting intellectual mayhem.
>
> In writing it we found we were not so much dramatists or intellectuals as two reporters in exile.[2]

The Front Page debuted in a time of controversy about tabloid news and the press's role in society. Hecht and MacArthur cared little about such debates; they and the Broadway professionals they worked with sought merely to entertain. Still they managed to encompass both what historian Ann Douglas calls "terrible honesty"—a tough, modern view of life holding contempt for sentimen-

"Two reporters in exile": Ben Hecht (standing) and Charles MacArthur late in their careers. (Courtesy of the Academy of Motion Picture Arts and Sciences)

tal naiveté[3]—and the view that journalism was a carefree existence that one left only reluctantly to do something more serious and grown-up. They presented a romantic, outlaw view of the press while also showing it to be a thoroughly disreputable trade. Thus, *The Front Page* was brilliantly ambivalent toward the press, mass culture, and middle-class virtues, yet in the end it still managed to be an old-fashioned valentine to journalism and American life.

BEN HECHT AND CHICAGO JOURNALISM

The play reflected the backgrounds and sensibilities of its authors. Ben Hecht was by far the more prolific of the two, a writer for hire for most of his life. He was born in 1893 to Russian Jewish parents. After graduating from high school in Wisconsin, he landed a job as a "picture chaser" on the *Chicago Daily Journal* in 1910. His job was to find images of those fortunate or unfortunate enough to make the news.[4]

Hecht entered the news business just as the heyday of the "New Journalism" pioneered by Pulitzer and Hearst was ending. It began in the 1880s and marked the development of a national system of communication, the transformation of the media into big businesses, and the emergence of the "professional communicator"—in particular, the reporter who hit the streets to find stories targeted at the cities' burgeoning immigrant and working-class populations.[5] In 1910, Chicago was a teeming metropolis with eight daily English-language newspapers. That year marked the beginning of a bloody circulation war between the *Chicago Tribune* and the city's Hearst papers, the *Examiner* (later the *Herald-Examiner*) and the *American*. The two sides recruited rival bands of hoodlums to commit mayhem and murder. When it was over, the *Tribune* had surpassed the Hearst papers in circulation, but twenty-seven news dealers were dead and only six dailies were still operating in the city.[6]

In short, Hecht was plunged into a rough environment. He later claimed that to keep the *Journal* afloat against its more successful competitors, editor-publisher John Eastman "was ready to jettison all the Ten Commandments."[7] That seems an exaggeration; another account says the paper was "extremely conservative in both its politics and its journalism,"[8] and there is no record of Eastman conspiring to commit homicide as the hired thugs of the *Tribune* and Hearst papers had done. Nevertheless, as the young Hecht discovered, the *Journal* was hardly dull.

"A Vote for the Loop Is a Vote against Subways; Watch Your Alderman and See if He Is a Grafter."[9] Those words ran above the *Journal*'s front page masthead on July 6, 1910, Hecht's third day on the job. At the bottom of the page was an editorial: "Chicago needs passenger subways. But city hall grafters, friends of the traction magnates, need not imagine that public funds can be diverted to construction of subways to be turned over as a gift to the traction companies." The controversy concerned a public transportation system that had grown hopelessly inadequate as growing throngs packed into downtown; the "traction magnates" ran the streetcars and the new elevated train loop. The magnates' coziness with city aldermen was well known, and the papers feared its impact on a proposed subway system.[10] The *Journal* similarly editorialized against municipal ownership of the city's docks because of the "danger of graft and scandal." Even on this supposedly conservative paper, an impressionable young man learned quickly that government and business leaders often were corrupt and should not be trusted—perhaps not even taken seriously.

The *Journal* mixed attacks on graft with human interest reporting in a style typical of New Journalism. The first week of July 1910, Jack Johnson beat Jim Jeffries for the heavyweight championship. The African American boxer's victory over his white opponent sparked unrest: "Fear of Race Riots Causes Chief of Police to Stop the Demonstration for Champion." The paper also reported scandal: "Willis F. Counselman, whose divorce from his insane wife was set aside after it had been learned that he had remarried five days after the decree was entered, sought vainly to defend his former attorney Milton L. Thackaberry today at the hearing of the disbarment proceedings against the lawyer."

And it reported blurbs of random violence and misfortune: "Maniac Kills His Father with Hammer While Asleep," "Two Burglars Choke Woman," "Woman Once Wealthy Now in Asylum as a Pauper," "Girl Killed under Auto That Leaped into Creek," and "Boy Killed in Tug of War." And in a longer, front page story, "Woman, Halted Often by 'Thou Shalt Not Kill,' Wounds Two, Then Succumbs to Poison." That was the tale of a woman whose husband apparently "'loved another'"; she overcame her "fear of eternal punishment" long enough to shoot both him and her baby daughter before committing suicide. The paper featured photographs of everyone involved, the kind Hecht would have been expected to obtain as a picture chaser.

He was up to the challenge, writing in his memoirs that the brawling world of big-city journalism "fitted me as water fits a fish." Hecht was the classic cub reporter who fled the University of Wisconsin for Chicago "with no thoughts yet in my head" other than a vague ambition of becoming a writer. His editor at the *Journal* sternly informed him that he must begin work on Independence Day: "There are no holidays in this dreadful profession you have chosen." He learned that profession on the streets, where the crowds, corruption, and calamity enthralled him. "Politicians were crooks," he wrote. "The leaders of causes were scoundrels. Morality was a farce full of murders, rapes and love nests. Swindlers ran the world and the Devil sang everywhere. These discoveries filled me with a great joy."[11]

Hecht's memoirs are suffused with nostalgia for his youth (as is the 1969 movie *Gaily, Gaily,* which was loosely based on one of those memoirs and purports to show young "Ben Harvey's" introduction to sex and other worldly delights). He claimed to have committed all manner of trickery as a picture catcher and later as a full-fledged reporter. In one case, he said he fabricated a front page story about an earthquake, digging a trench in Lincoln Park as evidence that the earth had split. Such stories must be taken with a grain of salt; Chicago is not noted for violent temblors, and his editors presumably were not imbeciles. What is striking is Hecht's delight in spinning yarns that would shake up people figuratively if not literally, a predilection he demonstrated from his earliest days as a writer. A critic of the 1920s called him a "romantic reporter, one to whom the meticulous accuracy of a stenographic report was abominable and uninspired, and who loved to let the imagination play over the dull, prosaic routine of a commonplace event."[12]

Hecht thus carried on what a historian calls "the sketch-hoax writer and the literary artisan" tradition of Chicago journalism. However, that tradition was starting to give way to "science, realism, and a growing facts-consciousness" in reporting.[13] Hecht acknowledged the presence of a few "very methodical sort" of journalists who "wore glasses and bought houses in the suburbs."[14] Some belonged to the Press Club of Chicago. Their aspiration was to improve journalism's image and status by becoming a true profession as opposed to the "dreadful" trade on which Hecht had been weaned. The reporter who scavenged for news wherever and however he or she could find it was, in James Carey's words, increasingly falling victim to "an attack on the style of the Bohemian reporter and on the sensational journalism that satisfied the cultural styles of the working class and immigrant."[15] In effect, the outlaw reporter was giving way to the official one.

Professionalism's rise coincided with that of the social sciences. A founder of the so-called Chicago school of sociology, John Dewey, found the city as wondrous and exciting as Hecht did. "Chicago is the place to make you appreciate at every turn the absolute opportunity which chaos affords," he wrote his wife. "Every conceivable thing solicits you; the town seems filled with problems holding out their hands & asking somebody to please solve them—or else dump them in the Lake."[16] There was the continuing influx of immigrants and African Americans that exacerbated ethnic tensions, culminating in the race riots of 1919; the poverty that Jane Addams and Ida B. Wells sought to alleviate; the scandalous conditions in the city's industrial plants, as exposed by Upton Sinclair in *The Jungle;* and the often bloody struggles of the labor unions to improve the working class's plight.[17]

Dewey and his colleagues cast their lot with those trying to solve such problems, whereas others—including some of the city's most prominent literary figures—favored more radical approaches. The editor of the *Little Review* literary journal, Margaret Anderson, wrote an anguished response to the 1915 execution of labor organizer Joe Hill: "For God's sake, why doesn't someone start the revolution?"[18]

Hecht was well acquainted with Anderson and others such as Carl Sandburg who held leftist sympathies, but he did not share in them. "We knew about the sins, about the hungry, jobless poor," he would write. "But we showed our metal in our derision. We sneered at all reformers, including those who worked for improvements among 'the great unwashed.' Perhaps this was because general poverty and a flourishing few were part of a show we liked."[19]

"We" referred to Hecht's reporter friends and fellow holdouts against the growing tide of scientific fact-gathering and suburban living. In the 1890s, their spiritual predecessors had met at Chicago's Whitechapel Club, decorated with skulls and a coffin-shaped bar. Journalist and essayist George Ade described it as "a little group of thirsty intellectuals who were opposed to everything."[20] In the early decades of the twentieth century, the new generation of thirsty intellectuals met in King's Restaurant and Schlogl's, where Hecht said they too "took gleeful part in the destruction of the world," heaping contempt on "the mayor, the chief of police, women, literature, politics and morality." That contempt extended to their editors, but according to Hecht in his memoirs, they still prided themselves on their choice of occupation: "A good newspaperman, of my day, was to be known by the fact that he was ashamed of being anything else. He scorned offers of double wages in other fields. He sneered at all the honors life held other than the one to which he aspired, which was a simple one. He dreamed of dying in harness, a casual figure full of anonymous power; and free."[21]

It is a succinctly romantic portrait of the journalist as outlaw, existential hero. It is also misleading, colored again by Hecht's nostalgia. While he was young, he did everything he could to ensure that he would not die anonymous or poor, which almost certainly would have been his fate had he remained a street reporter for the *Journal*. Like many of his fellow reporters, he sought a literary career beyond the confines of journalism while still using the press as subject matter. Also like many of his colleagues, he cast a mixed light on the press in his writings.

Some of Hecht's contemporaries dallied in journalism just long enough to garner experiences that they could translate into fiction. Theodore Dreiser drew on his Chicago reporting days to write *Sister Carrie*. However, such triumphs were the exception. Journalists turned out mediocre novels by the dozen, marked by superficial realism and what has been called the "twin defenses of cynicism and sentimentality."[22] Many of the stories and novels were marketed to a mass audience and therefore represent some of popular culture's first portrayals of the press. A common theme concerned an idealistic young reporter suffering a multitude of humiliations at the hands of his brutish editor before finally getting a big scoop and winning his true love. A gloomier theme was a reporter lingering too long in the newspaper business and gradually being worn down by its wretched working conditions and complete lack of ethics.[23]

It was inevitable that Hecht would write a journalism novel himself. From childhood he had "devoured books as if they were popcorn,"[24] and he published poems, stories, plays, and essays almost from his first days in Chicago. They were more successful than those of most of his peers, prompting no less than Ezra Pound to declare that "there is only one intelligent man in the whole United States to talk to—Ben Hecht."[25] In 1914, still barely out of his teens, Hecht moved to the newspaper with the highest circulation in Chicago, the *Daily News.* Its editor, Henry Justin Smith, was fond of literary men and wrote his own newspaper novel, featuring a character uncannily like Hecht: a reporter who was "death on pretenders, hypocrites, and optimists."[26]

When Hecht penned *Erik Dorn* in 1921, he also was death on journalism. The title character was a Chicago journalist who visited postwar Germany and was torn between his wife and another woman, just as Hecht had been. "A scavenger digging for the disgusts and abnormalities of life, is the press," Hecht wrote. "A yellow journal of lies, idiocies, filth." In the novel, Dorn escapes his newspaper to write for a learned journal of opinion, only to find a place of "intruding sterility" staffed by "a group of carefully tailored Abstractions bombinating mellifluously in a void."[27] The book seemed the work of a man finding journalism in all its forms—not just the outlaw version but also the official version—to be a dead end.

In fact, Hecht briefly abandoned the *Daily News* to work for a public relations firm. Although he made a lot of money, the firm collapsed (its owner, who had stolen some of the funds, committed suicide), and Hecht returned to the newspaper to write a daily series of ruminations on city life, "1001 Afternoons in Chicago." In one column he described people lying in Grant Park and staring at the sky, apparently waiting for something. Writing of himself in the third person, Hecht pondered what the people were waiting for:

> The newspaper reporter bit into his pencil. "Nothing, nothing," he muttered. "Yes, that's it. They aren't waiting for anything. That's the secret. Life is a few years of suspended animation. But there's no story in that. Better forget it."
>
> So he looked glumly out of his bedroom window, and, being a sentimentalist, the huge inverted music notes the telephone poles made against the dark played a long, sad tune in his mind.[28]

"1001 Afternoons" was the culmination of Hecht's career in Chicago and the "literary artisan" tradition of journalism he represented. At the time, a critic wrote of Hecht's potential, "Once he gets away from his journalistic ballyhoo, from his superficial estimates of people, from his desire to walk the tight rope and do acrobatic tricks in mid-air to the delight of a gaping mob, he will be able to dig deep and search for the really lasting treasures of literature."[29] However, Hecht's next novel was seized by the post office for obscenity, and the *Daily News* fired him. For a time he published his own literary journal, an issue of which featured a memorable parting shot at journalism: "Trying to

determine what is going on in the world by reading the newspapers is like trying to tell the time by watching the second hand of a clock."[30] In 1924, he followed the path of many other Chicago literary figures and headed for New
York.

HECHT AND MACARTHUR IN NEW YORK

"We were all fools to have left Chicago," Hecht wrote long after the fact.[31] Yet
his new home surely agreed with him in many ways. In Ann Douglas's words,
"For a few giddy and glorious moments in the 1920s, New York held out to its
new inhabitants an extraordinary promise of freedom and creative self-expres-
sion."[32] Its writers shared Hecht's contempt for the genteel Victorian literature of the previous century and his fascination with ironic realism. They similarly shared his devotion "to pleasure, particularly to the pleasure of not giving
a damn" and his "laughter at reformers and fanatics."[33]

The group included Gene Fowler, Damon Runyon, Dorothy Parker, Herman Mankiewicz, Samson Raphaelson, Nunnally Johnson, Marc Connelly,
Robert Benchley, George S. Kaufman, Maxwell Anderson, and Robert E. Sher-
wood. They contributed mightily to the theater at a time when Broadway produced an average of 225 plays a year;[34] soon they also made their mark on the
movies. All had worked in the news business. Pauline Kael wrote that they were
"ambivalently nostalgic about their youth as reporters, journalists, critics, or
playwrights, and they glorified the hard-drinking, cynical newspaperman."[35]

The plays they wrote reflected those qualities. As they had with novels, some
writers worked in journalism solely to garner material for the stage. Maurine
Watkins joined the *Chicago Tribune* in 1924 and quickly became a specialist in
comically lurid stories of women who murdered their husbands or lovers and,
more often than not, were acquitted of their crimes. After just six months, she
quit the paper and wrote *Chicago,* which premiered on Broadway in 1926. It
told of a woman who kills her illicit lover and whose trial turns into a feeding
frenzy for a cynical press corps.[36] The following year, another show written by
a former Chicago reporter premiered in New York. Bartlett Cormack's *The
Racket* focused on Chicago gangsters but prominently featured a wisecracking group of reporters hanging around a police station.

Both Watkins's and Cormack's plays were successes, and both portrayed the
press in the same ambivalent light that journalism fiction had. However, neither made journalism its primary subject. Just before *The Racket* opened, a
newspaper play called *Ink* flopped on Broadway. *New York Times* critic Brooks
Atkinson dismissed it as "rambling, ill-digested entertainment" and added, "By
an unwritten law, rarely violated, good plays cannot be written about the newspaper profession."[37]

That did not daunt Hecht. He had spent a brief sojourn in Hollywood to write his own gangster tale. (Herman Mankiewicz had lured him west with a telegram: "Millions are to be grabbed out here and your only competition is idiots."[38]) The silent movie *Underworld* earned Hecht an Oscar. Upon returning to New York, he began work on a newspaper play with a fellow ex-reporter from Chicago: Charles MacArthur.

MacArthur was a couple of years younger than Hecht.[39] He had left home in his teens and begun a newspaper career that was interrupted by the war. After fighting across France with the Rainbow Division, he landed a job on the *Chicago Herald-Examiner.* There he came under the tutelage—if one could call it that—of Walter Howey, who had been at the helm of the *Tribune* during its circulation war with the Hearst papers. In 1917, Howey fell out with the *Tribune*'s publishers and defected to the opposition, taking every opportunity from then on to scoop and swindle his former employer.

One observer noted that Howey "did not operate his paper by any code of ethics dreamed up at journalism school in an ivory tower full of idealistic professors."[40] He amassed scandalous tidbits on local officials to blackmail them into giving him what he wanted. Although small and innocuous-looking, he had a glass eye that some attributed to the circulation war and others to his drunkenly passing out and impaling himself on a copy spike. (Hecht famously declared that Howey's glass eye was the one that showed warmth.) It was also said that Howey stopped at nothing to discourage his staff from matrimony. One story holds that MacArthur boarded a train with a fellow *Herald-Examiner* reporter to try to persuade her to marry him. Howey contacted police and told them to arrest MacArthur, claiming that "the son of a bitch stole my watch."[41]

MacArthur eventually married the fellow reporter and escaped Howey and Chicago for New York, where he became a favorite of the artistic elite. His romantic life was complicated during his collaboration with Hecht. MacArthur sought to divorce his wife to marry stage star Helen Hayes. First, however, he wanted his own Broadway hit to match the success of his wife-to-be. Hecht recalled that "Charlie worked like a house afire" on their newspaper play.[42] But its tone and attitude toward the press were yet to be determined.

PRESS CRITICISM OF THE 1920S

The mass popular culture that was burgeoning in New York concerned many, with that concern extending to so-called jazz journalism. The city had three new tabloid newspapers: the *Daily News,* the *Mirror,* and the *Graphic.* Although the *Graphic* was the most outrageous of the three, the *Daily News* pulled off the biggest scoop. In a plot recalling that of *Chicago,* Ruth Snyder had conspired with her lover to murder her husband. Her trial was a media sensation that climaxed with Snyder sentenced to the electric chair. Just as the switch was thrown, a *Daily News* photographer snapped a picture with a hidden camera. The photo appeared under the headline "DEAD!" and boosted circulation by a million. Such stunts aroused particular vilification from those who branded the tabloid press a "danger-laden organ of vulgarity and evil."[43]

The critics included the new press associations that sought to solidify journalism's professional standing. The American Society of Newspaper Editors formed in 1922 and approved a code of ethics that it hoped would be binding on its members, only to find the code unenforceable.[44] Others charged that journalism's woes extended well beyond a lack of professionalism; in fact, the first decades of the twentieth century have been called "the Golden Age of press criticism."[45] Upton Sinclair wrote a ringing denunciation of the press's coziness with big business in *The Brass Check*. John Macy penned a similar critique in *Civilization in the United States,* a collection of essays lambasting the state of American culture. Walter Lippmann published *Public Opinion* and *The Phantom Public,* asserting that it was unrealistic to expect the average citizen to help shape public policy. John Dewey's *The Public and Its Problems* was more optimistic in its faith in a viable public but sketchy on how it might be brought into being.[46]

Much has been written about the differences between Lippmann's and Dewey's perspectives on the press during this period, but according to Michael Schudson, they "disagreed only over what might be done to save democracy from the devastation wrought by the increasingly urban, industrial, impersonal national society burgeoning around them."[47] Neither expressed particular hope that journalism could be that savior. Dewey and fellow sociologists Charles Horton Cooley and Robert Park (a former reporter) had at various times pondered trying to reform the press or even creating a paper to serve what Park called the "referential" function of reporting necessary facts and ideas to the public. They saw the existing press as mostly serving the "expressive" function of providing emotion and entertainment, much like other popular media. And in Daniel Czitrom's words, they "recoiled from the new popular culture engendered by modern media, treating it only insofar as they perceived it adding to the superficiality and strain of modern life."[48]

Hecht and MacArthur were certainly aware of such concerns. After all, Hecht in his novel had branded the modern urban newspaper a "yellow journal of lies, idiocies, filth." MacArthur had worked for Howey and the Hearst papers; if anyone knew how the press could manipulate and pander to the public, he did. The two men were part of the New York literati who prided themselves on their tough-minded sensibility. Therefore, it would not be surprising if the authors approached their new play intending to show their "intellectual disdain of and superiority to the Newspaper."

However, the writers and artists of the time were not at all averse to popular success; they were "eager to capture mass acceptance and elite adulation in a single stroke."[49] MacArthur had the added incentive of producing a hit that would make him in his eyes worthy of Helen Hayes. And there was another influence on the playwrights: the ambivalent nostalgia they shared with other ex-journalists. "We were both writing of people we had loved, and of an employment that had been like none other was ever to be," said Hecht. "Also, of a city we both called Avalon."[50]

THE CREATION OF THE PLAY

Even with love in their hearts, Hecht and MacArthur still had plenty of dirt to dish.[51] MacArthur's former editor Walter Howey became the play's Walter Burns, the last name purportedly changed out of fear of what Howey might do to the authors. They described Burns in their stage directions as "that product of thoughtless, pointless, nerve-drumming unmorality that is the Boss Journalist," the embodiment of every editor they had derided over drinks in Chicago's taverns.[52]

Burns's confederate and nemesis in the play was a *Herald-Examiner* reporter named Hildy Johnson, inspired by an actual *Herald-Examiner* reporter also named Hildy Johnson. However, he seemed based more on Hecht's and MacArthur's memories of themselves. "Hildy is of a vanishing type—the lusty, hoodlumesque half drunken caballero that was the newspaperman of our youth," they wrote—the outlaw type that journalism schools and the new professionalism were driving into extinction, much to the playwrights' dismay.[53]

At the same time, Hildy was desperate to escape his editor and get married as MacArthur had done, go into advertising and public relations as Hecht had done, and abandon Chicago for New York as both men had done. Hildy longed for the respectability he knew his current trade would never give him, as his words in the play indicate: "Journalists! Peeking through keyholes! Running after fire engines like a lot of coach dogs! Waking up people in the middle of the night to ask them what they think of Mussolini. Stealing pictures off old ladies of their daughters that get raped in Oak Park. A lot of lousy, daffy butt-inskis, swelling around with holes in their pants, borrowing nickels from office boys! And for what? So a million hired girls and motormen's wives'll know what's going on."

Hecht and MacArthur surrounded their protagonists with a motley crew also drawn from real life. The characters McCue, Bensinger, Murphy, Schwartz, and Duffy were all based on Chicago journalists with the same or similar names. The police officer "Woodenshoes" and gangster "Diamond Louie" also had actual Chicago counterparts. The authors heaped particular scorn on the characters of the mayor and sheriff. "Peter B. Hartman" was said to be based on a Chicago sheriff whose wrongdoing landed him in his own jail. And it was easy to recognize the unctuously sleazy mayor as Big Bill Thompson, Chicago's leader for most of the period between 1915 and 1931. The mayor's and sheriff's reelection slogan in the play—"Reform the Reds with a Rope!"—was not far removed from reality; during the "Red Scare" of 1919, Thompson had commissioned a police Bolshevik squad supposedly to prevent the creation of a Chicago soviet.

Significantly, the most sympathetic characters were a condemned prisoner and a prostitute; like Damon Runyon and other writers of the time, Hecht and MacArthur were far more benevolent toward so-called lowlifes or the dispossessed than anyone smacking of pretense or hypocrisy.[54] The character of Earl Williams was based on Bartolomeo Vanzetti, who had been convicted of murder with Nicola Sacco and executed in 1927. Vanzetti's eloquent pleas of innocence had helped trigger a vast outcry against the death sentences. In the play, Earl Williams declares, "I ain't important. It's humanity that's important, like I told you. Humanity is a wonderful thing, Mollie." He is speaking to "Mollie Malloy," a self-described "Clark Street tart" who is Earl's only friend and who delivers the play's angriest attacks on journalism. "God damn your greasy souls," she snarls at the reporters who have printed lies about her and Earl. "It's a wonder a bolt of lightning don't come through the ceiling and strike you all *dead!*"

Hecht and MacArthur finished their as-yet untitled play in the spring of 1928 and took it to New York's hottest producer, Jed Harris. Harris later wrote that he told the authors their script delighted him, but they would have to throw out the last two acts. Hecht called Harris a "son of a bitch" and stormed off with the script, only to be dragged back by MacArthur. Harris explained that they had a collection of funny scenes with no line of action holding them together. Instead, he proposed centering the play around a single theme: "Once you get caught in the lousy newspaper business you can never get out again." According to Harris, Hecht listened and then said, "I have to admit he's a son of a bitch with genius."[55]

Whether or not the story is totally true, it cannot be doubted that Harris was exactly what Hecht called him in the story: a theatrical genius with a vicious temper and a talent for alienating his colleagues. That eventually included George S. Kaufman, but in 1928 Kaufman was still on good enough terms with Harris to agree to direct the new play. Along with being a *New York Times* theater critic, Kaufman was a highly successful playwright and much in demand as a script doctor. He was noted for being able to strip a play to its bones and reconstruct it to extract maximum laughter from an audience. Kaufman worked with Hecht and MacArthur on rewrites and suggested the title.[56]

By the time *The Front Page* premiered on Broadway that August with Osgood Perkins (Anthony Perkins's father) as Walter and Lee Tracy as Hildy, it was thoroughly slick and commercial. Many years later, when it was revived in New York, critic Walter Kerr dubbed it "a watch that laughed," a smoothly running mechanism that delivered surprise and amusement like clockwork. Fellow critic Clive Barnes saw the same revival and called it a "positively great bad play," exaggerated and contrived but nevertheless breathlessly fun.[57]

In the play, Hildy fights Walter over Hildy's plans to leave journalism, marry his fiancée, Peggy, and leave Chicago for a New York advertising job. Then a sensational story falls into Hildy's lap. Earl Williams, sentenced to hang the following morning, escapes jail and collapses in the pressroom of the Criminal Courts building, where Hildy hides him in a rolltop desk. Mollie leaps out the pressroom window to distract the rival reporters who are about to uncover Earl. At that moment, Walter appears and badgers Hildy into writing the story of Earl's escape. Peggy, who has been unsuccessfully begging Hildy to leave town with her, runs off in tears.

In a feverish climax, the mayor and sheriff recapture Earl at gunpoint in the pressroom and arrest Walter and Hildy for hiding him. Then a man enters with a reprieve for Earl that the journalists learn the mayor and sheriff had planned to suppress. Walter and Hildy are released and have a huge scoop. Peggy reappears, and Walter magnanimously sends her and Hildy off to New York with a watch as a wedding present. The play ends with Walter plotting to have Hildy arrested for stealing the watch.

The plot follows the outline Jed Harris said he gave Hecht and MacArthur when they first met to discuss *The Front Page*. At the first act curtain, Earl's escape keeps Hildy from leaving journalism. At the second act curtain, Mollie's leap out the window and Walter's entrance keep him from leaving. At the final curtain, Walter's watch apparently will keep him from leaving. Walter's famous last line—"The son of a bitch stole my watch!"—may or may not have been a verbatim transcription of what Walter Howey said when he tried to prevent MacArthur from marrying. It also may have been an oblique reference to Jed Harris's not-so-secret desire to keep MacArthur and Helen Hayes apart.[58] Regardless, it was the culmination of the play's seemingly bitter theme: You never can escape the "lousy newspaper business," at least not without a heck of a fight.

Much of the play suggests that the business is indeed lousy. The reporters really are "daffy buttinskis" who are lazy, callous, and profane. Walter truly is a model of "thoughtless, pointless, nerve-drumming unmorality." In many ways, *The Front Page* shows the popular press to be every bit as bad as critics of the 1920s saw it as being.

Yet that is hardly the whole story. In giving the show a strong line of action and stark confrontations between the central characters, Hecht and Mac-

The climax of *The Front Page*, as seen in the 1931 film. Walter (Adolphe Menjou) guards the rolltop desk while Hildy (Pat O'Brien, standing third from left) and the other journalists watch. (Courtesy of the Academy of Motion Picture Arts and Sciences)

Arthur—and the seasoned Broadway pros Harris and Kaufman—managed not to stack the deck one way or another. If the play asks not only whether Hildy will leave journalism but also whether he *should* leave journalism, it very carefully leaves the second question unanswered (in contrast to *His Girl Friday,* the 1940 movie remake discussed in chapter 3).

The play uses the oppositions or dualisms around which popular texts are typically structured and that the characters' relationships express. The reporter, Hildy, is torn between the editor, Walter, and the love interest, Peggy. Hildy's and Walter's relationship represents an abiding and iconoclastic cynicism. In critic James Harvey's words, there is "no way to imagine them in anything but an adversary relation to any authority that human society could devise. . . . [T]hey are simply, permanently wised up."[59] That is a necessary defense in the corrupt urban milieu in which they operate, a world run by conniving crooks such as the mayor and sheriff. To be wised up is to know the score and not to be taken in, recalling Hecht's celebration of the journalist as "a casual figure full of anonymous power and free." It also reflects Hecht's assertion that the writers and artists of the 1920s sought to "remain orphaned from the smothering arms of society."[60]

In those ways, Hildy and Walter are classic outlaw characters. Robert Ray notes that such characters "try desperately to postpone responsibilities by clinging to adolescent lifestyles" and demonstrate a "distrust of civilization, typically represented by women and marriage."[61] That clearly is true of the protagonists; to an extent, it also was true of Hecht and MacArthur themselves.

But just as both playwrights aspired to leave journalism for something better, so Hildy seeks to leave for the middle-class status and comforts that Peggy and a professional advertising career represent.[62] "It's your chance to have a home and be a human being—and I'm going to make you take it," Peggy tells him. More pointedly, Hildy tells the other reporters that a journalist is a "cross between a bootlegger and a whore," adding that "you'll all end up on the copy desk: gray-headed, humpbacked slobs, dodging garnishees when you're ninety." That echoes the journalism novels of earlier years as well as Hecht's less romantic descriptions of journalism in works such as *Erik Dorn*. Despite the playwrights' disclaimer in the play's epilogue, *The Front Page* still reflects a fair share of educated scorn toward the newspaper.

Then there is Hildy's relationship with the story of Earl Williams and Mollie Malloy. Hildy treats them little better than the other reporters do: She is only a streetwalker; he is only an anarchist who killed a policeman (and an African American one at that; the journalists are not notably progressive as far as race is concerned). The reporters even badger the sheriff to move up Earl's hanging so they can include it in their early editions. When Earl escapes, Hildy and Walter hide the convicted murderer solely for a scoop; when the other reporters correctly guess that Mollie knows something about it, they hound and threaten her until she jumps out the window. The story is all that matters even if it is not true: A highlight of *The Front Page* is the reporters calling in grossly exaggerated and contradictory accounts of Earl's recapture in the pressroom. The outlaw journalist is thus depicted as disreputable, even inhuman.

For all that, Hildy and Walter triumph in the end. They get their scoop. They save Earl from execution. They thwart the mayor's and sheriff's criminally wicked plot. (If the press takes its lumps in *The Front Page,* it is nothing compared with those sustained by municipal government.) Yet their triumph results from a series of comic, cosmic accidents: Earl escaping from jail and then sneaking into the pressroom at just the right time, Mollie jumping out the window at just the right time, the man entering with the reprieve at just the right time. Small wonder that Walter speaks exultantly of an "unseen power" watching over the paper in times of peril.

Of course, the real powers watching over *The Front Page* were masters of theatrical timing and craft, as critics of the time recognized. Brooks Atkinson noted that the play was "shrewdly contrived to avoid that superiority in mind and manners which frightens audiences away."[63] It was not intended as a sermon about journalism's failings. Nor was it intended as art, the kind of "lasting treasure of literature" Harry Hansen had said he hoped Hecht would write. Instead it was in keeping with precisely what Hansen had criticized Hecht for: "journalistic ballyhoo" and "the desire to walk the tight rope and do acrobatic tricks in mid-air to the delight of a gaping mob." In short, it was designed to be popular. Atkinson praised "the color, the pace, the incidents and the lusty humor that make it so vibrantly entertaining." Another reviewer of the time declared that "such a night in a press room never was, on sea or land. But what a gorgeous excitement, what a magnificent riot, what a set of good fellows, what times, what stories, what extraordinary characters, what *bon mots*—Why, of course, what days those good old days WERE!"[64]

For that critic, Hecht's and MacArthur's play had achieved what the authors said was its purpose, to be "a Valentine thrown to the past." As for the "stern and uncompromising intellects" of the day who looked down on the popular press, the authors expressed not just their apologies but also their amused contempt. Nothing more or less could be expected from two reporters in exile.

THE MOVIE VERSION

When Hollywood producers read or saw *The Front Page,* they had concerns about its profanity; apart from Walter's curtain line, there were numerous "hells" and "God damns" along with racist invective that is more disturbing today than it apparently was then. Producers also worried about a possible backlash from the newspapers on which they depended for advertising. At the same time, they salivated over the play's potential as a movie. Silent films also had dealt with the press, but *The Front Page* appeared just as talking pictures were starting to be produced. The play's rapid-fire dialogue and dramatic sound effects made it a natural for the new medium.[65]

Howard Hughes bought the film rights from Jed Harris for $125,000 and assigned the screenplay to ex-journalists Charles Lederer and Bartlett Cormack, the author of *The Racket.* Lewis Milestone, winner of an Oscar for *All Quiet on the Western Front,* directed. Milestone later said Hughes rejected James Cagney as Hildy (because Cagney was a "runt") and Clark Gable as Walter (because his ears were too big). Instead, Pat O'Brien played Hildy and Adolphe Menjou took over as Walter after the first actor cast in the role suddenly died. Menjou proved to be a suave and shifty Burns, all but twirling his mustache as he cooked up his nefarious schemes.

The filmmakers negotiated with the Hays Office, in charge of censoring

Hollywood films, to soften the language and depiction of journalism. The profanity and racist talk were largely eliminated, and a title card—"This story is laid in a Mythical Kingdom"—was added to the start to deflect criticism that the film defamed Chicago and its press. Fortunately for Hughes and Milestone, a new production code that would tightly restrict Hollywood cinema was not yet being enforced. So they were able to get away with things that would not be possible a few years later, and the 1931 movie retains much of the play's bite.[66]

It begins with a close-up of a sack labeled "SUNSHINE FLOUR INSURES DOMESTIC HAPPINESS." The camera pulls out to show the sack tied with a noose above the trap door of a gallows. Three men best described as "mugs" are testing the gallows for the Earl Williams hanging. The film cuts from close-ups of the mugs wolfing down food and spitting tobacco to a shot of the sack plunging through the trap. One of the mugs is strolling away from the gallows when an empty liquor bottle shatters at his feet. He looks up to see a reporter glaring down at him from the pressroom window. The reporter tells the mug to quit making noise with the gallows and then spits water at him. The mug threatens the reporter and storms off, and the reporter laughs, "Ain't much respect for the press around here."

The film thus immediately announces itself as tough and ironic; its "Mythical Kingdom" is an outlaw world not far removed from the frontier towns of movie Westerns in which morality has a similarly tenuous hold. The reporters who inhabit it are still lazy and callous, if not quite as profane as in the play (although one actually gives the mayor the finger under the guise of checking his nails). They play cards while impatiently waiting for Williams to be hanged, they sneer at the sheriff, and they leer at Mollie and shove her out of the pressroom when she berates them.

If anything, the movie portrays Hildy's dilemma in starker terms than the play. Here, journalism literally stinks. "You ever come up out of a sewer and have the cool fresh air hit you?" Hildy tenderly asks Peggy. "Well, I did. And honey, you're the cool fresh air; you made a fresh-air fiend out of me, dear. And I'm not going back there unless you send me." However, Walter will not let Hildy go without a fight. Seen much earlier than in the play, he dispatches his cronies to search for Hildy in the city's brothels. Finally he pulls a fire alarm on the street, confident that his star reporter—always a sucker for a big fire—will come running. Sure enough Hildy does, and Walter drags him into a speakeasy.

They drink, with Walter craftily seeing to it that Hildy guzzles a lot more than he does. "So you're leaving me for marriage," he tells Hildy. "It must be grand. None of this idiotic jumping around at all hours and having to be on the inside of all the crazy excitement in this town. Ah—the 5:15 out to some quiet suburb, a home-cooked dinner every night exactly at seven, and by ten in bed—unless after the tapioca the wife has a few friends in for a neighborly

Walter (Adolphe Menjou) and Peggy (Mary Brian) eye each other suspiciously before an oblivious Hildy (Pat O'Brien) in *The Front Page*. (Courtesy of the Academy of Motion Picture Arts and Sciences)

chat." A miserable Hildy slumps over the bar, and Walter claps him on the back: "I don't blame you, Hildy; it sounds *great.*" In fact, it sounds even worse than the outlaw world Hildy is trying to escape. He finally catches on to what Walter is doing and sneaks out the bathroom window.

Ultimately, the film leaves Hildy's dilemma unresolved, just as the play did. Walter's closing line is the same as in the play, although he hits a typewriter carriage to mask the word "bitch." The film concludes with a giant question mark superimposed over "The End" as a train is heard grinding to a halt over Walter's maniacal laughter.

THE LEGACY

The Front Page was a highly influential film. Milestone demonstrated the visual possibilities of talking pictures by employing a much more mobile camera than most early talkies did.[67] More importantly, the movie presented a vision of the urban reporter and the wicked, glamorous big city that shaped pictures for years to come. It was a city, Andrew Bergman has written, where high society rubbed shoulders with shady lawyers and politicians in swanky nightclubs. Meanwhile, "on the sidewalk below were men with pads, pencils, and snap-brim hats who told other men holding cameras to 'Get ready, here he comes.' These people were newspapermen, who 'phoned in' to 'the chief' (a man they hated but loved) and made a great many wisecracks."[68] Small wonder that many journalists entered the business after they saw movies such as those and decided it looked like fun.[69]

At the time, though, the press—at least the part that prided itself on its professional standing and looked down on the tabloids—was not appreciative. Significantly, there had been no "official" model of journalism to which Hildy could turn; working for a paper such as the *New York Times* did not enter the equation. Thus, even though his theater critic had praised the stage version of *The Front Page, Times* publisher Adolph Ochs considered refusing advertising for it. Instead, the paper's attorney, George Gordon Battle, wrote an editorial attacking the play: "Managing editors are not all conscienceless and cruel. The standards of all newspaper men are not those of the gutter."[70] About the time the film version appeared, John Drewry told fellow journalism professors in a speech titled "The Journalist's Inferiority Complex" that the movies made "the reporter more nearly resemble a gangster than even a moderately well-off business or professional man."[71] *American Press* went so far as to condemn Hollywood for having "created a false and degraded impression of the newspaper business in the minds of millions."[72]

The intellectuals whom Hecht and MacArthur tweaked in the play's epilogue could not have been particularly happy either, whether or not they had ever heard of *The Front Page.* In 1916, Randolph Bourne had written an essay decrying the "insipidity" of "the American culture of the cheap newspaper, the 'movies,' [and] popular song" that was turning the masses into "cultural half-breeds, neither assimilated Anglo-Saxons nor nationals of another culture."[73]

The film of *The Front Page* that appeared fifteen years later was an apotheosis of the very things Bourne had attacked. Its roots were in the newspapers that the likes of Pulitzer and Hearst had targeted at the growing immigrant populations of cities such as Chicago. It drew inspiration from short stories and novels peddled to a mass audience and penned by the "professional communicators" to whom the New Journalism had given rise.[74] It debuted on the New York stage when Broadway enjoyed its widest popularity and the tabloids represented what could be considered either a new high or new low for the popular press. Finally it burst into cinemas with what seemed a markedly sour depiction of American life just as the movies were beginning to exert their strongest grip on the public imagination. It appeared to confirm the worst fears of those who looked down on mass culture and questioned how democratic society could be sustained in the modern age.

Yet for critic James Harvey, that is what was wonderful about it. He says its sops to social conscience (such as Earl's assertion that "humanity is a wonderful thing") only detracted from its success in getting "close—as almost no work before it had done so well—to a certain complexity, and even mystery, of the American consciousness and character: the combination of an absolute cynicism about public and social life with a kind of innocence and even hopefulness." For Harvey, *The Front Page* exalted "a particularly American idea of community: a world of private skepticisms and public energies—where no one wants to be cut off from either the energy or the clarity of the skepticism. A community of wiseacres—in a larger society of fakes and fools (as we all at times believe all larger societies to be). . . . America—in this vision—is the land of the privately wised up, of the quietly sardonic. A community of secret smilers."[75]

All that is to say that *The Front Page* reproduced myths wholly congruent with American ideology. On the surface, the play seemed uncompromising enough for Tennessee Williams to claim that it uncorseted the American theater;[76] underneath it was ready and eager to please. It paid lip service to social ruptures and failings—class inequities, racial tensions, government and media corruption—but ultimately made them all fodder for farce. The grimmer realities the playwrights may have experienced in their Chicago days were subsumed by nostalgia, consistent with the critic who labeled the original production "Ben Hecht's and Charles MacArthur's romance of journalism as they would like to remember it; a sort of memory of youth."[77] As Richard Slotkin notes, nostalgia is characteristic of American myth and ideology: the "yearning for a lost innocence, regret for the condition or sentiment of belief that (we like to imagine) existed in simpler and 'better' times." It also is characteristic of journalistic mythology, which Michael Schudson says often centers around "recalling and dramatizing one's past" in terms of a "struggle between a young eager reporter and a wizened, cynical editor" in "the big city."[78]

There also is the characteristic notion that irreconcilable values somehow can be reconciled: that one can be both "privately wised up" and at the same time connected to the "public energies" of the community or that (like Hildy in the play) one does not have to pick one over the other. Robert Ray argues that "when faced with a difficult choice, American stories resolved it either simplistically (by refusing to acknowledge that a choice is necessary), sentimentally (by blurring the differences between the two sides), or by laughing the whole thing off."[79] *The Front Page* is the quintessential example of laughing the whole thing off.

Nostalgic or not, *The Front Page* should be recognized as more than just a period piece (the way it was largely presented in Billy Wilder's 1974 movie remake). As Ann Douglas writes, "The 1920s could be said to have patented the idea of history as a form of instant irony, as a funhouse mirror revealing every distortion and falsity in things once held timeless and true."[80] In a contemporary world in which the lines between high and low culture are increasingly blurred and irony is everywhere, Hecht's and MacArthur's opus seems more relevant than ever, not so much modern as postmodern. However, its embrace of classic American myth—"absolute cynicism" tempered by "innocence and even hopefulness"—makes it timeless.

The Front Page also inspired a raft of movies that continued to explore journalism's place in American life. Some are jewels of the cinema. As will be seen, though, not all are so obviously full of "Heim Weh and Love" for the press.

NOTES

1. For a discussion of "initiating" works in film genres, see Richard Slotkin, "Prologue to a Study of Myth and Genre in American Movies," *Prospects: The Annual of American Cultural Studies* 9 (1984): 407–32.

2. Ben Hecht and Charles MacArthur, *The Front Page* (New York: Covici-Friede, 1928), pp. 191–92.

3. Ann Douglas, *Terrible Honesty: Mongrel Manhattan in the 1920s* (New York: Farrar, Straus and Giroux, 1995).

4. Biographical information on Hecht comes from William MacAdams, *Ben Hecht: The Man behind the Legend* (New York: Charles Scribner's Sons, 1990); Doug Fetherling, *The Five Lives of Ben Hecht* (Toronto: Lester and Orphen, 1977); Ben Hecht, *Child of the Century* (New York: Simon and Schuster, 1954); Ben Hecht, *Gaily, Gaily* (Garden City, N.Y.: Doubleday, 1963); Jeffrey Brown Martin, *Ben Hecht: Hollywood Screenwriter* (Ann Arbor, Mich.: UMI Research Press, 1985). Some sources give Hecht's birth date as 1894.

5. George Everett, "The Age of New Journalism," in *The Media in Society: A History*, 3rd ed., ed. David Sloan and James D. Startt (Northport, Ala.: Vision, 1996), pp. 275–304; James W. Carey, "The Communications Revolution and the Professional Communicator," in *James Carey: A Critical Reader*, ed. Eve Stryker Munson and Catherine A. Warren (Minneapolis: University of Minnesota Press, 1997), pp. 128–43; Michael Schudson, *Discovering the News* (New York: Basic, 1978), pp. 88–120; Kevin G. Barnhurst and John Nerone, *The Form of News: A History* (New York: Guilford, 2001).

6. Elizabeth Dewey Johns, *Chicago's Papers and the News* (Unpublished Ph.D. dissertation, University of Chicago, 1942), pp. 2–54; W. A. Swanberg, *Citizen Hearst* (New York: Bantam Matrix, 1967), pp. 321–26.

7. Hecht, *Gaily, Gaily*, p. 80.

8. Johns, *Chicago's Papers and the News*, p. 38.

9. This quote and those that follow come from the *Chicago Daily Journal*, July 5, 6, and 10, 1910.

10. For more on the traction controversies, see Perry Duis, *Challenging Chicago* (Urbana: University of Illinois Press, 1998), pp. 3–41; Donald L. Miller, *City of the Century* (New York: Touchstone, 1996), pp. 254–300.

11. Hecht, *Child of the Century,* pp. 119, 143.

12. Harry Hansen, *Midwest Portraits* (New York: Harcourt, Brace, 1923), p. 327.

13. Norman Howard Sims, *The Chicago Style of Journalism* (Unpublished Ph.D. dissertation, University of Illinois at Urbana-Champaign, 1979), pp. 44, 253–75.

14. Hecht, *Child of the Century,* p. 149.

15. James W. Carey, "A Plea for the University Tradition," *Journalism Quarterly* 55 (Winter 1978): 852. See also Norma Green, Stephen Lacy, and Jean Folkerts, "Chicago Journalists at the Turn of the Century: Bohemians All?" *Journalism Quarterly* 66 (1989): 813–21; Schudson, *Discovering the News,* pp. 121–59; Barnhurst and Nerone, *The Form of News,* p. 17.

16. Louis Menand, *The Metaphysical Club* (New York: Farrar, Straus and Giroux, 2001), pp. 318–19.

17. Douglas Bukowski, *Big Bill Thompson, Chicago, and the Politics of Image* (Urbana: University of Illinois Press, 1998); Duis, *Challenging Chicago;* Miller, *City of the Century.*

18. Dale Kramer, *Chicago Renaissance* (New York: Appleton-Century, 1966), p. 256.

19. Hecht, *Gaily, Gaily,* p. 185.

20. Miller, *City of the Century,* p. 519. See also Alfred Lawrence Lorenz, "The Whitechapel Club: Defining Chicago's Newspapermen in the 1890s," *American Journalism* 15:1 (1998): 83–102; Sims, *Chicago Style of Journalism,* pp. 207–52.

21. Hecht, *Child of the Century,* pp. 143, 191.

22. Larner Ziff, *The American 1890s: Life and Times of a Lost Generation* (Lincoln: University of Nebraska Press, 1966), p. 152.

23. See Thomas Elliott Berry, *The Newspaper in the American Novel* (Metuchen, N.J.: Scarecrow, 1970); Loren Ghiglione, *The American Journalist: Paradox of the Press* (Washington, D.C.: Library of Congress, 1990); Howard Good, *Acquainted with the Night* (Metuchen, N.J.: Scarecrow, 1986); Thomas C. Leonard, *News for All* (New York: Oxford University Press, 1995); Miller, *City of the Century.*

24. Bret Primack, ed., *The Ben Hecht Show* (Jefferson, N.C.: McFarland, 1993), p. 22.

25. MacAdams, *Ben Hecht,* p. 43.

26. Henry Justin Smith, *Deadlines* (Chicago: Covici-McGee, 1923), p. 47.

27. Ben Hecht, *Erik Dorn* (New York: G.P. Putnam's Sons, 1921), pp. 82, 215–16.

28. Ben Hecht, *1001 Afternoons in Chicago* (Chicago: University of Chicago Press, 1992), p. 289.

29. Hansen, *Midwest Portraits,* p. 357.

30. Hecht, *Child of the Century,* p. 331.

31. Ben Hecht, *Charlie: The Improbable Life and Times of Charles MacArthur* (New York: Harper and Brothers, 1957), p. 69.

32. Douglas, *Terrible Honesty,* p. 26.

33. Hecht, *Child of the Century,* pp. 357, 359.

34. Douglas, *Terrible Honesty,* p. 60.

35. Pauline Kael, "Raising Kane," in *The Citizen Kane Book,* by Pauline Kael, Herman J. Mankiewicz, and Orson Welles (New York: Limelight, 1984), p. 25.

36. Louise Kernan, "Murder, She Wrote," *Chicago Tribune,* July 16, 1997, sec. 2, pp. 1, 7. *Chicago* enjoyed a long and successful life. It was made into a silent film and later into the 1942 movie *Roxie Hart.* It then became a Broadway musical in the 1970s and finally an Oscar-winning movie musical in 2002.

37. J. Brooks Atkinson, "Shocking Exposure of Journalism," *New York Times,* November 2, 1927, p. 24.

38. MacAdams, *Ben Hecht,* p. 5.

39. Biographical information on MacArthur and Walter Howey comes from Helen Hayes and Katherine Hatch, *My Life in Three Acts* (San Diego, Calif.: Harcourt Brace Jovanovich, 1990); Hecht, *Charlie;* MacAdams, *Ben Hecht;* George Murray, *The Madhouse on Madison Street* (Chicago: Follett, 1965); Fetherling, *Five Lives of Ben Hecht.*

40. Murray, *Madhouse on Madison Street,* p. 180.

41. Ibid., p. 282.

42. Hecht, *Charlie,* p. 135.

43. Simon M. Bessie, *Jazz Journalism* (New York: E.P. Dutton, 1938), p. 20; John D. Stevens, *Sensationalism and the New York Press* (New York: Columbia University Press, 1991), pp. 118–54.

44. Bruce J. Evensen, "Journalism's Struggle over Ethics and Professionalism during America's Jazz Age," *Journalism History* 16:3–4 (1989): 54–63.

45. Robert W. McChesney and Ben Scott, "Introduction," in Upton Sinclair, *The Brass Check: A Study of American Journalism* (Urbana: University of Illinois Press, 2003), p. xx.

46. See Sinclair, *The Brass Check;* John Macy, "Journalism," in *Civilization in the United States,* ed. Harold Stearns (New York: Harcourt, Brace, 1922), pp. 35–51; Walter Lippmann, *Public Opinion* (New York: Macmillan, 1922); Walter Lippmann, *The Phantom Public* (New York: Harcourt, Brace, 1925); John Dewey, *The Public and Its Problems* (New York: Henry Holt, 1927). For analyses of the press criticism of this period, see James W. Carey, "The Chicago School and the History of Mass Communication Research," in *James Carey: A Critical Reader,* ed. Eve Stryker Munson and Catherine A. Warren (Minneapolis: University of Minnesota Press), pp. 14–33; Jay Rosen, *What Are Journalists For?* (New Haven, Conn.: Yale University Press, 1999), pp. 64–67; Schudson, *Discovering the News,* pp. 121–59; McChesney and Scott, "Introduction."

47. Michael Schudson, "What Public Journalism Knows about Journalism but Doesn't Know about 'Public,'" in *The Idea of Public Journalism,* ed. Theodore L. Glasser (New York: Guilford, 1999), p. 124.

48. Daniel J. Czitrom, *Media and the American Mind* (Chapel Hill: University of North Carolina Press, 1982), p. 93.

49. Douglas, *Terrible Honesty,* p. 70.

50. Hecht, *Charlie,* p. 135.

51. Information on the writing of the play comes from *The Front Page* (1974) Production/Clippings file, Margaret Herrick Library, Academy of Motion Picture Arts and Sciences (AMPAS), Beverly Hills, Calif.; MacAdams, *Ben Hecht;* Hecht, *Charlie;* Wil-

liam T. Moore, *Dateline Chicago* (New York: Taplinger, 1973); Martin, *Ben Hecht;* Jhan Robbins, *Front Page Marriage* (New York: G.P. Putnam's Sons, 1982); John J. McPhaul, *Deadlines and Monkeyshines* (Englewood Cliffs, N.J.: Prentice Hall, 1962); Murray, *Madhouse on Madison Street;* Bukowski, *Big Bill Thompson;* Arthur Schlesinger Jr., "The Front Page," in *Past Imperfect: History According to the Movies,* ed. Mark C. Carnes (New York: Henry Holt, 1995), pp. 200–203.

52. Hecht and MacArthur, *The Front Page,* p. 129.

53. Ibid., p. 31.

54. John J. Pauly, "Damon Runyon," in *A Sourcebook of American Literary Journalism,* ed. Thomas B. Connery (New York: Greenwood, 1992), pp. 169–77. See also Robert B. Ray, *A Certain Tendency of the American Cinema* (Princeton, N.J.: Princeton University Press, 1985), pp. 60–61.

55. Jed Harris, *A Dance on the High Wire* (New York: Crown, 1979), pp. 117–18.

56. Scott Meredith, *George S. Kaufman and His Friends* (Garden City, N.Y.: Doubleday, 1974), pp. 342–67.

57. Walter Kerr, "After 41 Years, It's Still Page One," *New York Times,* May 25, 1969, sec. 2, p. 1; Clive Barnes, review of *The Front Page, New York Times,* May 12, 1969, p. 54.

58. Hayes and Hatch, *My Life in Three Acts,* p. 54.

59. James Harvey, *Romantic Comedy* (New York: Alfred A. Knopf, 1987), p. 89.

60. Quoted in Douglas, *Terrible Honesty,* p. 27.

61. Ray, *A Certain Tendency of the Hollywood Cinema,* pp. 59–60.

62. Burton J. Bledstein, *The Culture of Professionalism: The Middle Class and the Development of Higher Education in America* (New York: W.W. Norton, 1976).

63. J. Brooks Atkinson, review of *The Front Page, New York Times,* August 26, 1928, sec. 7, p. 1.

64. Ibid.; Francis R. Bellamy, "The Theatre," *Outlook,* August 29, 1928, p. 705.

65. Stephen Vaughn and Bruce Evensen, "Democracy's Guardians: Hollywood's Portrait of Reporters, 1930–1945," *Journalism Quarterly* 68 (1991): 829–38; *The Front Page* Production Code Administration (PCA) File, AMPAS; Richard R. Ness, *From Headline Hunter to Superman: A Journalism Filmography* (Lanham, Md.: Scarecrow, 1997); Joe Saltzman, *Frank Capra and the Image of the Journalist in American Film* (Los Angeles: Image of the Journalist in Popular Culture, 2002). Talking pictures dealing with journalism were released before the film of *The Front Page,* including 1929's *Big News,* which borrowed a great deal from Hecht's and MacArthur's play.

66. *The Front Page* PCA File, AMPAS; Tony Thomas, *Howard Hughes in Hollywood* (Secaucus, N.J.: Citadel, 1985), pp. 65–70.

67. Joseph R. Millichap, *Lewis Milestone* (Boston: Twayne, 1981), pp. 53–60.

68. Andrew Bergman, *We're in the Money* (New York: Harper Colophon, 1971), pp. 20–21.

69. Loren Ghiglione, *The American Journalist: Paradox of the Press* (Washington, D.C.: Library of Congress, 1990), pp. 8–9; Don Hewitt, *Tell Me a Story* (New York: Public Affairs, 2001), pp. 14–15.

70. George Gordon Battle, "Stage Profanity Again under Fire," *New York Times,* September 9, 1928, sec. 10, p. 2; Meredith, *George S. Kaufman,* p. 365.

71. John E. Drewry, "Presidential Address: The Journalist's Inferiority Complex," *Journalism Quarterly* 8 (1931): 14.

72. Frank Parker Stockbridge, "Public Gets False Picture of Journalism," *American Press*, November, 1931, p. 2.

73. Menand, *The Metaphysical Club*, p. 403.

74. For a discussion of the relationship between early journalism fiction and *The Front Page*, see Norma Fay Green, *"The Front Page" on Film as a Case Study of American Journalism Mythology in Motion* (Unpublished Ph.D. dissertation, Michigan State University, 1993).

75. Harvey, *Romantic Comedy*, pp. 88–90.

76. Anne Klarner, "Best Bet: 'Front Page' Follies," *Los Angeles Times*, November 12, 1992, p. J2.

77. Bellamy, "The Theatre," p. 705.

78. Richard Slotkin, *Gunfighter Nation: The Myth of the Frontier in Twentieth-Century America* (Norman: University of Oklahoma Press, 1998), p. 640; Schudson, *Discovering the News*, p. 84.

79. Ray, *A Certain Tendency of the American Cinema*, p. 67.

80. Douglas, *Terrible Honesty*, p. 483.

❦ 3

Screwball Comedy and Frank Capra

Screwball comedies, the wisecracking romances that Hollywood produced for a short period beginning in the mid-1930s, are among the best-loved American films.[1] Many feature journalists in what have been described as "morality tales in which the morals are notably absent."[2] As in *The Front Page,* a certain moral code exists—the story and the paper above all else—but moralizing has no place. The movies show a corrupt, big-city world in which being a smart-aleck is the ultimate form of "sanity and resistance."[3]

The element that screwball added to the newspaper film was sophisticated romance via a group of uncommonly smart and funny women who would have had no place in the boys' club of *The Front Page.* In changing Hildy into a woman, *His Girl Friday* (1940) resolves the conundrum of the original play to make love and work synonymous. Tabloid journalism in these films is an equalizer, allowing men and women and haves and have-nots to meet on a more level playing field. Official pieties and pretension are undercut; autonomy and self-determination are celebrated.

However, not everyone bought into the screwball ethos and the press's privileged place in it. Frank Capra's *Mr. Deeds Goes to Town, Mr. Smith Goes to Washington,* and *Meet John Doe* present a sharper critique of journalism. Here smart and funny women are unhappily involved in schemes to injure the innocent and serve the official powers that be; the tabloid press becomes an instrument of mass manipulation. If screwball comedies largely transcend whatever doubts *The Front Page* expressed about journalism, the Capra pictures extend them into a whole new realm. Yet both sets of movies extol democratic ideals and the power of the individual, and even in the Capra films there is the sense that journalists can make a positive difference in society.

THE DEVELOPMENT OF SCREWBALL

The years immediately after *The Front Page* saw a flurry of pictures featuring fast-talking journalists. A particularly vivid example was *Picture Snatcher*

"He's got it, and it's GOOD!" Danny (James Cagney, standing second from left) returns with his scoop in *Picture Snatcher*. (Courtesy of the Academy of Motion Picture Arts and Sciences)

(1933), which combined the gangster and newspaper themes that were Warner Brothers specialties.[4] James Cagney plays Danny, a gangster just out of Sing Sing who goes straight with a newspaper job. Like Ben Hecht, he establishes himself by snatching a photograph of a cuckolded firefighter's dead wife. He meanwhile falls for journalism student Patricia, whose father is a cop who once shot Danny six times. How Danny survived is not clear, but never mind: A woman is about to be executed at Sing Sing, and Danny returns to the prison with a camera hidden under his pant leg (an obvious take-off on Ruth Snyder and the *New York Daily News*). He photographs the electrocution, but police and rival reporters discover his ploy just as he is about to make his getaway.

A wild chase ensues. Danny leaps from his speeding car, steals back to the city, evades more pursuers on the subway, climbs the newspaper's fire escape, bangs on the window (the startled society editor screams and faints), and tumbles inside. The photo is developed ("He's got it . . . *and it's GOOD!*" the publisher shouts) while Danny dictates his story with arms flailing. "Am I talking too fast?" he barks. No matter; a reporter named Allison who lusts after Danny translates him into proper tabloidese. Before the movie ends, Danny goes on a binge after Patricia dumps him, sobers up in time to get another scoop (a former gangster pal is gunned down in front of his screaming family), and gets back Patricia.

Such movies had little time to ruminate about journalistic ethics. They were in the spirit of what James Harvey has called the "tough comedy" of the early 1930s, with Cagney specializing in the kind of sardonic outsiders that *The Front Page* had helped make familiar on screen.[5] Whatever expressions of conscience there were came from the female characters, who seemed obligatory plot devices not allowed to slow down the action for long.

That was in keeping with outlaw hero mythology in which women were depicted as domesticating threats.[6] It also was in keeping with Hildy's fiancée, Peggy, in *The Front Page*. "In her unconscious and highly noble efforts to make what the female world calls 'a man' out of Hildy, Peggy has neither the sympathy nor acclaim of the authors, yet—regarded superficially, she is a very sweet and satisfying heroine," Hecht and MacArthur wrote.[7] Sweet she might have been, but she was also dull and teary and clingy, and her mother (who made no secret of her disdain for Hildy) was far worse. In *Picture Snatcher,* Patricia tells Danny that in his new job he is "just a thug, doing the same thing you always did": He is no better than the crook he once was. Still Danny wins her heart while fending off Allison's advances. Both women are stereotypes—the "good girl" and the "bad girl"—and Danny shoves Allison around a lot, with Cagney in his *Public Enemy* grapefruit-in-the-face mode.

Screwball comedy created stronger female roles, thanks partly to the enforcement of the Production Code starting in 1934. It was Hollywood's response to the concerns of clergy, social scientists, and others that the violence and sexual frankness of films such as *Picture Snatcher* threatened children and public morality, an official condemnation of popular culture similar to the condemnations of the tabloid press at about the same time. Fearful of government regulation and a threatened boycott, the studios agreed to censor themselves by submitting scripts to a Production Code Administration (PCA). The PCA called for the elimination of anything appearing to encourage sympathy "to the side of crime, wrongdoing, evil or sin," including showing married couples in the same bed.[8]

As quaint as the restrictions now seem, film scholars argue that in some ways they helped the movies. With overt sexuality prohibited, sexual tension took the form of a battle of wits. It helped that the films were scripted by a legendarily witty group of writers, such as Ben Hecht, who had been part of the New York literary scene in the 1920s and had migrated to Hollywood. Pauline Kael wrote, "They one and all experienced it as prostitution of their talents—joyous prostitution in some cases." Despite or because of that, they "changed movies by raking the old moralistic muck with derision," including the moralistic impulses that had led to the code's imposition in the first place.[9] It also helped that the movies starred some of Hollywood's most glamorous stars working with some of its most gifted directors.

An early and influential screwball film was *It Happened One Night* (1934), directed by Frank Capra and written by Robert Riskin. Capra had dealt with journalism as early as 1928 in the silent *The Power of the Press*.[10] Three years later, in *Platinum Blonde* (also written by Riskin), reporter Robert Williams was torn between fellow reporter Loretta Young and heiress Jean Harlow. Williams married Harlow but soon saw himself as a "bird in a gilded cage," and he left her and her mansion to write plays in a modest apartment with Young.

It Happened One Night used many of the same plot elements. In the original script, the male protagonist was an artist. Capra later said his friend Myles Connolly, an ex-journalist, urged him and Riskin to "forget that panty-waist painter. Make him a guy we all know and like. Maybe a tough, crusading reporter—at outs with his pig-headed editor."[11] So it was in the film: Reporter Clark Gable is fired from his paper, meets runaway heiress Claudette Colbert on a bus, and tries to exploit her as a scoop to get his job back. The exploitation is mutual; she needs him to help her join her husband, an aviator whom her father loathes (his opposition to her still-unconsummated marriage has prompted her to run away). Exploitation gives way to mutual learning. The "spoiled brat" heiress is taught to live like common folk, and the cynical reporter is redeemed through love.

Thus, *It Happened One Night* added new ingredients to the *Front Page* formula: The reporter fell in love with the scoop he was pursuing; the story and love interest became one. The love interest was not the usual ingenue (the "sweet and satisfying heroine" of whom Hecht and MacArthur patronizingly wrote) but a stronger and more fully developed character. Particularly noteworthy was Colbert's proving herself Gable's equal in the hitchhiking scene in which the heiress stops a car after the reporter fails to do so. Although she resorts to stereotypical "feminine wiles" by hiking up her skirt, she *wins,* showing the wise-aleck reporter he is not nearly as smart as he thinks he is. The movie thus contained a subtle critique not only of the spoiled, idle rich but also of the outlaw, *Front Page*–like reporter. However, Capra and Riskin did not use *It Happened One Night* to question more directly the press's methods or explore the contrast between the frenzied city newsroom and the idyllic countryside where the reporter and heiress fell in love; that would come later. For the moment, social criticism was subordinated to laughter and romance.

The same formula appeared in *Libeled Lady* (1936) and *Nothing Sacred* (1937). In the first film, hardboiled editor Spencer Tracy is torn between his paper and the fiancée he desperately tries to avoid marrying. Superficially the fiancée is another version of Peggy, but as played by Jean Harlow she is far more funny and formidable. ("The things I do for that *newspaper!*" she fumes as Tracy corrals her into one outlandish scheme after another.) Myrna Loy plays an heiress who has filed a libel suit against Tracy's paper and spars with cynical journalist William Powell. Powell tries to blackmail her into dropping her suit, but he falls for her instead and naturally is much the better for it. *Nothing Sacred* features yet another cynical reporter (Fredric March) trying to get back into the good graces of his tyrannical editor by exploiting the story of Hazel Flagg, a young woman supposedly dying of radium poisoning. It turns out she is using him every bit as much as he is her (she is in perfect health and only wants a free trip to New York), but Carole Lombard makes her utterly charming, and "Wally," the reporter, is soon smitten. Everyone cashes in on Hazel's apparent ill fortune, and even after they learn the truth, they beg her to keep playing the doomed heroine so that they may continue to benefit. Eventually Hazel fakes her demise and steals away with Wally on a boat to the tropics.

Nothing Sacred exemplifies the subversive derisiveness that Pauline Kael said characterized screwball comedy. Ben Hecht's screenplay begins with a set of titles superimposed on the Manhattan cityscape: "THIS IS NEW YORK/Skyscraper Champion of the World . . . where the Slickers and Know-It-Alls peddle gold bricks to each other . . . and where Truth, crushed to earth, rises again more phony than a glass eye." If the big city is portrayed much as it was in *The Front Page,* populated by corrupt and sanctimonious scoundrels, Hazel's small hometown comes off no better. No one will talk to Wally unless he pays them, and a small child darts from behind a white picket fence and bites him on the leg.

As for the film's treatment of the press, Hazel's doctor greets Wally as follows: "I think you're a newspaperman. I can *smell* 'em. Excuse me while I open the window." Still, the press is no more satirized than anything else in the aptly titled *Nothing Sacred.* Rather than condemning the city slickers and know-it-alls of whom the tabloid reporter is an exemplar, it celebrates them; the picture is an ironic tribute to phoniness. There is no semblance of official virtue. The movie is an extension of the outlaw ethos of *The Front Page,* implying that cynicism does not necessarily have to be cured and that one can get away with double-crosses and fakery. At the same time, it remains at heart a romantic comedy like *Libeled Lady* and *It Happened One Night,* albeit one in which the protagonists express mutual devotion through deceit and fisticuffs (much to the dismay of the PCA, which nevertheless finally approved the film).[12] Even then, there is parity: After Wally delivers a roundhouse to Hazel's chin, she retaliates with one of her own and then blows lightly on him to make him topple.

SCREWBALL AND WOMEN JOURNALISTS

The apotheosis of the screwball newspaper comedy was *His Girl Friday,* the 1940 *Front Page* remake that made Hildy a woman. By then, women journalists already had become prominent on screen. In *The Mystery of the Wax Museum* (1933), Glenda Farrell was a wisecracking reporter who ended the film in a clinch with her editor; she then played much the same character in Warner's "Torchy Blane" serial.[13] *There Goes My Girl* (1937) copied *The Front Page*'s plot of a fanatical editor trying to stop his star reporter from marrying, but with a female reporter (Ann Sothern) and a male love interest (Gene Raymond). Raymond seemed the one who really wanted to get married—indeed, he was almost a Peggy type—whereas Sothern seemed more interested in chasing the story at any cost, including a gunshot wound. Joan Blondell in *Back in Circulation* (1937) was even more formidable playing opposite Pat O'Brien as her boss and love interest. Whereas O'Brien reproduced the Walter Burns stereotype of the ogreish editor, Blondell created a livelier character combining glamour (the star reporter has a live-in maid and expensive wardrobe) with news savvy (she punctuates her frequent scoops with shouts of "Hotdiggity!").

Back in Circulation was based on a story by Adela Rogers St. Johns, who worked for Hearst newspapers and served as a model for female journalist characters in movies.[14] She was billed as "The World's Greatest Girl Reporter" despite being in her forties, and like many others she branched into fiction and movie writing. However, she paid a price that included alcoholism and two failed marriages. Many years later she wrote that she had often viewed "Modern Woman" as a failure who had "spread herself too goddam thin," adding that she herself had found it almost impossible to drive the "three mules" of career, marriage, and children all at once.[15]

Her travails were not unique. Other women reporters of the era found it difficult to balance home and work, assuming they were able to make any headway in their careers at all. Newspapers laid off many women during the Depression, and those who remained on the job lagged far behind men in salary and quality of assignments. Their lives were well removed from those of the glamorous heroines of screwball romances.[16]

His Girl Friday hinted at the price women journalists paid by making its female protagonist face the same dilemma the male Hildy had faced: continuing a newspaper career or forsaking it for marriage and family. But the film's creators made comic fodder of that dilemma by making the domestic alternative utterly ridiculous.

Although scholars and critics almost universally call *His Girl Friday* a classic, they disagree over who deserves the most credit. Many say it is consistent with the other films of director Howard Hawks, who was noted for creating strong female characters and who claimed it was his idea to turn Hildy into a woman. Others note that screenwriter Charles Lederer developed the key plot device of making Hildy Walter's ex-wife. It was not an original notion to pit a female reporter against a male editor; *The Mystery of the Wax Museum, There Goes My Girl,* and *Back in Circulation* already had done the same. *Wedding Present* (1936) was another such film, and it had starred Cary Grant, who played Walter in *His Girl Friday.* Perhaps even more influential was *The Awful Truth* (1937), another screwball classic in which Grant tried to win back his ex-wife, Irene Dunne, from her dim beau, played by Ralph Bellamy.[17]

Regardless, no film yet had featured a newswoman quite like Hildy as embodied by Rosalind Russell. It begins with her returning to the newsroom after a long vacation, dressed in a snappy striped suit (Adela Rogers St. Johns was known for such outfits). She strides past her colleagues, trading good-natured greetings and jibes with them. In tow is her fiancé, insurance man Bruce Baldwin (Ralph Bellamy again). Hildy has come to tell Walter that she is quitting the paper, marrying Bruce, and moving with him and his mother to Albany. She divorced Walter after he constantly put the paper before her. "I intended to be with you on our honeymoon, Hildy, honest I did," he says. He wants her to cover the Earl Williams hanging for him. "Scram, Svengali," she retorts. Walter persists: "You're a newspaperman!" "That's why I'm quitting," she replies. "I want to go someplace where I can be a woman."

However, Walter will not give up. He takes Hildy and Bruce to lunch, where Bruce is no match for the journalists who sit together blowing clouds of cigarette smoke in his face. Bruce is not exactly dumb; he is simply too slow in word, thought, and deed to keep up. It is as though the filmmakers have seized on Peggy's blandness and ingenuousness in the original play and amplified it a hundredfold (especially in casting Bellamy, whose presence would have indicated to audiences of the day what sort of character he was). He is a parody of safe, comfortable, official niceties, a man devoted to his mother and surrounded by insurance policies, who takes both an umbrella and galoshes at the slightest chance of rain. Walter calls him a "paragon" and does not mean it as a compliment; paragons are meant to be derided and abused by streetwise types such as Walter. As editors always seem to do in films of this era, he has on call assorted thugs and floozies whom he deploys against Bruce. Hildy will not be able to leave with her fiancé even if she wants to do so.

Over lunch, however, she is still determined to do just that, and she agrees to interview Earl Williams in exchange for Walter buying a $100,000 insurance policy from Bruce. The idea is to show that Earl is insane, stop his execution, and score a scoop. The warden forbids the interview at first. However, Hildy drops a twenty-dollar bill on the floor, picks it up to show to the warden ("is this your money?"), and soon is talking to Earl. "My name's Johnson," she says, lighting a cigarette for him and apologizing for the lipstick. In short order, Hildy persuades the befuddled Earl that he shot the policeman because of the phrase "production for use" ringing in his brain: Guns are produced to be used, after all. "It's simple, isn't it?" he asks her. "*Very* simple," she says quietly.

If the movie shows Hildy as less than a model of journalistic virtue, it also shows her as a master tabloid reporter; apart from his romantic designs on her, Walter knows what he is doing when he persuades her to do the interview. In *The Front Page,* Hildy's big scoop literally tumbled through the window behind him. In *His Girl Friday,* Hildy gets and writes the story with eloquent dispatch, a task none of the rival male reporters could have accomplished—and they know it. After Hildy writes her story in the pressroom, the men gather around to sneak a peek. One emits a low whistle of admiration, and another asks, "Can that girl write an interview?"

Hildy is also easily the movie's most humane presence. She demonstrates the characteristic outlaw code of honor—sticking up for the dispossessed—while giving it a distinctly feminine twist. When the male reporters abuse Mollie Malloy, Hildy comforts and escorts her from the room. "They ain't human!" Mollie cries. "I know," says Hildy. "They're newspapermen." After the two women leave, there is a long, embarrassed silence before Hildy returns alone. She stares for a moment at the men and issues a quiet reproach: "Gentlemen of the press." She then furiously tears up her Earl Williams story after she discovers that Walter has double-crossed her by setting up her fiancé to be arrested. "I'm gonna be a woman, not a news-getting machine," she tells her colleagues. "I'm gonna have babies and take care of them and give them cod liver oil and watch their teeth grow—and oh dear, if I ever see one of them look at a newspaper again, I'm gonna *brain* them!" Just then, Earl Williams escapes, and immediately Hildy is chasing down and tackling a sheriff's deputy to get yet another exclusive.

The ending of *His Girl Friday* has proved controversial in some quarters. After Earl's escape, the film closely follows *The Front Page*'s plot up to the journalists' triumph over the crooked mayor and sheriff. Walter then sends Hildy after Bruce, saying Bruce can give her the kind of life he never could. As Hildy is very reluctantly about to leave, the phone rings: Bruce is in jail again, thanks to Walter. Hildy begins to cry: "I thought you were really sending me away!" "What do you think I was, a chump?" Walter replies. They will remarry and take a real honeymoon. But then the newspaper sends them to Albany to cover a strike. "I wonder if Bruce can put us up?" chortles Walter as he strides out of the room, with Hildy running behind him with the suitcases.

One critic has written that "the only morally acceptable ending would be

Hildy (Rosalind Russell) is greeted by her press room colleagues in *His Girl Friday.*
(Courtesy of the Academy of Motion Picture Arts and Sciences)

to have Hildy walk out on *both* men, or to present her capitulation to Walter as tragic."[18] Cary Grant's magnetic charm helps disguise that Walter, in contrast to Bruce, is not a particularly nice fellow. As Hildy herself says, "Walter, you're wonderful, in a loathsome sort of way."

Largely because of that wonderful loathsomeness, *His Girl Friday* retains its satirical edge even though it had been softened from the original play and film. Among other things, the PCA objected to repeated references to journalists as "scum."[19] The film was released with an opening title card declaring that "It all happened in the 'Dark Ages' of the newspaper game" and adding that "you will see in this picture no resemblance to the men and women of the press of today." Still, the film contains contemporary references to LaGuardia, Hitler, and the Polish Corridor. And Walter is just as gleefully unscrupulous as in the original, showing nary a hint of conscience or remorse. Why should he? In *His Girl Friday,* journalism is a wonderful game that is won by playing dirty, and in David Thomson's words, the movie "remains the fiercest proof that if the fun or the game ever stops then we'll die like rats in poisonous boredom."[20]

It is also a screwball movie, though, and that means the fun includes romance. Like other cynical journalists in these movies, Walter is redeemed, at least a little, by his love for his ex-wife and star reporter. Hildy is tough but vulnerable and a little klutzy, and her tears at the end seem not out of place; she is capable of weeping for joy as opposed to hysteria or fear.

A similar denouement occurs in *Woman of the Year* (1942), the first pairing of Katharine Hepburn and Spencer Tracy. He plays down-to-earth sportswriter Sam Craig; she plays celebrated political journalist Tess Harding. The milieu is more earnest than that of *His Girl Friday,* drawing inspiration not from Hearst-style tabloid reporting but the serious journalism of the *New York Herald-Tribune* and its columnist Dorothy Thompson. Thompson was renowned for her incisive commentary on world affairs, but her romantic life was even more tumultuous than Adela Rogers St. Johns's; she took both men and women as lovers and endured an unhappy marriage to an alcoholic Sinclair Lewis.[21]

Nothing like that makes it into *Woman of the Year,* but the marriage between the two principals is still rocky. This time it is the woman, Tess, who puts her career ahead of her husband, Sam, and matters worsen when she takes in a war orphan without Sam's knowledge and then ignores the child. After Sam leaves her, she tries to win him back by proving herself a good wife, but her attempts to fix him breakfast wreck the kitchen. "I don't want to be married to Tess Harding any more than I want you to be just Mrs. Sam Craig," the exasperated Sam tells her. "Why can't you be Tess Harding Craig?" "I think it's a wonderful name," she replies tearfully as they embrace.

As with Hildy crying in *His Girl Friday, Woman of the Year*'s ending has had its critics.[22] The first script drafts concluded with Sam telling Tess that "being your husband is the most important thing in my life" and "being married to you will make me a better writer." After numerous rewrites, the movie's original close was shelved, and the new one with Tess's apparent humiliation in the kitchen was filmed.[23]

However, it hardly matters that Tess cannot operate a toaster. Throughout most of the film, she is a model of witty sophistication and conscientious reportage, anticipating the more "official" and respectable depiction of journalism that emerged in postwar movies. Not for Tess are the antics of *His Girl Friday;* when she accompanies Sam to the baseball game, she asks why the newspaper has sent two reporters to cover the event when it has only one in Vichy.

In the end, Sam has to set Tess's priorities straight, just as Walter set Hildy's straight. The result is the same, though: The woman retains her independence and vitality by remaining in the professional world. Thus, Tess, like Hildy, is a quintessentially American romantic heroine. "Her talk was sexy and smart and high-spirited," Maria DiBattista writes of such characters, "yet the pugnacity and energy of her speech made her an exemplary rather than anomalous figure for democratic culture. She was at home in reality and spoke its language, a vivid vernacular."[24] And that finally is what makes Hildy and Tess ideal matches for Walter and Sam, for the men (who of course are also journalists) speak the same language. Hildy's stated desire to leave journalism to "go someplace where I can be a woman" is as misguided as Tess's attempt at being a domestic servant; they are most fully themselves when they are working along with their partners in the newsroom.

In such ways, screwball comedies present a mythic view of romantic and democratic possibilities. True to myth, they smooth away social rifts and contradictions. The wrenching economic misery of the Depression is glossed over in stories of common reporters meeting and marrying heiresses.[25] The harsh realities that most female journalists of the time faced are largely ignored in tales of women simultaneously finding true love and professional fulfillment.

Whatever their ideological functions, the movies still bracingly provide what one critic has called "deliverance from cant": the bland homilies to which the world's Bruces and their mothers subscribe.[26] They also provide a tantalizing glimpse of gender equality. *His Girl Friday* has been praised for showing a "new kind of marriage, one of mutuality, one in which the turn-on is work, one in which male and female do not occupy separate spheres but lose themselves (and their romantic self-consciousness) in a unifying, energizing, and eternally engaging profession."[27] Thus the movies make women—and journalists— models for what American life could and should be.

PRESS CRITIQUES AND CAPRA'S SOCIAL PROBLEM FILMS

Such cheery takes on love and journalism were not the only ones to come out of Hollywood, however. From start of the sound era, the movies also presented a harsher portrait of the press. In *Scandal Sheet* (1931), a hardboiled editor goes to prison for murdering his wife's lover. In *Scandal for Sale* (1932), another hardboiled editor becomes so involved in boosting his tabloid's circulation that his wife leaves him and his son dies of neglect. In *Merrily, We Go to Hell* (1932), an alcoholic journalist and playwright manages to get his show produced but takes up with the show's star while his wife gets pregnant with another man.

Toughest of all was Warner's *Five Star Final* (1931), which directly attacked the tabloid ethos that other Warner Brothers films celebrated. The movie was based on a Broadway play by Louis Weitzenkorn, a one-time managing editor of the *New York Graphic* that wags dubbed the PORNO-graphic. Along with his unhappy experiences at the tabloid, Weitzenkorn appeared to draw on the

Edward G. Robinson as the conscience-haunted tabloid editor in *Five Star Final*. (Courtesy of the Academy of Motion Picture Arts and Sciences)

Hall-Mills double murder case that had been a media sensation in the 1920s. Hearst's *New York Mirror* claimed to have uncovered new evidence several years after the murders, leading to a trial that ended with the acquittal of the woman the *Mirror* had fingered as the killer. Another inspiration for Weitzenkorn's play may have been New York tabloid editor Emile Gauvreau. He had written the novel on which *Scandal for Sale* was based and was a learned but troubled man who never fully reconciled himself to the tabloid world.[28]

Five Star Final centers around an editor named Randall (Edward G. Robinson). His publisher, Hinchecliffe, and his sales managers are alarmed over a circulation decrease. At their urging, Randall dredges up an old scandal concerning Nancy Voorhess, who had killed her boss after he made her pregnant and refused to marry her. Now, twenty years later, Nancy is married and living in perfect bliss; her daughter is about to wed. Then the tabloid begins publishing its series about her past. In short order, Nancy and her husband take poison, and the daughter bursts into the newspaper office seeking revenge with a gun. After the daughter's fiancé disarms her, Randall—who has been increasingly plagued with guilt—quits the paper with a memorable speech. "I've had ten years of filth and blood," he snarls into the phone. "Take your love nest killings to Hinchecliffe with my compliments! And tell him to *shove it up his. . . .*" With that, he hurls the phone through the plate glass window of the publisher's door. If anyone still misses the point, the film ends with a tabloid front page being splattered with mud and swept into the gutter.

Such movies, even more so than *The Front Page,* alarmed real-life journalists. The Hearst papers vigorously campaigned against *Five Star Final* (probably because it struck too close to home), and others worried that film audiences would not be able to distinguish between tabloids and more responsible newspapers.[29] However, Louis Weitzenkorn took pains to separate the outlaw-style journalism that his play indicted from the respectable press for which he used to work. He dedicated the play to his former boss at the *New York World,* Herbert Bayard Swope: "The ethics of journalism learned from him made the author of FIVE STAR FINAL a failure as a tabloid editor." In return, Swope wrote that Weitzenkorn's cynical exterior hid "a pitying sympathy, an understanding and kindliness, quick to respond to those who struggle, to those who suffer, to the underdog."[30]

It was to much the same subjects—the suffering underdog struggling against the powerful, the cynical journalist finally revealing "understanding and kindliness"—that Frank Capra was about to turn. Alongside *Platinum Blonde*'s and *It Happened One Night*'s comparatively benign depictions of the press, Capra directed *Forbidden* (1932), which ended with an advice columnist pumping her editor husband full of bullets. That movie was inspired less by *The Front Page* than "weepers" such as *Back Street,* focusing on the illicit romance between a long-suffering woman and a married man. (The director later dismissed it as "two hours of soggy, 99.44% pure soap opera.")[31]

However, not long after *It Happened One Night* swept the Oscars, Capra fell seriously ill. He later claimed that a "faceless little man" visited him at the time and told him he was "an offense to God" for making films that sought merely to entertain. Capra said he was convinced: "Beginning with *Mr. Deeds Goes to Town,* my films had to *say* something."[32] Although the "little man" story has been debunked, unquestionably 1936's *Deeds* marked a shift toward more serious themes in the director's work, thanks partly to his continuing collaboration with screenwriter Robert Riskin.[33]

The title character (Gary Cooper) is a small-town businessman, tuba player, and writer of homely verse. He inherits $20 million from a late uncle and heads to New York to administer the estate. Reporter Babe Bennett (Jean Arthur) poses as an unemployed woman who befriends Deeds while writing stories that mock him. The stories wound Deeds, but he does not know Babe has written them, and he falls for her. The conscience-stricken Babe loves him in return and vows to reveal all. Before she can, Deeds learns the truth and prepares in disillusionment to return to his small town. An encounter with a destitute farmer inspires him to give away most of his fortune. Lawyers representing other relatives of the late uncle conspire to have Deeds declared legally insane. At a hearing, Deeds hears Babe declare her remorse and love for him. He easily refutes the insanity charges against him and embraces Babe.

Babe starts off very much like Hildy in *His Girl Friday:* cool and calm in her work and better at it than her male colleagues; she even has won a Pulitzer Prize. She is first seen abstractedly playing with a string while her Walter Burns–like editor berates the staff for not finding news on Deeds. (The men stalk out grumbling, and when the editor demands to know what one said, the man points to the ceiling: "You have *dirty plaster!*") The editor finally gets Babe's attention by promising her a month's paid vacation if she gets a story about Deeds. She tells him to leave four columns open on the next day's front page.

When Deeds emerges from his mansion that night, Babe and a carload of photographers are waiting. "I suppose it'll be the same old thing," one photographer says. Evidently Babe habitually poses as an unemployed woman to get stories, almost parodying what Adela Rogers St. Johns had done in a well-publicized series on such women's plight.[34] She paints Deeds as a rube without him knowing she is responsible. "What puzzles me is why people get so much pleasure out of hurting each other," he tells her. "Why don't they try *liking* each other once in a while?" Meanwhile, Babe expresses her qualms regarding Deeds to her roommate. "He's got goodness, Mabel. Do you know what that means? No, of course you don't. We've forgotten. We're too busy being smart alecks."

The world of big-city newspapers in *Deeds* is much the same as in *Nothing Sacred* and *His Girl Friday,* with the smart-aleck journalists butting up against shady lawyers and pompous fools while peddling hyped-up stories to a gullible public. The movie's basic plot is also familiar: *It Happened One Night* with a gender switch, a female reporter exploiting and then falling for a male millionaire. But much has changed. The pompous fools are New York literati who make fun of Deeds's poetry. The real-life literati who did so much to shape the Broadway and Hollywood comedy of the era would have taken special pleasure in ridiculing the likes of Deeds, but here their surrogates get socked in the jaw. The pleasure that the cynical journalists get from exposing pretense and inanity is explicitly condemned. They hurt people. Although they do the same in *His Girl Friday,* Mollie is a comparatively minor character; in *Deeds,* the wounded party is the protagonist. The indictment of the press and its tactics is not so far removed from that of *Five Star Final.*

However, this is a Frank Capra film, meaning it ends in celebration instead of death. Deeds wins them over—not just Babe but also her editor and a sour-puss press agent named Cobb. Their faith in goodness, a quality foreign to pictures such as *Nothing Sacred,* is restored. As for Babe, her fate is significantly different from that of Hildy and Tess. Deeds was immediately attracted to her because she seemed a "damsel in distress." Although she thought she was only posing as an impoverished woman, the movie shows her as being spiritually impoverished, and it lays much of the blame on her ties to journalism and the big city. Deeds rescues her from it all. The result is that Babe forfeits work and her screwball, outlaw mentality for romance and an idealized small-town America that again is well removed from that in *Nothing Sacred* (in which children bite strangers).[35]

Jean Arthur acted much the same role in Capra's *Mr. Smith Goes to Washington* (1939), written by Sidney Buchman. She plays Saunders, a cynical aide to newly appointed Senator Jefferson Smith (James Stewart). Smith idolizes his fellow senator Joseph Paine (Claude Rains), but he gradually learns that Paine is beholden to Jim Taylor (Edward Arnold), a political boss who is push-ing through a dam project to net a fortune in graft. When Smith tries to ex-pose the plan, the Taylor machine frames him to make it seem as though he is the one guilty of graft. In a last-ditch effort to get out the truth, Smith stages a filibuster in the Senate with coaching from Saunders, who has fallen in love with him and quit her job. The Taylor machine suppresses news of what he says and stirs up public opinion against him. Finally Smith collapses in exhaus-tion, but Paine breaks and reveals all.

The film's most prominent reporter character is Diz (Thomas Mitchell), who spends most of his time dozing, flirting with Saunders, and tippling. Still he and his colleagues play a critical role in wising up Smith. Much as in *Mr. Deeds Goes to Town,* they have written stories making fun of the hero. The enraged Smith slugs some of them and chases another into the National Press Club, where the reporters restrain him. "If you thought as much about being honest as you do about being smart . . ." snarls Smith. "Honest?" retorts Diz. "Why, we're the only ones who can *afford* to be honest in what we tell the vot-ers! We don't have to be reelected like *politicians!*" The other reporters laugh and pat Diz on the back, and another chimes in, "For instance, we tell them when phonies or crackpots come here to make their laws!" "You're not a sen-ator," Diz sneers. "You're an honorary stooge!" A chastened Smith, realizing they are right, asks Paine for a more active role in the Senate, and the result—much to Paine's chagrin—is Smith discovering the fraudulent dam project.

To a degree, the reporters are screwball types who know the score and de-ride those who do not. However, Diz is a pitiable character, too fond of Saun-ders (who rebuffs him) and of the bottle. The drunken journalist was a famil-iar enough movie type;[36] Clark Gable's reporter was intoxicated when he first appeared in *It Happened One Night*. As a screwball hero, though, Gable's character found redemption through romance, whereas Diz seems unlikely to enjoy such luck.

Furthermore, once the reporters have alerted Smith to his "honorary stooge" status, they cease being of much help. On the contrary, as the Taylor machine produces a damning pile of "evidence" purportedly showing that Smith has committed graft, Diz mutters to a fellow journalist, "Beautiful, that Taylor machine!" They know full well what is happening but write down every phony word, Diz's claims to honesty forgotten. In this movie, phoniness is nothing to celebrate.

Just as in *Deeds,* the reporters finally convert to the hero's cause, but when they try to report the truth about him, Taylor's use of money and intimidation squelches stories about Smith in his home state. Saunders hears of the "Taylor-made" public opinion and snorts, "Freedom of the press!" Then she has an inspiration: Smith has a little newspaper for his "Boy Rangers" back home. In a dramatic montage, children use a hand-operated press to print a banner headline ("JEFF TELLS TRUTH!"), while motorized presses in full menacing roar print their own headline ("SMITH LIES, SAYS SENATE"). When the children start distributing their paper, thugs beat them up and run them off the road. Attempted political coercion of the press had been featured in *The Front Page* but was played for laughs. In *Mr. Smith,* it seems to render press freedom moot.

At the time he wrote the movie, Sidney Buchman belonged to the Communist party. The press's depiction as a tool of concentrated political and economic forces is consistent with a Marxist viewpoint or at least an antifascist one; Buchman later said he saw Communism as the best vehicle to fight fascism. In contrast, Capra was a conservative Republican (as was Myles Connolly, who had an uncredited assist with the script). Yet the director also criticized the press. He attended a Washington news conference while doing research for *Smith* and afterward said the reporters were a "terrible" bunch of "yes men" who relied on government handouts.[37]

Thus it is not surprising that many professional journalism organizations objected to *Mr. Smith Goes to Washington,* claiming among other things that one man could not control the news of an entire state.[38] More damning in the film is that characters such as Diz are no longer at the center of the story. Nobody scores a big scoop; nobody nails a bad guy. There are "broken-down opposition papers" as Taylor calls them, but he easily muzzles them. H. V. Kaltenborn, a well-known radio commentator of the day, does a cameo. But although he provides a dramatic blow-by-blow of Smith's filibuster ("those tired Boy Ranger legs are buckling!"), he never relates any details of Smith's charges against Paine and Taylor. When Smith emerges victorious, there is no guarantee that the details ever will be published in his home state given that Taylor is still in power.

However, just as the movie finally is optimistic toward the Senate—Smith *does* win, Paine *does* break, Taylor (it is suggested) *will* topple—the film also implicitly is optimistic toward the press, for a journalistic voice of conscience helps make the happy ending possible. It belongs to Smith's late father, a small-town newspaper editor who inspired his son to start the "Boy Rangers" newspaper. Absent small-town patriarchs are Capra fixtures; in *Mr. Deeds Goes to Town,* Babe tells Deeds how much he reminds her of her father. Such characters can be seen as another representation of the director's fond nostalgia for a more simple and virtuous life outside the big city. (Small-town editors were recurring characters in early journalism fiction, allowing readers to "escape the mounting problems of the present and vicariously satisfy their nostalgia for a vanished golden world."[39]) The characters also can be seen as male equivalents of what has been called the "Good Mother" myth: "the ordinary individual" who "offers people a model of goodness in times when goodness may seem in short supply" and proves that "individuals *can* make a difference."[40]

In Smith's father's case, he was a crusading journalist beholden to and afraid of no one, always ready to fight for seemingly lost causes in the face of entrenched power. He stood for official virtues—truth and justice and reform—but did so by bucking an official system that had grown incorrigibly corrupt. Paine had been his closest friend and shared the same ideals. Then Smith's father was fatally shot in the back while defending a single miner against a syndicate, and Paine started down the ruinous road to sell-out and vice. Just before Smith collapses in the film's climax, he invokes his father's memory to shame Paine. He reminds his fellow senator that Paine himself had once fought for lost causes "for the only reason that any man ever fights for them, because of just one plain simple rule: 'Love Thy Neighbor.' . . . And you know that you fight for the lost causes harder than for any others. Yes, you even die for them—like a man we both knew, Mr. Paine."

That speech finally extracts the truth from Paine and transforms the Senate into happy bedlam. It also underscores Capra's defense of *Mr. Smith Goes to Washington* against its critics: He said its purpose "was to idealize American democracy, not to attack it."[41] Both Smith and his late father represent democratic ideals. Smith is the model for what a public servant should be even as his colleagues appear hopelessly crooked; his father is the model for what a good neighbor and journalist should be even as the press appears hopelessly compromised.

If possible, the prospects for the press seem even more grim in Capra's *Meet John Doe* (1941). Robert Riskin returned as screenwriter and wrote of a newspaper that foists a fake upon the public: "John Doe," a man who says he will protest social conditions by committing suicide on Christmas Eve. The paper employs ex–baseball pitcher John Willoughby (Gary Cooper) to play Doe and columnist Ann Mitchell (Barbara Stanwyck) to write speeches for him. Soon the John Doe movement sweeps the country, promoting neighborliness and self-sufficiency. But the paper's publisher, D. B. Norton (Edward Arnold again), plans to exploit the movement to impose a totalitarian order. When John discovers this, he tries to reveal the truth, only to be crushed by Norton. John then attempts to commit suicide for real, but Ann loves John and rises from her sickbed to stop him. They set off with a handful of others to start the Doe movement anew.

Few journalism movies start so powerfully—or unsubtly—as *Meet John Doe.* A building plaque is seen: "The BULLETIN/'A free press means a free people.'" In close-up, a pneumatic chisel blasts the words "free press" into dust. A new plaque is installed: "THE NEW BULLETIN/A STREAMLINED NEWSPAPER FOR A STREAMLINED ERA." Norton has bought the paper, and the "streamlining" is in full swing in the newsroom. One by one, longtime employees get the axe as an office boy whistles at each and draws his finger across his throat. Among the victims is Ann. When she begs the new editor, Connell (James Gleason), for her job, he replies that her column is "lavender and old lace" and that he wants "fireworks" instead. Ann obliges him with one more column, purportedly about the aggrieved John Doe. It creates a sensation, but because Doe does not actually exist, the paper stands to be embarrassed. Ann shrewdly blackmails Connell into rehiring her and continuing the Doe hoax to boost circulation. She handpicks Willoughby for the role: "That face is wonderful. They'll believe *him!*"

On the surface, Ann and Connell are classic screwball sharpies: the cynical reporter and editor, unconcerned with the truth but very much concerned with circulation and money (Norton keeps Ann in line with expensive gifts). Underneath their tough, outlaw exteriors is desperation and grief: Ann is sole supporter of her family and apparently will do anything to stay employed; Connell saw his father killed on the battlefield in the Great War. The editor plays the same role that Diz and the other reporters did in *Mr. Smith,* wising up the hero to the scheme against him. Instead of doing it with wisecracks, though, Connell does it in a haze of alcohol while expressing heartfelt devotion to Washington, Lincoln, and the national anthem.

As for Ann, she seems smarter than most of the men in the film, just as Hildy and Babe did. The John Doe scheme is her idea, and Barbara Stanwyck is well suited to portray her cunning. But once Doe becomes more than a circulation stunt, Ann feeds him not her own words but those of her late father. (Thus, once more—and as also is true of Connell—an absent, beloved patriarch plays a significant role.) Her falling in love with John smacks of incestuousness. And

"They'll believe *him!*" Ann (Barbara Stanwyck) grooms John (Gary Cooper) for the press in *Meet John Doe*. (Courtesy of the Academy of Motion Picture Arts and Sciences)

although she saves him from suicide and helps persuade him to revive the Doe movement, she can do so only after she leaves her job, and then only in a fit of delirium that ends with her collapsing at John's feet.

The contradictions in the characters extend to the film as a whole. Capra and Riskin had a famously difficult time ending *Meet John Doe*. They tried a number of climaxes, including one in which John actually committed suicide and another in which Norton converted to the Doe cause. Capra called the ending they eventually settled on "the best of a sorry lot" and added: "What our film said to bewildered people hungry for solutions was this, 'No answers this time, ladies and gentlemen. It's back to the drawing board.'"[42]

One thing that clearly emerges is that the press as represented by the *New Bulletin* is the last institution to rely on for solutions or answers. Its sins go beyond even those in *Deeds* and *Smith*. Here it commits deliberate fakery to promote fascism. When John tries to tell a political rally the truth about Norton, Norton interrupts by calling Doe a fake (which on the surface he is, of course), and the publisher's henchmen saturate the crowd with newspapers doing the same. It is the first time the papers have been truthful concerning

Doe—or at least accurate—and they have done it for a despicable cause. The crowd turns on Doe and pelts him with the wadded-up, rain-soaked papers. Just as *Mr. Smith Goes to Washington* could not obliterate the specter of a *truly* lost cause—the fear that a free press and free people just might be beyond salvation—*Meet John Doe* cannot obliterate the specter of a nation permanently subjugated by propaganda and mob rule.

Still, the movie does its best to do just that. Again consistent with myth, and contrary to Capra's own claims, *Meet John Doe*'s climax smooths away the contradictions the film's plot and characters have raised. It asserts that individuals can resist institutional abuses, that idealism can redeem cynicism, that truth can defeat falsehood. Once more it is journalists who help bring about the happy ending—or, more accurately, ex-journalists, because Ann is unemployed and it seems probable that Connell is as well. With reawakened consciences, Ann beseeches John "not to give up, but to keep on fighting," and Connell joins in reorganizing the Doe movement while delivering the movie's final line: "There you are, Norton! The people! Try and lick *that!*"

Capra's *Deeds-Smith-Doe* trilogy has been criticized for being politically naive at best and dangerous at worst,[43] but the movies raise provocative questions regarding the nature of mass-mediated truth. *Meet John Doe*'s political rally is only one example. Although Babe's newspaper stories about Deeds were accurate in depicting him as an eccentric bumpkin, they omitted any mention of his true wisdom and goodness. The tales of Smith being a stooge were factually correct, but cynical journalistic convention and naked political pressure prevented the greater truth from being reported.

Truth also was problematic in screwball comedies, but no great social ill came from the lies and posturing that took place. Certainly there was no concern with "answers" or "solutions"; that implied reform, and those such as Ben Hecht held reformers in contempt. Screwball journalists took the world as they found it and made no pretense of trying to perfect it.

The journalists in Capra's films have no hope of improving things either, at least not working for the press as it currently exists. Indeed, they may inhibit change by being part of an oppressive institutional machinery that deliberately confuses appearance with reality in misinforming the all-too-susceptible masses. Their outlaw stances and the officially sanctioned "truth" they manufacture lead to nothing but lies and disillusionment.

So the journalists, particularly the female ones, must forsake their identities as professional smart-alecks. The reporter-source relationship so prone to exploitation must give way to helping others speak truly and honestly for themselves, as Deeds, Smith, and Doe finally are able to do.[44] When at last that happens, the contemporary failings of America and its journalism cease to matter much. What matters is that its time-honored ideals have been reaffirmed and its cause reinvigorated, with due thanks to journalists both past and present.

Film historian Jeanine Basinger notes that when people are asked to define a Western, they recite a list of things such as good guys in white hats, gold-hearted saloon women, and big, climactic shootouts. "A simple test for any genre is whether or not you can, in fact, generate such a list," she writes. "If you can, it's a genre. If you can't, it probably isn't."[45]

Such a list can be generated for journalism movies: aggressive, wisecracking reporters; tough, bellowing editors; fabulous, press-stopping exclusives. The screwball era built on *The Front Page* in fixing that list in the public consciousness. The era's films also presented sophisticated portrayals of American culture and journalism.

Journalists in classic screwball comedies were romantic heroes; their cynicism resisted society's balderdash. The screwball heroine was "an icon of American individualism, bold and imaginative in her pursuit of happiness."[46] Frank Capra's films similarly celebrated the individual, but in opposition to the existing mass media and their cynical, if not criminal, manipulation of public opinion. The women in those films were no less bold or imaginative, but they achieved happiness only when they renounced that cynicism that their lives in big-city journalism or government had engendered.

Latter-day critics have tended to view screwball more favorably than Capra. One laments Capra's propensity to force his female protagonists "to repent [their] freedom and wit" and to feed his audiences the same feel-good platitudes that the screwball pictures mocked.[47] Capra's movies often were steeped in nostalgia, much as *The Front Page* had been, and thus they could seem more sentimental and prone to wishful thinking than the screwball films were.

However, both screwball and Capra reproduced democratic myths and used journalists as their tools for doing so. Even in presenting a dire portrait of the contemporary press according to journalism's own professional standards, the movies typically portrayed journalists themselves in hopeful, upbeat ways.

There was one last flowering of the spirit of 1930s movie comedy in Orson Welles's cinematic debut. At the same time, the film pointed the way to a more sober depiction of the journalist in the decades to come.

NOTES

1. For overviews of screwball comedy, see Maria DiBattista, *Fast-Talking Dames* (New Haven, Conn.: Yale University Press, 2001); James Harvey, *Romantic Comedy* (New York: Knopf, 1987); Elizabeth Kendall, *The Runaway Bride* (New York: Knopf, 1990); Thomas Schatz, *Hollywood Genres* (New York: McGraw-Hill, 1981), pp. 150–85; Ed Sikov,

Screwball (New York: Crown, 1989); and Gerald Weales, *Canned Goods as Caviar* (Chicago: University of Chicago Press, 1985).

2. Sikov, *Screwball,* p. 158.

3. Harvey, *Romantic Comedy,* p. 669.

4. Nick Roddick, *A New Deal in Entertainment: Warner Brothers in the 1930s* (London: British Film Institute, 1983), pp. 73–98.

5. Harvey, *Romantic Comedy,* pp. 83–103.

6. Robert B. Ray, *A Certain Tendency of the Hollywood Cinema, 1930–1980* (Princeton, N.J.: Princeton University Press, 1985), pp. 60–61.

7. Ben Hecht and Charles MacArthur, *The Front Page* (New York: Covici-Friede, 1928), p. 78.

8. Thomas Doherty, *Pre-Code Hollywood* (New York: Columbia University Press, 1999), p. 361.

9. Pauline Kael, "Raising Kane," in *The Citizen Kane Book,* by Pauline Kael, Herman J. Mankiewicz, and Orson Welles (New York: Limelight, 1984), pp. 10, 19.

10. For a discussion of Capra's early journalism films, see Joe Saltzman, *Frank Capra and the Image of the Journalist in American Film* (Los Angeles: Image of the Journalist in Popular Culture, 2002).

11. Frank Capra, *The Name above the Title* (New York: Belvedere, 1982), p. 183.

12. Thomas Schatz, *The Genius of the System* (New York: Pantheon, 1988), pp. 196–97.

13. Howard Good, *Girl Reporter* (Lanham, Md.: Scarecrow, 1998).

14. Kael, "Raising Kane," p. 48. Another model was fellow Hearst reporter Dorothy Kilgallen, whose stunt journalism inspired the Torchy Blane film *Fly-Away Baby;* see Good, *Girl Reporter,* p. 51.

15. Adela Rogers St. Johns, *The Honeycomb* (Garden City, N.Y.: Doubleday, 1969), pp. 13–34, 304; Dennis McLellan, "Writer Adela Rogers St. Johns Dies at 94," *Los Angeles Times,* August 11, 1988, p. 3.

16. Good, *Girl Reporter,* pp. 48–50; Ishbel Ross, *Ladies of the Press* (New York: Harper and Brothers, 1936); Linda Steiner, "Stories of Quitting: Why Did Women Journalists Leave the Newsroom?" *American Journalism* 15:3 (1998): 89–116.

17. Manny Farber, "Howard Hawks," in *Focus on Howard Hawks,* ed. Joseph McBride (Englewood Cliffs, N.J.: Prentice Hall, 1972), pp. 28–34; Gerald Mast, *Howard Hawks, Storyteller* (New York: Oxford University Press, 1982), pp. 189–242; Todd McCarthy, *Howard Hawks* (New York: Grove, 1997), pp. 278–87; Jeffrey Brown Martin, *Ben Hecht: Hollywood Screenwriter* (Ann Arbor, Mich.: UMI Research Press, 1985), pp. 90–96; Kael, "Raising Kane," p. 48; DiBattista, *Fast-Talking Dames,* pp. 268–97.

18. Robin Wood, *Howard Hawks* (Garden City, N.Y.: Doubleday, 1968), p. 77.

19. McCarthy, *Howard Hawks,* p. 281; Stephen Vaughn and Bruce Evensen, "Democracy's Guardians: Hollywood's Portrait of Reporters, 1930–1945," *Journalism Quarterly* 68 (1991): 833–34.

20. David Thomson, *Beneath Mulholland* (New York: Vintage, 1998), p. 26.

21. Peter Kurth, *American Cassandra: The Life of Dorothy Thompson* (Boston: Little, Brown, 1990).

22. See for example Andrew Britton, *Katharine Hepburn: Star as Feminist* (New York: Continuum, 1995), p. 203; Barbara Leaming, *Katharine Hepburn* (New York: Crown, 1995), p. 395.

23. For information on the making of *Woman of the Year,* see Ring Lardner Jr., *I'd Hate Myself in the Morning* (New York: Thunder's Mouth Press/Nation Books, 2000), pp. 91–97. Script drafts of the film are in the George Stevens Collection, Margaret Herrick Library, Academy of Motion Picture Arts and Sciences (AMPAS), Beverly Hills, Calif.

24. DiBattista, *Fast-Talking Dames,* p. 37.

25. Schatz, *Hollywood Genres,* pp. 155–57. Along with the movies already discussed, *The Philadelphia Story* (1940) pairs Katharine Hepburn's wealthy young woman with James Stewart's tabloid journalist, although Hepburn finally rejects Stewart for her ex-husband, Cary Grant.

26. Harvey, *Romantic Comedy,* p. 443.

27. Molly Haskell, *Holding My Own in No Man's Land* (New York: Oxford University Press, 1997), pp. 115–16.

28. See Herbert Bayard Swope, "Preface," in *Five Star Final,* by Louis Weitzenkorn (New York: Samuel French, 1931), pp. vii–viii; Louis Pizzitola, *Hearst over Hollywood* (New York: Columbia University Press, 2002), pp. 270–76; Emile Gauvreau, *My Last Million Readers* (New York: Arno, 1974; originally published 1941); Samuel Fuller, "News That's Fit to Film," *American Film,* October, 1975, pp. 22–23; Neal Gabler, *Winchell* (New York: Vintage, 1995).

29. *Five Star Final* Production Code Administration (PCA) File, AMPAS; David Nasaw, *The Chief: The Life of William Randolph Hearst* (Boston: Houghton Mifflin, 2000), pp. 445–46; Pizzitola, *Hearst over Hollywood,* pp. 270–76; George F. Custen, *Twentieth Century's Fox: Darryl F. Zanuck and the Culture of Hollywood* (New York: Basic, 1997), pp. 147–48.

30. Weitzenkorn, *Five Star Final,* p. v; Swope, "Preface," p. viii.

31. Capra, *The Name above the Title,* p. 149.

32. Ibid., pp. 196, 205.

33. Joseph McBride, *Frank Capra: The Catastrophe of Success* (New York: Simon and Schuster, 1992), pp. 317–24.

34. St. Johns, *The Honeycomb,* pp. 239–64.

35. Harvey, *Romantic Comedy,* pp. 155–56.

36. See Howard Good, *The Drunken Journalist: The Biography of a Film Stereotype* (Lanham, Md.: Scarecrow, 2000); Saltzman, *Frank Capra and the Image of the Journalist in American Film,* pp. 28–30.

37. McBride, *Frank Capra,* pp. 411–15, 418.

38. Ibid., pp. 418–22; Saltzman, *Frank Capra and the Image of the Journalist in American Film,* pp. 27–28; *His Girl Friday* PCA File, AMPAS.

39. Howard Good, *Acquainted with the Night* (Metuchen, N.J.: Scarecrow, 1986), p. 76.

40. Jack Lule, *Daily News, Eternal Stories: The Mythological Role of Journalism* (New York: Guilford, 2001), pp. 24, 118–19.

41. McBride, *Frank Capra*, p. 411.

42. Capra, *The Name above the Title*, p. 339.

43. See for example Herbert Biberman's review in *Meet John Doe*, ed. Charles Wolfe (New Brunswick, N.J.: Rutgers University Press, 1989), pp. 231–35; Harvey, *Romantic Comedy*, pp. 159–66; David Thomson, *A Biographical Dictionary of Film*, 3rd ed. (New York: Knopf, 1996), pp. 107–8.

44. See Ray Carney, *American Vision: The Films of Frank Capra* (Hanover, N.H.: University Press of New England, 1986).

45. Jeanine Basinger, *The World War II Combat Film* (New York: Columbia University Press, 1986), p. 15.

46. DiBattista, *Fast-Talking Dames*, p. 38.

47. Harvey, *Romantic Comedy*, p. 154. Capra continued to feature journalists prominently in his postwar pictures, although with the exception of *It's a Wonderful Life* the movies are not considered to be on a par with his earlier efforts. For a discussion of those pictures, see Saltzman, *Frank Capra and the Image of the Journalist in American Film*.

4

Citizen Kane

Citizen Kane has been called "the film that routinely tops all critical polls, the motion picture used most frequently in film classes to show young filmmakers how to create their art," and "the apotheosis of the newspaper film."[1] As such, it deserves separate treatment here. It is the story of Charles Foster Kane, who as a child inherits a fortune and as a young man decides "it would be fun to run a newspaper." On the front page of the *Inquirer*, he publishes a Declaration of Principles pledging he will "tell all the news honestly" and be "a fighting and tireless champion" of the people. Gradually he abandons his principles and uses his media empire to push a political career that ends in scandal. Two marriages crumble, and he dies bitter and alone. Kane's story is told in flashbacks as a reporter tries to learn the secret of Kane's dying word, "Rosebud." The reporter eventually abandons his quest: "I don't think any word can explain a man's life."

Citizen Kane and its director and star, Orson Welles, have been regular subjects of analysis.[2] In the present context, three aspects of the movie are of interest. The first is how it marks a transition from the screwball journalism films of the 1930s to the journalism noir films of the two decades to come. The second is how it relates to William Randolph Hearst, both as a purported exposé of his life and a purported target of his wrath. The third is how it presents a distinctly ambiguous stance toward the press, reproducing the myths of the journalism movie genre while highlighting the contradictions at their cores.[3]

FROM SCREWBALL TO NOIR

When film critic Pauline Kael wrote about *Kane* in the early 1970s, she heaped praise on Herman Mankiewicz, who was listed with Welles as co-author of the screenplay. Welles directed and starred in *Kane* while still in his twenties, and in the years hence, admirers had lionized him as the film's sole auteur. In contrast, Kael saw the film as the culmination of screwball newspaper comedy thanks to Mankiewicz, whom she asserted had written the script by himself.

Charles Foster Kane (Orson Welles) at once standing on his principles and putting the boot to them in *Citizen Kane*. (Courtesy of the Academy of Motion Picture Arts and Sciences)

He had worked for the *Chicago Tribune,* the *New York World,* and the *New Yorker.* He also was a *New York Times* theater critic who was nearly fired after drunkenly passing out while writing a negative review. Soon after that, he left for Hollywood to write movies (inviting Ben Hecht to do the same and helping start the flood of ex-journalists out west), and he occasionally was a guest at the home of Hearst's mistress, Marion Davies.

Kane does include elements familiar from screwball. There is Thompson, the reporter dispatched by his boss to track down a hot tabloid-like story: "Rosebud dead or alive!" There are buffoons such as Carter, the *Inquirer*'s editor when Kane takes charge. There is the conflict between home and work in the celebrated breakfast table scene in which Kane drifts apart from his first wife. (When she asks him what he does at the newspaper at night, he replies, "My dear, your only co-respondent is the *Inquirer*.")

Finally there is the love-hate relationship between Kane and his right-hand man, Jed Leland (Joseph Cotten), which has something of Walter and Hildy in it. Leland is based partly on Mankiewicz; he drunkenly passes out while writing a negative review of Kane's wife's opera debut. One historian says Mankiewicz also developed the story frame and characters, wrote much of the dialogue, and contributed the Rosebud plot device. Yet Welles "added the narrative brilliance—the visual and verbal wit [and] the stylistic fluidity."[4] That included Kane leaning into darkness to sign his Declaration of Principles and the visualization of Thompson, who stays in the shadows with his face mostly unseen.

Such expressionistic touches came to characterize film noir, as did *Kane*'s complicated time structure, with its flashbacks and flash-forwards. Also characteristic of noir was the film's treatment of journalism. If the screwball reporter was a fast-talking urban type who fell in love with the story or the editor, the noir reporter often was a detective searching for clues to a mystery. So it is with Thompson, who collects clues concerning the publisher's checkered life and career.[5]

KANE VERSUS HEARST

Kane's life and career paralleled William Randolph Hearst's, which naturally was no accident. Stage plays in the previous decade already had satirized the publisher; one even starred Orson Welles. So there was precedent for Mankiewicz's borrowing liberally from Hearst's life in the first script drafts for *Citizen Kane*. Although the completed film eliminated much of that material, plenty remained: The dilettante Kane (having been expelled from college) takes control of the *Inquirer,* just as the dilettante Hearst (having been expelled from Harvard) took control of the *San Francisco Examiner;* Kane sends a telegram to a reporter in Cuba instructing him to "provide the prose poems; I'll provide the war," just as legend holds that Hearst sent a cable to Frederic Remington instructing him to "furnish the pictures, and I'll furnish the war"; Kane builds a media empire via a mix of sensationalism, populism, and then reactionism, just as Hearst did; Kane takes up with "Susan Alexander," whose performing career he pushes through his papers, just as Hearst took up with Marion Davies, whose movie career he pushed via his papers; Kane fails in his bid for governor, just as Hearst failed; Kane dallies with Hitler, just as Hearst hired both Hitler and Mussolini as writers; Kane retreats to his "Xanadu" estate filled with "the loot of the world," just as Hearst built his San Simeon estate filled with "the wholesale transmigration of art and antiques to his New World."[6]

As a result, Hearst's biographer sued for plagiarism, and the Hearst press launched a campaign against *Citizen Kane* and RKO, the studio that produced it. That campaign has taken on mythic proportions. A made-for-cable TV movie, *RKO 281* (2000), shows Hearst himself trying to intimidate Hollywood into killing the film, dropping anti-Semitic hints to studio heads and ordering gossip columnist Louella Parsons to circulate photos of stars in compromising situations.

Nothing concrete proves that Hearst personally did such things. News reports at the time said his minions, including Adela Rogers St. Johns, were threatening to investigate "the alien situation in Hollywood" and Welles's "romantic adventures." Hearst's staff also prepared a report on Welles's "Leftist" leanings and suggested a broader exposé of Communist influence in the movies. Hearst apparently saw the report but did nothing with it. The Hearst press banned all mention of *Citizen Kane* and for a time refused ads for all RKO movies. Hearst himself had led such actions before against *Five Star Final* and Mae West's films, but there is no indication he did so here. What can be said is that he did nothing to stop the effort against *Kane* once it began.[7]

That effort ultimately failed. One of Welles's biographers notes that the director's career to that point had been "meteorically advanced" by the newspapers "to whom he pandered shamelessly,"[8] and *Time* publisher Henry Luce and others in the press staged a vigorous counteroffensive to save the movie. It was finally released to critical acclaim. Although it did poorly at the box office, that seems due less to Hearst than to the film's break with traditional Hollywood techniques and happy endings; audiences simply did not know what to make of it. As for it being Hearst's story, one of his biographers writes that unlike Kane he "never regarded himself as a failure, never recognized defeat, never stopped loving Marion or his wife," and never withdrew "from the world to entomb himself in a vast, gloomy art-choked hermitage." (He also never was signed away as a child by his mother, as Kane was; on the contrary, Hearst's mother was a central and "rarely absent" figure in his life.)[9]

If the movie was poor history, it was intentionally so. The filmmakers changed many details of Hearst's life to try to deflect his wrath. The projection room scene early in the film explicitly differentiates Kane from Hearst, and the movie draws on several other journalistic models. The "News on the March" sequence is a parody of the *March of Time* newsreels and so-called "*Time*-speak" ("for forty years appeared in Kane newsprint no public issue on which Kane Papers took no stand!"), ironic given Henry Luce's support of the film. Kane's "Declaration of Principles" in some ways echoes Joseph Pulitzer's credo for the *New York World*. The photograph of the staff that Kane hires away from a rival newspaper was based on a nineteenth-century photo of James Gordon Bennett's staff at the *New York Herald*. *Chicago Tribune* publisher Robert McCormick and electricity magnate Samuel Insull also provided inspiration; both men had dalliances with mediocre opera singers, much as Kane did in the film.[10] In a letter unsuccessfully trying to convince Louella Parsons that the movie was not about Hearst, Welles cited most of the names just listed as well as that of newspaper publisher Frank A. Munsey. He added, "Not that it matters; *Kane* isn't any of them."[11]

Regardless of whom it is or is not about, *Citizen Kane* remains one of the movies' richest portrayals of the press. It is less an exposé of Hearst than of journalistic hubris, not just Kane's but that of Thompson and his cronies. At the same time, the movie stops well short of a wholesale condemnation of journalism.

CITIZEN KANE'S DEPICTION OF JOURNALISM

Orson Welles said the filmmakers "wished to show a man with an urge to assume a position of responsibility in public affairs but himself having no sense of responsibility. . . . Such men as Kane always tend toward the newspaper and entertainment world. They combine a morbid preoccupation with the public with a devastatingly low opinion of the public mentality and moral character."[12] That is reflected in Kane's trajectory from "fighting liberal" to embittered reactionary, one that could be said to match not only that of Hearst but of Robert McCormick and other media moguls of the era. Kane professes to believe sincerely in his Declaration of Principles at first, saying he will "see to it that the decent, hard-working people of this community aren't robbed blind by a pack of money-mad pirates." The *Inquirer* leads fights against the traction trust (recalling the traction controversies in Chicago during Ben Hecht's day) and against slums and police corruption.

Still, Leland recognizes a paternalistic and megalomaniac undercurrent as he grows disillusioned with his boss. "As long as I can remember, you've talked about giving the people their rights as if you could make them a present of liberty," he tells Kane. "You just want to persuade people that you love them so much that they ought to love you back." Kane is singularly unsuccessful in that regard; he cannot dictate opinion or command affection as he fancied he could. The people defeat him at the polls after a rival paper prints stories of his extramarital "love nest," thus making him a victim of his own brand of journalism, just as critics have suggested that *Citizen Kane* painted Hearst with his own yellow brush.[13] Eventually Kane tears up the scrap of paper on which he had first written his principles, declaring it an "antique."

In such ways, the movie can be read as a morality tale: the idealistic young journalist losing his way and paying the price later in life, akin to Senator Joseph Paine in *Mr. Smith Goes to Washington*. Indeed, *Citizen Kane* is imbued with nostalgia not unlike that in the Capra films and *The Front Page*. Kane's melancholy memory of his childhood sled, Rosebud, is the most obvious manifestation, but there also is what David Thomson describes as the film's "vast, melancholy nostalgia for self-destructive talent."[14] A central tenet of journal-

"You talk about the people as though you *own* them!" Leland (Joseph Cotten, right) confronts Kane (Orson Welles) in *Citizen Kane*. (Courtesy of the Academy of Motion Picture Arts and Sciences)

istic mythology is that public service and the profit motive can go hand in hand. The young Kane appears to embody that myth: the talented editor-publisher who is both a model citizen and model businessperson, serving democratic interests while enriching himself and his company. From that perspective, his subsequent fall from grace (betraying his journalistic ideals while almost willfully destroying his political career and personal life) seems a tragedy.

However, that by itself does not adequately explain Kane. Welles would say "the point of the picture is not so much the solution of the problem as its presentation,"[15] the "problem" being who exactly Kane was. The opening newsreel offers one solution, but Thompson's boss declares that it misses the mark. "What it needs is an angle," he says. He tells Thompson to take "a week, two weeks if you have to" and find out Rosebud's identity: "It'll probably turn out to be a very simple thing."

Thompson does what most reporters would do; he interviews people and reads documents. Finally he recognizes he is no closer to a solution than when he started. "I guess Rosebud is just a piece in a jigsaw puzzle, a missing piece," he says. Although viewers at the end discover Rosebud's identity, that fails to explain the man; the "NO TRESPASSING" sign that opens and closes the movie underscores the futility of such explanations. Journalism's glib renderings of reality through newsreels and story "angles" are thus discredited.

The movie also highlights the contradictions within journalistic mythology by suggesting that Kane never possessed strong convictions or principles even at the start of his career when he asserts that "if the headline is big enough, it makes the news big enough." Additionally, it hints that such a lack of conviction extends to journalism as a whole. Leland hoped that Kane and the *Inquirer* could promote lasting reform; when they disappoint him, he descends quickly into cynicism and drink. Thompson and his colleagues are little more than hired guns for a big *Time*-like company. The press's assertion that it is the people's "fighting and tireless champion" seems just a pretense. Peddling products—whether papers or politicians—is its true mission.

That still does not adequately summarize the movie's treatment of Charles Foster Kane and the press, though. For Kane is not just an evil boogeyman like the villains in Capra's films, nor just an example of "nerve-drumming unmorality" like Walter Burns.[16] Welles said of Herman Mankiewicz and himself that "one of the authors hated Kane and one of them loved him," and not surprisingly Welles was the one in love (he played Kane, after all, and had much in common with the character). He also said he wanted to give Kane an "elegance of attitude which, even when it was self-regarding and vain, was peculiarly chic."[17] Welles was speaking of when Kane finishes the devastating review of his own wife's performance, a scene in which the publisher resembles the screwball-like newshound who derides and deflates all he sees, gleefully pounding out "WEAK" on his typewriter.

Kane's "elegance of attitude" is also embodied in his offhand remark, "I think it would be fun to run a newspaper." It is a damning comment—the press seen as personal plaything, as vanity project—yet it also shows breathtaking chutzpah (no wonder it leaves his guardian sputtering). And when the movie shows not just the *Inquirer*'s crusades against corruption but its risible misrepresentations of the truth ("FRAUD AT POLLS!" its headline reads after Kane loses the governorship), it does all look like fun.

In the end, much as Thompson is, *Citizen Kane*'s viewers are left with only the fragmented and contradictory impressions of Kane's life and career that the movie has given them. As Orson Welles indicated, that is precisely the point. The man the movie was supposedly about was considered an enigma in his own time; as early as 1906, Lincoln Steffens asked, "Who, what, where is the reality behind the mystery of William Randolph Hearst, the unknown?" Welles himself reveled in such mysteries, his own as well as everyone else's: "We are made of oppositions; we live between two poles. There's a philistine and an aesthete in all of us, and a murderer and a saint. You don't reconcile the poles. You just recognize them."[18]

Citizen Kane's refusal to "reconcile the poles" probably contributed to its initial box office failure. Robert Ray has argued that its "dramatization of the irresolvable conflict between American myths of success (celebrating energy and ambition) and of the simple life (warning that power and wealth corrupt) made audiences uneasy." At the same time, its recognition of fundamental opposites is part of the greatness of what Roger Ebert describes as a film whose "depths surpass understanding."[19]

If it is a classic American movie, it is also a classic journalism movie. Ebert says its "surface is as much fun as any movie ever made," consistent with Pauline Kael's description of it as "a *shallow* masterpiece."[20] The movie mixes sassy disrespect toward its subject with nostalgic sentiment, moralizing about the shirking of personal and public responsibilities and at the same time winking at it. Its love-hate portrayal of Kane and journalism exudes what Orson Welles approvingly called "a kind of controlled cheerful virulence."[21] Hecht and MacArthur themselves could not have done better.

❦

If *Citizen Kane*'s screwball qualities constituted a *Front Page*–like valentine to journalism (unmasking the press's arrogance and pretensions while reveling in them), its noir-like qualities pointed to a bleakness underlying screwball's comic ethos. That ethos had idealized what James Harvey described as being part of "the community of wiseacres."[22] Kane, on the other hand, died alone. The women who were central to screwball and to Capra were not a part of his world. His alienation—the same alienation that Capra's heroes faced in their darkest moments before everything was miraculously made right again— proved irredeemable.

These darker elements continued to be prominent in the journalism movies to come. At the same time, Hollywood came under increasing pressure to improve its depictions of the press. The result was films that were just as ambivalent toward truth and morality as screwball had been, and at the same time even more enthusiastic in their embrace of journalism's mythic place in American life.

NOTES

1. Harlan Lebo, *Citizen Kane: The Fiftieth Anniversary Album* (New York: Double-day, 1990), p. 186; Simon Callow, *Orson Welles: The Road to Xanadu* (New York: Penguin, 1997), p. xv.

2. For a brief critical overview of this work, see Jonathan Rosenbaum, "The Battle over Orson Welles," *Cineaste* 22:3 (Summer 1996): 6.

3. Information on Hearst, Welles, and the making of *Kane* comes primarily from W. A. Swanberg, *Citizen Hearst* (New York: Bantam Matrix, 1967); David Nasaw, *The Chief: The Life of William Randolph Hearst* (Boston: Houghton Mifflin, 2000); Pauline Kael, "Raising Kane," in *The Citizen Kane Book,* by Pauline Kael, Herman J. Mankiewicz, and Orson Welles (New York: Limelight, 1984); Robert L. Carringer, *The Making of Citizen Kane*, Rev. Ed. (Berkeley: University of California Press, 1996); Lebo, *Citizen Kane;* David Thomson, *Rosebud: The Story of Orson Welles* (New York: Vintage, 1997); Callow, *Orson Welles;* Louis Pizzitola, *Hearst over Hollywood* (New York: Columbia University Press, 2002), pp. 389–405. Jonathan Rosenbaum, for one, sharply criticizes much of this work for being unfair to Welles and concentrating too heavily on *Kane* at the expense of his later films; see Rosenbaum, "The Battle over Orson Welles."

4. Carringer, *The Making of Citizen Kane,* p. 35. Harlan Lebo writes that "Welles created an exacting personal vision for *Citizen Kane,* but he reached his goal by encouraging the people around him to take the lead and show him what they could accomplish together." David Thomson—whose attitude toward Welles is mixed at best—still asserts that "no one who has seen the film as often as it deserves to be seen would dream that Welles is not its only begetter." See Lebo, *Citizen Kane,* pp. 196–97; David Thomson, *The New Biographical Dictionary of Film* (New York: Knopf, 2002), p. 924.

5. For more on *Kane*'s relationship to noir and detective films, see Thomas Schatz, *Hollywood Genres* (New York: McGraw-Hill, 1981), pp. 116–26.

6. Nasaw, *The Chief,* pp. 127, 296.

7. For more on Hearst's campaign against *Kane* and other films, see Nasaw, *The Chief,* pp. 445–46, 564–74; Lebo, *Citizen Kane,* pp. 130–52; Callow, *Orson Welles,* pp. 530–59; Emile Gauvreau, *My Last Million Readers* (New York: Arno, 1974; originally published 1941), pp. 159–62; Pizzitola, *Hearst over Hollywood,* pp. 274–77, 395–405.

8. Callow, *Orson Welles,* p. xv.

9. Nasaw, *The Chief,* p. 574; William Deverell, "Poor Little Rich Boy," *Reviews in American History* 30 (March 2002): 95.

10. Roger Ebert and Peter Bogdanovich audio commentaries, *Citizen Kane* DVD, Warner Home Video, 2001; James W. Barrett, *The World, the Flesh, and Messrs. Pulitzer* (New York: Vanguard, 1931), p. 8; Carringer, *The Making of Citizen Kane,* p. 114; Richard Norton Smith, *The Colonel: The Life and Legend of Robert R. McCormick* (Boston: Houghton Mifflin, 1997), pp. 122, 394–98.

11. Callow, *Orson Welles,* p. 531.

12. Ibid., p. 497.

13. Kael, "Raising Kane"; Pizzitola, *Hearst over Hollywood.*

14. Thomson, *The New Biographical Dictionary of Film,* p. 925.

15. Callow, *Orson Welles,* p. 531.

16. Ben Hecht and Charles MacArthur, *The Front Page* (New York: Covici-Friede, 1928), pp. 191–92.

17. Callow, *Orson Welles,* p. 494.

18. Nasaw, *The Chief,* p. 205; Callow, *Orson Welles,* p. xi.

19. Robert B. Ray, *A Certain Tendency of the Hollywood Cinema, 1930–1980* (Princeton, N.J.: Princeton University Press, 1985), p. 57; Roger Ebert, "Citizen Kane," *Chicago Sun-Times,* May 24, 1998, Show sec., p. 5.

20. Ibid., p. 5; Kael, "Raising Kane," p. 4.

21. Callow, *Orson Welles,* p. 494.

22. James Harvey, *Romantic Comedy* (New York: Alfred A. Knopf, 1987), p. 90.

❦ 5

News in a Noir World

Cinema scholars argue that film noir was as creative an artistic response to Cold War paranoia as screwball comedy had been to the Depression. Screwball's exuberance and connectedness gave way to dread and alienation; "sanity and resistance" gave way to madness and inexorable doom.[1] Truth and morality were just as much up for grabs, but whereas screwball had been preoccupied with phonies—unmasking them, making fun of them, even reveling in them— noir was preoccupied with confusion, blind alleys, and traps. Noir also targeted hubris as *Citizen Kane* had; efforts to commit the perfect crime or escape one's past were ruthlessly exposed and punished. Strong women were again on hand as they had been in screwball, but instead of empowering men through their own wise example, they helped destroy them.

The movies showed journalists in the noir world playing two basic roles that hewed to the outlaw-official dichotomy. In the first, they were outcasts caught in the darkness, unable or unwilling to conform to prescribed social roles. In the second, they were conscientious reporters who ventured into the darkness only to try to solve a mystery (as Thompson had in *Citizen Kane*) or right a wrong.

Both sets of portrayals reproduced the myths of the journalism movie genre. The first underscored rules of proper professional and personal conduct by using the outcast to show the costs of unbridled ambition and the abuse of power. The second used a pseudodocumentary approach that celebrated professional principles and ideals. It was often suffused in nostalgia, drawing inspiration from the venerated editor-publishers of the past.

ROOTS OF NOIR

The journalism movie in the 1940s was not simply a logical progression from *Citizen Kane*. That film had successfully resisted the efforts of the Hearst press to kill it while embodying a host of stylistic innovations that Hollywood was unlikely to imitate slavishly. In contrast, journalism films immediately before and during the war responded to pressure from press associations and the government while proving to be much more conventional in story and technique.

Journalists had complained about the movies' portrayals of them from at least the time of *The Front Page*. By the end of the 1930s, more systematic lobbying by organizations such as the American Newspaper Publishers Association and the American Society of Newspaper Editors had had some effect because the studios were mindful of the power of both good and bad press. Some movies presented a more idealistic and "official" depiction of the news media. The historical drama *Dispatch from Reuters* (1940) began with a dedication to "the great men of journalism . . . the gentlemen of the Fourth Estate" and ended with a ringing declaration from Reuters himself, played by Edward G. Robinson: "A censored press is the tool of a corrupt minority. A free press is the symbol of a free people. The truth is freedom!" By 1942, *St. Petersburg Times* publisher Nelson Poynter and the Office of War Information were working with the movie studios to portray the journalist as a "civic servant" who helped promote the war effort.[2]

Foreign correspondents were already familiar figures on screen by then. Before America's entry into the war, they were often screwball types, as exemplified by Clark Gable's journalist in *Comrade X* (1940). Ben Hecht and Charles Lederer began their screenplay by calling Stalinist Russia "the never never land of steppes, samovars and spies—beards, bears, bombs and borscht—where almost anything can happen—and usually does."

Alfred Hitchcock's *Foreign Correspondent* (1940) marked a turning point. Its roots were in Vincent "Jimmy" Sheean's 1935 memoir *Personal History,* concerning his reporting experiences in Europe and the Far East. Although Sheean had screwball qualities of his own (he confessed being prone to "dreams, visions, struggles and trances" and once swore he saw a flying saucer), he also was a pioneer of reflective, interpretive journalism.[3] Hitchcock helped fashion a script around a *Front Page*–like crime reporter who is sent to Europe because his editor wants a "fresh, unused mind" there. After a series of adventures involving Nazi spies, kidnapped diplomats, and shot-down airplanes, the reporter is transformed into an Edward R. Murrow–like correspondent broadcasting from a London air raid: "Hello, America! Hang onto your lights! They're the only lights left in the world!"[4] War had no place for screwball shenanigans.

Some screenwriters tried to use the war to promote social ideals, which in retrospect critics such as Pauline Kael saw as unfortunate: "The comedy writers who had laughed at cant now learned to write it and were rehabilitated as useful citizens of the community of mediocrity."[5] Regardless, Donald Ogden Stewart (with input from the Office of War Information) wrote *Keeper of The Flame* (1942), starring Spencer Tracy as a dedicated journalist who uncovers the story of an American fascist planning a national coup. Arthur Miller worked with Ernie Pyle to try to turn Pyle's book *Here Is Your War* into a film that Miller hoped would highlight the better world the war would bring. Lester Cole and Alvah Bessie co-wrote *Objective, Burma!* (1945), extolling the Allied fight against fascism abroad.[6]

Journalists fit well into the formula of the World War II combat film, which typically focused on an ethnically diverse group of soldiers following a heroic leader on an important mission while accompanied by an observer.[7] The observer in both *Objective, Burma!* and the movie that finally emerged from Ernie Pyle's book, *The Story of G.I. Joe* (1945), was a newspaper journalist. In neither picture did he espouse politically progressive sentiments. Arthur Miller's collaboration with Pyle failed because the journalist was leery of big, idealistic statements; others wrote the film instead. It focused on the men at the front and, in the words of Pyle's biographer, "blended myth and reality in about the same proportion as the column that inspired it."[8] As for *Objective, Burma!*, Cole and Bessie complained vehemently about a speech another writer gave the film's journalist. The character witnesses enemy atrocities and becomes hysterical, calling the Japanese "stinking little savages" and yelling, "Wipe 'em all out! Wipe 'em off the FACE OF THE EARTH!" Despite the objections, the speech—since called "the worst example of anti-Japanese rhetoric [ever] to appear on the screen"—remained.[9] In such movies, the journalist as wisecracking outsider had vanished to be replaced by the patriotic (if racist) public servant the newspaper industry and government wanted.

After the Japanese surrender, the Soviet Union that had been depicted so whimsically in *Comrade X* became the enemy, and progressive sentiments became suspect as the Communist witch hunts in Hollywood began in earnest. Lester Cole and Alvah Bessie went to prison along with others of the so-called Hollywood Ten including Ring Lardner Jr., who had co-authored *Woman of the Year.* Donald Ogden Stewart and Philip Stevenson (a contributor to *The Story of G.I. Joe*) were blacklisted. In the coming years, even seemingly innocuous pictures such as *Roman Holiday* (1953) were affected. The movie about a reporter who romances a princess in Rome won a screenwriting Oscar for Ian McLellan Hunter, but he was a front for Dalton Trumbo, another member of the Hollywood Ten. Paramount removed producer Lester Koenig's name from the film after he refused to cooperate with the House Un-American Activities Committee, and he too was blacklisted.[10]

Such was the air of fear and suspicion lurking beneath the surface of American movies. The Hollywood studios faced not only the witch hunts but a Supreme Court decision stripping them of the big-city theaters where they exhibited their films; they also were rapidly losing their traditional audience to television.[11]

Scholars have argued that film noir responded to the suppressed anxiety and paranoia of the times, and indeed movies of this era often painted the journalist with a much darker hue than had been customary during the war. However, they moralized more than other noir pictures did while also tending toward more of a realist than an expressionistic mode.[12] As a result, the movies typically stopped short of attacking journalism as an institution while endorsing the notion that it could be a force for social good.

NEWSPAPER NOIR

The classic film noir tells of a man who is alienated from conventional society and finds himself in a trap. He is lured or kept there by a femme fatale. The dialogue is hardboiled and nonnaturalistic; real people do not talk that way. The look is filled with shadow and rain. The story centers around mystery, suspense, and violence, with the conventional happy ending nowhere to be found.

Ace in the Hole (1951), also known as *The Big Carnival,* is a prominent example of newspaper noir. Billy Wilder co-wrote and directed the film. As a young man, Wilder reported for tabloids in Vienna and Berlin, once working as a dance hall gigolo to get material for a story. In Berlin he wrote scripts for the German film studios. When the Nazis assumed power, Wilder—a Jew—fled to Hollywood. He spoke little English when he arrived, but he soon mastered the language so thoroughly that his scripts became marvels of razor-sharp American vernacular. Frustrated with how directors butchered his screenplays, he began directing himself and by 1950 had created the classics *Double Indemnity, The Lost Weekend,* and *Sunset Boulevard.*[13]

Wilder and Walter Newman wrote about a reporter who exploits a man stuck in a cave. It was loosely based on two actual incidents. The first in 1925 concerned Floyd Collins, who was trapped in a Kentucky cave he had been exploring in hopes of finding a tourist attraction that would make him rich. He lay there for two weeks as rescuers vainly tried to reach him, while outside throngs gawked at the proceedings and the press made him nationwide front-page news. Finally Collins died and his cash-strapped father sold his corpse to be displayed at another cave nearby. The second incident occurred in 1949 just before Wilder and Newman began writing their script. Three-year-old Kathy Fiscus fell down a well near her California home. Again a huge crowd rushed to the scene, again the newspapers and the new medium of television made it a nationwide story, again it ended sadly: The girl died before rescuers could reach her.

Although journalists had figured prominently in both cases, they certainly had not tried to prolong the incidents to turn them into better stories. On the contrary, reporter William "Skeets" Miller had crawled into the cave several times to feed Floyd Collins milk and whiskey and help lead efforts to pull him free. And while the scene near where Kathy Fiscus was trapped was carnival-like in some respects—a group of dwarf circus clowns volunteered to go down the well—the thousands of others who showed up were somber and quiet, and the rescuers worked long, dangerous hours for no pay.[14]

Wilder and Newman told a more acidic tale in *Ace in the Hole.* Unemployed New York reporter Chuck Tatum (Kirk Douglas) lands at an Albuquerque newspaper. His editor, Mr. Boot (Porter Hall), has hung embroidered signs reading "Tell the Truth" on the newsroom walls. Tatum pays no heed. When he comes across the story of Leo Minosa trapped in a cave, he plays it big. Telling Leo that he will be freed soon, Tatum convinces the local sheriff to draw out the rescue effort so that Tatum can parlay it into a lucrative New York newspaper job while the sheriff exploits it in his reelection campaign. Meanwhile, Tatum beds Leo's slatternly wife, Lorraine (Jan Sterling). She hires the circus to perform for the hordes of curiosity-seekers outside the cave. Then everything falls apart. Tatum and Lorraine fight, and she stabs him; Leo contracts pneumonia and dies. Bleeding but still ambulatory, the guilt-stricken Tatum returns to the Albuquerque newsroom. "How'd you like to make yourself a thousand dollars a day, Mr. Boot?" he asks the editor. "I'm a thousand-dollar-a-day newspaperman—you can have me for *nothing*." With that, he topples over dead.

Ace in the Hole demonstrates many of the characteristics of noir. The brilliantly punning title alludes to Leo as the reporter's ace card trapped in the literal hole of the cave and Tatum as the ace reporter trapped in the figurative hole he has dug for himself. Both men are alienated, even if Leo does not fully realize it. He is a war veteran (a familiar noir figure) married to a woman who holds him in contempt and bound by circumstances he cannot change or understand. He is ripe for exploitation. Tatum is exiled from the world of big-city newspapering he longs to return to, a man who is ruled by his utter contempt for humanity and who views "tell the truth" as an empty-headed homily.

Both Leo and Tatum fall victim to Lorraine, who helps doom Leo by being an accomplice to keeping him trapped in the cave. She also dooms Tatum by stabbing him (although only after he has slapped and choked her). The story is one of suspense (will Leo be freed in time?) and ultimately murder (near the end, Tatum calls his New York office to claim that he has killed Leo by keeping him buried). The dialogue features some of Wilder's most hardboiled one-liners: "I don't go to church," says Lorraine. "Kneeling bags my nylons." The harsh white light of the desert exteriors contrasts sharply with the murky darkness of the cave, and when Tatum collapses in the film's climax, he plummets head-first toward the camera with his dead, staring face blackened by shadow. To put it mildly, the ending is not happy.

Chuck Tatum (Kirk Douglas) rides the road to perdition in *Ace in the Hole*. (Courtesy of the Academy of Motion Picture Arts and Sciences)

In many respects, then, *Ace in the Hole* was a classic noir exploration of the dark side of American life and myth. Billy Wilder said characters such as Tatum embodied "the American mania for making it even if it has to be made on someone's personal tragedy"[15]—in other words, the viciousness underlying "official" myths celebrating personal ambition and self-striving. Faith in the community was also undercut via the specter of an easily manipulated mob, and official America as represented by the Fourth Estate and law enforcement took its licks as well.

The movie was a box office failure. "We were shafted unmercifully by most of the newspapers," said Walter Newman.[16] Some of the press reviews were highly negative, unsurprising given that the film was a far cry from the likes of *Dispatch from Reuters* and its veneration of the "great men of journalism." The *Hollywood Reporter* branded *Ace in the Hole* "a brazen, uncalled-for slap in the face of two respected and frequently effective American institutions— democratic government and the free press." The *New Yorker* reviewer called it "a compound of unjelled satire [and] half-baked melodrama" and said Tatum was "the most preposterous version of a reporter *I've* ever seen." Others, though, called the movie "powerfully disturbing," "extraordinarily potent," "remarkably compelling," "a superior melodrama," and "a brilliant film." The problem, as *Variety* diagnosed it, was that "the very nature of its plot" ensured that *Ace in the Hole* would have "limited appeal," adding that it would need "shrewd exploitation and selling" to succeed.[17]

Paramount tried to save its movie by changing the title to *The Big Carnival* and, in an exquisite irony, creating ads aimed at the same sensation-hungry audience the film condemned: "Can you take it? Can you stand pulse-pounding suspense? Can you take bold, tense drama? Can you stand daring realism? If you can, 'The Big Carnival' is your meat."[18] Nothing worked, although the film did well overseas despite concerns about how it portrayed America during the Cold War. Wilder came to call it "the runt of my litter," and film scholars labeled it—not unadmiringly—"one of the most grimly cynical motion pictures ever to emerge from Hollywood."[19]

Although the film is undeniably grim, it is in many ways less cynical and more pious than screwball movies. Tatum is a screwball-like character in many ways, a self-schooled urban newshound who represents an outlaw mentality and is obsessed with tabloid tales. Driving to a rattlesnake hunt with Herbie (the impressionable cub reporter who idolizes him), Tatum describes what he sees as the ideal story: fifty rattlers loose in the city and gradually rounded up except for the one left in Tatum's desk drawer: "Stashed away, only nobody knows it, see? The story's good for another three days. Then when I'm good and ready, we come out with a big extra: '*Sun-Bulletin* Snags Number 50'!" Such a story is essentially no different from Hildy and Walter hiding Earl Williams in the rolltop desk. Tatum's casual acceptance of political corruption is also in keeping with pictures such as *His Girl Friday:* "So there'll be one more crooked sheriff in the world—who cares?"

Similarly, the grossly exploited and distorted story fed to an insatiable, sucker public recalls *Nothing Sacred.* So does a scene in which Tatum slaps Lorraine to make her look the part of the grief-stricken wife, just as Wally struck Hazel in the earlier movie to make her look the part of the mortally ill young woman.

Unlike in most screwball films, though, there is a voice of official, professional conscience in *Ace in the Hole.* The editor, Mr. Boot, struggles to keep young Herbie from following Tatum's path of sin and damnation while condemning Tatum for his "phony, below the belt journalism." Phoniness is not a source of amusement as in screwball; much as in Capra films, it is branded as dishonest and unfair. Mr. Boot is admittedly bland compared with Tatum, who mocks the editor for wearing both a belt and suspenders (similar to Walter mocking Bruce for carrying both an umbrella and galoshes in *His Girl Friday*). Tatum also rejects Mr. Boot's admonitions concerning his style of journalism: "Not below the belt. Right in the gut, Mr. Boot! Human interest!"

Soon enough, though, Tatum's screwball-like scoop goes noir on him. His attempt to pull off the perfect story, similar to efforts to commit the perfect crime in other noir movies, ends in disaster. Tatum tries to call in a different human interest story—the story of how Leo was murdered, with the headline "Reporter Keeps Man Buried for Six Days"—but his New York office will not accept it. The thousand-dollar-a-day reporter has been rendered worthless.

The noir world is significantly different from the screwball world. Romantic comedy's iconoclastic outsiders find redemption and belonging through love. After Wally knocks out Hazel in *Nothing Sacred,* she knocks him out in return, and it is portrayed as an exotic courtship ritual. In contrast, noir's outsiders pay a steep price as their encounters result not in romance but perfidy: When Tatum slaps and chokes Lorraine, she stabs him, and he bleeds to death. In *His Girl Friday* and *Nothing Sacred,* the audience is invited to laugh and applaud as journalists get away with fraud and deceit; in *Ace in the Hole,* the audience is invited to reflect on its own heartlessness as the wayward reporter is made to confess and then die for his sins.

As those who act beyond the pale are punished, order is restored. Myth in popular culture often tells "scapegoat" stories, "affirming and defending social consensus" by doling out "dark consequences for those who deviate."[20] Tatum's deviant cynicism is clearly marked as outside the boundaries of social consensus, and Mr. Boot's upstanding idealism is affirmed. That is reinforced by Tatum's last living deed: He returns Herbie to the side of the upstanding editor, telling the young man that is where he belongs. If newspaper screwball films are morality tales that are short on morals,[21] *Ace in the Hole* is a more traditional tale that places the truth-telling journalist at its moral center and graphically illustrates what happens to those who lie and cheat to get to the top.

The noir classic *Sweet Smell of Success* (1957) is considered by some to be "*the* hip American movie,"[22] but it too moralizes in its conclusion while providing another instructive contrast to older films. In the tradition of *Citizen Kane,* it is a veiled portrait of a real-life journalist. However, whereas *Kane* was deliberately ambivalent toward its title character, *Sweet Smell* eviscerates its Walter Winchell–like protagonist.

Early talkies lionized fast-talking, big-city columnists such as Winchell. *Blessed Event* (1932) starred Broadway's original Hildy, Lee Tracy, as a newspaper advertising flunky who becomes a famous columnist as the paper's circulation soars. By the 1950s, however, Walter Winchell was growing ever more paranoid and reactionary, not unlike Charles Foster Kane. Ernest Lehman wrote a novella based on his unhappy experiences as a press agent toady who chased down gossip for Winchell and others in return for plugs for clients. Burt Lancaster's production company adapted the novella for the screen with Lancaster as columnist J. J. Hunsecker and Tony Curtis as Sidney Falco, the press agent who curries the columnist's favor. Clifford Odets, who went to prison for contempt of Congress before the Hollywood Ten did and then named names, incorporated what he had learned about fear, retaliation, and capitulation into the screenplay he co-wrote with Lehman.

Hunsecker is a New York columnist with a nationwide audience for his column and television show. He has seemingly unlimited power to make or break entertainers and politicians. Falco, a smooth pretty boy whom Hunsecker calls a "cookie full of arsenic," stops at nothing to stay in the columnist's good graces. He arranges for thugs to beat up the jazz musician boyfriend of Hunsecker's sister, Susan, to whom the columnist has a virtually incestuous attachment. In the end, Falco—who has finally stood up to Hunsecker—is himself beaten up and dragged away, and Hunsecker's sister abandons him.

For most of the picture, *Sweet Smell of Success* is a devastating portrait of all-encompassing amorality and corruption. News, such as it is, is the product of desperately ambitious young men prostrating themselves before a monster in hopes of garnering a few miserable crumbs of fluff hyping their hack clients. If that requires them to destroy people by branding them as Communists and dope fiends, it is all in a night's work. Even orchestrating physical assault is not out of line if it feeds the monster's megalomania. "I want that boy taken apart," says Hunsecker of Susan's boyfriend. "[He] wiped his feet on the choice and predilection of sixty million men and women."

Again, though, the protagonists are clearly marked as deviants and scapegoats. Falco is the same kind of outlaw hustler that Tatum was in *Ace in the Hole,* and he receives the same censure. "You're a real rascal, Sidney," Hunsecker's secretary tells him. "An amusing boy, but you haven't got a drop of respect in you for anything alive. You're so immersed in the theology of making a fast buck." Hunsecker is a similarly alienated outlaw, but he masquerades as an official pillar by spouting empty platitudes on his TV show: "You know and I know that our best secret weapon is D-E-M-O-C-R-A-C-Y!" A rival columnist tells Falco that he sees through Hunsecker's facade. "Your man prints anything," he says. "Use[s] any spice to pepper up his daily garbage. You tell him I said so. Tell him that like yourself he's got the scruples of a guinea pig and the morals of a gangster!"

Falco is seemingly unmoved by such attacks: "What do I do now? Whistle 'Stars and Stripes Forever'?" Truth, honor, and all related concepts have no utility in his and Hunsecker's world. When the columnist asks Falco what Susan sees in her boyfriend, Falco replies, "Integrity: acute, like indigestion." "What does this mean—*integrity?*" says Hunsecker.

Finally, just as in *Ace in the Hole,* justice and morality are served; the snappy and streetwise ethos of movies such as *Blessed Event* is condemned. It dawns on Falco that he is trapped in the same sort of incestuous relationship with Hunsecker that Susan is: a Walter-Hildy bond gone very bad. ("You're in jail, Sidney," Hunsecker has coolly informed him.) When the columnist lies to Susan about his complicity in the assault on her boyfriend, Falco strikes back at him: "You big *phony!*" Again, phoniness is a brand of shame. Before Falco pays for his sins at the hands of Hunsecker's henchmen, he delivers a final riposte to the columnist—"You've got such contempt for people it makes you stupid!"—and vows to reveal everything he knows. Hunsecker thus faces not only the loss of his sister but also his own imminent downfall. Susan goes so far as to express her pity for him, and Hunsecker forlornly watches her walk away from him into the dawn.

LIBERALISM AND NEOREALISM

Alongside movies' depictions of the likes of Chuck Tatum and J. J. Hunsecker was a more ennobling set of depictions. They carried on the idealistic portraits of journalism that had appeared during the war while avoiding the overt jingoism of pictures such as *Objective, Burma!* Indeed, they showed journalists systematically exposing evil and making the world a better place, the sort of portrayals that press organizations had been pressing for all along.

Part of the impetus was an influx of new films from Europe. Roberto Rossellini made *Open City* (1945) as the Germans were pulling out of Rome. He used black market film stock and a mostly amateur cast. The result was called "neorealism," a gritty, documentary-like style that, unlike most American movies, sought to show what war and its aftermath were truly like. Other Italian films such as *Shoeshine, The Bicycle Thief,* and *La Terra Trema* garnered critical acclaim in the United States.[23]

Some in Hollywood responded with movies that attempted to confront the problems facing postwar America, taking advantage of a brief window of opportunity before the witch hunts and blacklist slammed it shut. The films were "characterized by a manifest seriousness which [was] frequently italicized by the incorporation of the narrational conventions of the documentary."[24] The result was not full-fledged neorealism, however. It reproduced traditional Hollywood formula and myth, such as the celebration of "official" heroes that included journalists.

At the forefront was the head of Twentieth Century Fox, Darryl F. Zanuck. While production chief at Warner Brothers in the early sound era, he oversaw the ripped-from-the-tabloids feel of that studio's gangster and newspaper pictures as well as such socially conscious films as 1932's *I Am a Fugitive from a Chain Gang*. Now he saw a similar opportunity. He would claim that he made *Gentleman's Agreement* (1947) so that if America ever went fascist, he could tell his children he at least had done something to try to stop it.[25]

The movie was based on the novel of the same name by Laura Z. Hobson, the daughter of the editor of a Jewish newspaper. She drew inspiration from an incident in which the notorious bigot John Rankin called Walter Winchell a "little kike" on the floor of the House of Representatives. Hobson's novel centered around magazine writer Phil Green, whose editor wants him to write a series on anti-Semitism. Green is reluctant until he decides to pose as a Jew to experience the problem firsthand. That drives a wedge between him and his fiancée, who does not recognize her own prejudice. For the movie, Zanuck recruited Moss Hart to adapt the screenplay, Elia Kazan to direct, and Gregory Peck to star as Phil.

Gentleman's Agreement won the Academy Award for Best Picture of 1947. Despite a certain obviousness in the writing and acting ("I'll be *Jewish!*" exclaims Peck when he finally realizes the device that will make the story work), its earnestness had to please those who lamented the screwball portrayal of the press.

If anything, Peck-as-Phil is the *anti*-screwball: "I'm always weighing and judging; I'm such a solemn fool," he says. He is serious, sober, adult—a widower raising his son with his mother's help. His editor is a paragon of principle and good intentions; it is he who urges the anti-Semitism series on the reluctant Phil, and when he learns that his magazine discriminates against Jews in its hiring, he is aghast and orders immediate change. Phil's fiancée is not an obligatory and ultimately irrelevant voice of conscience but a refined woman of means whose own conscience needs awakening. The reporter does not get his scoop via comic accident but through soul-searching, false starts, and hard work. The scoop is not a trivial tabloid yarn but an impassioned exposé of a societal ill, as quoted from by Phil's mother: "They, those patient stubborn men who argued and wrote and fought and came up with the Constitution and the Bill of Rights, they knew that the tree is known by its fruit and

The anti-screwball: Phil (Gregory Peck) struggles to find the right angle on his story in *Gentleman's Agreement*. (Courtesy of the Academy of Motion Picture Arts and Sciences)

that injustice corrupts the tree—that its fruit withers and shrivels and falls at last to that dark ground of history where other great hopes have rotted and died. For equality and freedom remain still the only choice for wholeness and soundness in a man or in a nation."

It is a speech that could have come from a Capra film: an appeal to American democratic ideals invoking the mythic heroes of the past. (Also reminiscent of Capra is the figure of the beloved late patriarch; Phil's mother remarks how proud his father would have been of him.) Unlike in Capra, though, the speech comes straight from the journalist's (mother's) mouth. Phil is an official hero rather than an outlaw villain. His personal and professional relationships are supportive, a marked contrast to *Ace in the Hole*. The main exception is his fiancée, and his good example finally brings her around. Meanwhile, the magazine's wisecracking fashion editor (Celeste Holm), a screwball throwback of sorts who not-so-secretly lusts after Phil, is cast off by both him and the movie.

Gentleman's Agreement was not by any conventional definition a film noir. The movie depicted noir-like ugliness, but it was a polite, discreet, upper-class ugliness. The most violent moment was marked not by gunfire but a desk clerk ringing a bell to have Phil escorted from a restricted hotel. Although the film was seen as progressive in its time, one critic notes that it "attacked anti-Semitism purely in terms of derogatory phrases and restricted ski resorts, without the slightest mention of the fact that millions of Jews had just been massacred in Europe."[26] It addressed intractable social problems in individual terms, suggesting that the journalist had the power to confront and potentially solve those problems.

Another Fox picture released the following year was more in the film noir tradition but again focused on a journalist hero fighting and righting wrongs. *Call Northside 777* (1948) stemmed from the real-life case of a Chicago police officer killed in a speakeasy in 1932. With the city's "Century of Progress" exposition soon to open, the mayor declared a "war on crime" to quell the impression that killers were roaming the streets. Two men were fingered for the murder, including Joe Majczek. His lawyer was drunk during his trial, and Majczek was sentenced to life in prison. After he had served eleven years, his mother placed an ad in the *Chicago Times* asking for information about the real killers and offering a $5,000 reward that she had raised by scrubbing floors. *Times* reporters James McGuire and John McPhaul produced evidence that the police and speakeasy owner had framed Majczek. He was pardoned in 1945 amid still more allegations of wrongdoing. The state awarded Majczek $24,000 in compensation, and he claimed that an Illinois lawmaker had demanded a $5,000 kickback for helping arrange the payment.[27]

It was a tale of official incompetence and corruption worthy of *The Front Page*, but the filmmakers were determined to tell a more dignified story. "James Stewart plays the new, modern type of Chicago newspaper reporter," Fox boasted in its publicity materials for the film. "The old, whiskey-bottle-on-hip, Capone-type reporter of 'Front Page' and other newspaper pictures of the 1929 period is definitely 'cut.'"[28] Fox also made much of the movie's realism. It was shot at the Chicago locations and the state prison where the actual events occurred.

The resulting style came to be called "documentary noir," although it was not the best example of either documentary or noir. One cinema scholar argues that noir's "richest offerings [were] oblique, deliriously slanted" and located in "a twilight zone shakily suspended between reality and nightmare." They were powerfully expressionistic in the manner of *Citizen Kane.* In contrast, documentary noir tended "toward simplicity, directness, reportorial accuracy."[29] Some of its most prominent examples were produced by Louis de Rochemont, who was responsible for the *March of Time* newsreels that *Citizen Kane* had gleefully satirized. Documentary noir was not designed to be purely accurate or reportorial, however. It used "conventional plotting strategies" and a "dynamic hero-centered narrative as a means of providing a suitable Hollywood-style ending."[30]

So it was with *Call Northside 777.* The first screenplay draft was co-authored by Quentin Reynolds, a noted journalist who like many others before him was having a go at movie writing. Reynolds largely stuck to the facts of the Majczek case, and Darryl Zanuck pronounced himself "gravely disappointed." He acknowledged that although "it is our intention to tell a hard-hitting, factual, semi-documentary story," it needed an injection of old-fashioned movie drama if it were not to end up "as impersonal as a *March of Time.*" The reporter should have a "friendly feud" with the city editor; he should be transformed from a "rather formless puppet" into a "fighting newspaperman." When a subsequent draft still did not meet Zanuck's expectations, he assigned different writers.[31]

In the completed film, the reporter "McNeal" did have a "friendly feud" with his editor. Much as in *Gentleman's Agreement,* the editor pushed the story onto the reluctant reporter, the opposite of what had occurred in reality. McNeal had a loving wife who encouraged him in his moments of doubt. As played by James Stewart in an effort to toughen his screen persona, he also had an attitude. ("All that cynical and sarcastic stuff is movie nonsense," James McGuire's daughter later said about the film's depiction of her father. "My father was mainly a worrier."[32]) Most dramatic was a completely fabricated climax in which a decades-old newspaper photo was magnified hundreds of times to prove that "Frank Wiecek" was innocent.

The movie ends with McNeal and Wiecek standing outside the prison gates. McNeal's cynicism has given way to conviction; his dangerous ventures into the Chicago netherworld have paid off with Wiecek's release. "It's a big thing when a sovereign state admits an error," McNeal tells Wiecek. "And remember this: There aren't many governments in the world that would do it." "It's a good world outside," Wiecek happily replies. "Yes, it's a good world outside," a narrator intones. "And Frank Wiecek is free: free because of a mother's faith, the courage of a newspaper, and one reporter's refusal to accept defeat." Wiecek embraces his son, and McNeal strolls off alone. His job is done.

Call Northside 777's melding of realism and melodrama produced a potent portrayal of the "press as guardians of morality," as one critic puts it.[33] Realism, whether in journalism or cinema, "implicitly argues that what we see is a dependable, truthful view of the world." It presumes that the world can be objectively and accurately rendered and grants particular authority to those such as journalists who are in charge of the rendering.[34] In *Citizen Kane,* the reporter Thompson abandoned his quest to find the truth about Kane by declaring that "Rosebud is just a piece in a jigsaw puzzle, a missing piece"; in *Call Northside 777,* McNeal's wife uses the same puzzle analogy in telling him, "Pieces never make the wrong picture. Maybe you're looking at them from the wrong angle." The reporter redoubles his quest and finally solves the puzzle by finding the "right" picture, a newspaper photo conclusively proving Wiecek's innocence.

Hollywood's dramatic conventions also underlined the journalist's role as upholder of the moral order. The movie gave the reporter an initially skeptical edge before gradually having him convert to the inmate's cause. As in Capra, the cynic-turned-idealist is as powerful a voice for morality as the sinner-turned-repentant. Like *Gentleman's Agreement, Call Northside 777* reproduced Hollywood's "traditional mythological dependence on individual solutions" and "reassured that hard work could correct societal injustices—the basic assertion of the official rhetoric."[35] It said that even with its glitches, the American system of justice and fair play worked, in contrast to those of other "governments in the world." Furthermore, it said journalists helped make it work, effectively equating them with Mom and apple pie.

NEWSROOM ELEGIES

If *Gentleman's Agreement* and *Call Northside 777* celebrated the "new, modern type" of professional journalist who was more adult and serious than that of the *Front Page* era, other movies celebrated the press by looking wistfully toward the past.

In Ben Hecht's and Charles MacArthur's day, reporters had been "an unlikely collection of itinerant scribblers . . . without much education and certainly without much refinement." Professionalization via journalism schools and press associations was an effort both to raise the standards of the craft and to harness "a workforce that [was] moral, orderly, habitual, and conservative."[36] Thus did Hecht and MacArthur lament that journalism schools had "nearly extirpated the species" of the "lusty, hoodlumesque half drunken caballero that was the newspaperman of our youth."[37]

Joseph Pulitzer was a major force behind that effort, endowing one of the nation's first journalism schools at Columbia University. Like Charles Foster

Kane, Pulitzer defied categorization. "Which was the real man—the front-page sensationalist or the schoolmaster-idealist of the editorial page?" wrote his biographer. "Could one really reconcile the millionaire capitalist, the palace-dweller, with the Pulitzer who attacked capitalists and trusts?" Pulitzer's credo for his flagship newspaper, the *New York World,* declared that it would "always fight for progress and reform" and "never be afraid to attack wrong, whether by predatory plutocracy or predatory poverty." At the same time, his paper served up "a gritty procession of headless corpses, adulterous clergy, and circulation-boosting stunts."[38]

Whatever his contradictions, they reconciled themselves over time in transforming Pulitzer into a mythic figure. One journalist hailed him as "the Great Emancipator of American journalism. He freed the American newspapers from the slavery of party and personal yoke and made them slaves to nothing except the truth and the facts."[39] The movies reproduced such myths in presenting Pulitzer-like figures. (*Citizen Kane* was an exception, but as already has been described, even that film did not reject the myth entirely.)

Park Row (1952) was as reverential as Pulitzer's most fervent disciples had been. It was written, directed, and produced by Samuel Fuller, who was no muddle-headed sentimentalist. He had reported for the *New York Graphic,* the most outlandish of the city's tabloids. His novel *The Dark Page,* about a homicidal newspaper journalist, helped inspire the noir films *The Big Clock* (1948) and *Scandal Sheet* (1952). However, *Park Row* was an homage to the birth of Pulitzer-like "New Journalism" in the 1880s.

It begins with hundreds of newspaper mastheads scrolling up the screen and a series of titles superimposed over them: "These are the names of 1,772 daily newspapers in the United States. One of them is the paper you read. All of them are the stars of this story." And finally, amid a thunderous volley of drums: "Dedicated to American journalism." Then viewers are introduced to the hero, Phineas Mitchell, the closest thing to a journalistic superhero next to Superman. As Fuller said, "I wanted one character to combine all the great newspaper editors of the period": James Gordon Bennett, Horace Greeley, Charles A. Dana, Henry J. Raymond, and Pulitzer.[40] So Mitchell starts his paper, the *Globe,* and in short order prints the story of Steve Brodie jumping off the Brooklyn Bridge, leads the fund drive for the Statue of Liberty's pedestal, and introduces the Linotype to newspapers thanks to Ottmar Mergenthaler himself (the inventor is understandably so impressed by Mitchell that he devotes all his energies to the *Globe*).

All does not go smoothly, however. The *Globe*'s publisher sees his staff beaten up and run over by wagons and his newsroom ransacked and bombed. The villain is the rival *Star*'s publisher, whom Mitchell calls "a frustrated journalistic fraud" even though he is powerfully attracted to her. Finally he assumes the role of outlaw hero and takes the law into his own hands by punching a *Star* thug down the street and smashing his skull repeatedly against a statue of Benjamin Franklin. As one critic writes of the film, "Good and evil are having one hell of a scrap and Fuller is reporting straight from the front line."[41]

Naturally, good wins. The mythic fighting editor stands up to all that would destroy him and his journalistic principles. The rival female editor kills the *Star* so that the *Globe* might live, and the movie ends with the image of the Statue of Liberty, an appropriate bookend to the film's start. *Park Row*'s message is clear: Contemporary newspapers carry on the legacy that men like Phineas Mitchell bequeathed them, one of liberty and professionalism.

Samuel Fuller originally had hoped to make *Park Row* for Darryl Zanuck at Fox, but he claimed that the studio chief wanted him to turn it into a musical with Mitzi Gaynor as "the first barmaid in New York."[42] As it turned out, Zanuck's studio produced a newspaper movie the same year that Fuller's appeared. *Deadline, USA* (1952) also was written and directed by a hardboiled ex-journalist, and it showed what eventually might have happened to Phineas Mitchell's *Globe* while it gave Mitchell a worthy heir.

Richard Brooks was born to immigrant parents who had learned English reading the *Philadelphia Bulletin*.[43] He attended journalism school at Temple University and worked as a sportswriter and radio commentator. After writing a successful novel, he worked in Hollywood first as a screenwriter and then as a director. He had wanted for years to do a film about the sort of newspaper his parents had read, gaining further inspiration from one that had folded two decades earlier: Pulitzer's *World*.

After Pulitzer's death in 1911, the *World* had increasingly targeted a more educated and middle-class readership, boasting a staff that at various times included Alexander Woolcott, Maxwell Anderson, Walter Lippmann, Heywood Broun, David Graham Phillips, and Herbert Bayard Swope. However, it was unable to compete with the *New York Times* and *Herald-Tribune* on one side and the city's new tabloids on the other. The paper ceased publication in 1931 to widespread dismay. City editor James W. Barrett wrote a tribute:

> It was the kind of newspaper that attracts newspapermen, makes them want to work for it, makes them glad to sacrifice for it, makes them willing to stay with the paper year after year on low salary, getting little or no recognition from the so-called higher-ups, doing the dirty work while others get the "by-lines" and the contracts, doing whatever came along, losing grip on home life, losing wife, children, family, just for the sake of being able to say: "I am working for *The World*."[44]

Brooks borrowed freely from the legend of the *World* and Pulitzer as he set out to create what he called "the first real HONEST movie about newspapers."[45] His screenplay called the paper the *Day* and gave it a fighting editor named Ed Hutcheson who struggled to keep it alive. In the first script drafts, Hutcheson's efforts paid off; the *Day* survived even as the editor left the paper.

As one of his friends later wrote, Brooks was "gruff yet unafraid of idealistic sentiment" and "retained the old-fashioned belief that rationality could, would eventually answer irrationality."[46] That surely resonated with the Darryl Zanuck who had made *Gentleman's Agreement.* By the early 1950s, however, even the comparatively mild liberalism of that film had come to seem dangerous in light of the witch hunts. During the production of *Deadline, USA,* Zanuck took pains to avoid raising the ire of the newspaper industry as well as that of the Breen Office, in charge of censoring Hollywood films.[47]

Thus, when he reviewed Brooks's initial drafts, Zanuck praised Hutcheson's character as being "a genuine original without being either Leftist or 'holy' about it" and suggested Gregory Peck ("awfully good as the reporter in *Gentleman's Agreement*") or Richard Widmark for the part. He did object to a barroom scene, saying "because of all the hell that newspapers have raised about drunken reporters and unethical newspaper men in *Ace in the Hole* I am frankly a trifle sensitive on this point." He also complained about a speech in which Hutcheson decried the decline in newspaper competition: "This is probably true but this picture we hope will play in Europe and I don't think we have the right to substantiate Communistic propaganda."

Most seriously, Zanuck said the ending lacked sufficient "suspense and jeopardy." Apart from Hutcheson trying to save the paper, the story focused on his efforts to win back his ex-reporter and ex-wife, Nora, while also trying to link a murder to a gangster named Rienzi. "What we need to get over here," said Zanuck, "is that there will always be a Rienzi unless there is somebody or some newspaper to stop him." Finally, the studio head called for a "hard-hitting" title.

Called *Deadline, USA* and starring Humphrey Bogart as Hutcheson, the movie showed the editor winning back his wife and proving the gangster's guilt with help from the immigrant mother of the young woman Rienzi has murdered. However, the paper is sold out from under him. It prints one last issue, leading to the stronger climax Zanuck called for and a memorable closing line. Hutcheson is in the pressroom to see the final edition printed when Rienzi telephones to threaten him. The editor responds by holding up the phone to the presses in full roar, and when Rienzi demands to know what the noise is, Hutcheson replies, "That's the press, baby. The press. And there's nothing you can do about it. Nothing!"

Whereas the world outside was good in *Call Northside 777,* it is not in *Deadline, USA.* The movie opens with Rienzi testifying before something like the Kefauver Committee on organized crime; that committee's hearings formed a backdrop to contemporaneous journalism films such as *The Captive City* (1952) and *The Turning Point* (1952) that have been categorized as noir.[48] One occasionally glimpses what seems to be a B-grade film noir happening just outside the newspaper's doors. The murdered young woman, "Sally," is pulled from the river nude except for a fur coat. Sally was being kept by Rienzi in return for her keeping hot money for him. She refused to return the money, apparently because she was stuck on him and thought that by holding the cash she also could hold him nearby. Rienzi then leaned on Sally's sweaty, bugeyed brother to reveal where she was; the brother stood aside as the gangster's henchmen beat and killed her. All that information starts to emerge after a *Day* sportswriter tracks down the brother in a dark corner of the city where foghorns sound and "Mood Indigo" plays.

In contrast, the newspaper office is a much more sedate, white-collar place. Ed Hutcheson at first is less concerned about gangsters than he is explaining the impact of a new tax program on the average citizen. When a young reporter asks to pursue the Rienzi story, the editor demurs: "It's not our job to prove he's guilty. We're not detectives and we're not in the crusading business."

After Rienzi's goons beat up the reporter, however, and after the *Day*'s prospective demise is made public, Hutcheson goes on the offensive. He is not the morally compromised protagonist of *Ace in the Hole* or *Sweet Smell of Success;* if Tatum, Falco, and Hunsecker have no conception of integrity, Hutcheson is the living embodiment of it. He readily quotes from the *Day*'s credo that Richard Brooks lifted word for word from Pulitzer and the *World.*

At the same time, Hutcheson is played by Bogart, which proved a crucial casting decision. In contrast to Gregory Peck or Richard Widmark (whose respective screen personas at the time were those of respectable citizen and giggling maniac), Bogart could be upstanding and insolent at once: a tough, sardonic good guy taking on tough, sardonic bad guys in the big city. Predictably, the editor character has his flaws. His marriage to his reporter wife has failed, and he makes a half-hearted Walter Burns–like attempt to break up her engagement to an advertising executive. He also gets drunk, but only at a wake for his dying paper (which Darryl Zanuck deemed permissible). When Rienzi tries to ply him with alcohol, he refuses.

Small wonder that Hutcheson's ex-wife finally returns to him and that the rest of the *Day*'s staff is devoted to him and the paper, no matter the personal cost. A reporter at the wake says after fourteen years on the paper that she has "eighty-one dollars in the bank, two dead husbands—and two or three kids I always wanted but never had." But, she adds tearfully, "I wouldn't change those years, not for anything in this world." Even while drunk, Hutcheson gives fatherly advice to a prospective young journalist, telling him that journalism is

The power of the press behind him, Ed Hutcheson (Humphrey Bogart) stands up to bad guys in *Deadline, USA*. (Courtesy of the Academy of Motion Picture Arts and Sciences)

"a performance for public good" and adding, "It may not be the oldest profession, but it's the best."

Just as in *Call Northside 777*, then, the newspaper is a righter of wrongs, a pillar of society, a haven of professionalism even when the noir world outside intrudes (the sweaty brother is shot by Rienzi's goons and plunges to his death on top of the newspaper presses). The woman who played the mother in *Call*

Northside 777 plays an identical role in *Deadline, USA,* one Brooks based on his own mother. She delivers damning evidence against Rienzi to Hutcheson, and when the editor tells her she may be endangering herself and asks why she has not gone to the police, she responds, "Police? I do not know police. I know *newspaper*. . . . You're not afraid. Your paper's not afraid. *I* am not afraid." Hutcheson and the *Day* print their exposé of Rienzi, and when the gangster issues his threat—"Sooner or later you'll catch it!"—Hutcheson retorts, "People like you have tried it before—with bullets, prisons, censorship—but as long as even one newspaper will print the truth, you're finished." Then comes the "that's the press" line as the *Day's* presses roll to the strains of "Battle Hymn of the Republic."

Still, that is the last hurrah; the battle hymn is also a funeral dirge. It already has been heard during the wake scene in its "John Brown's Body" version, sung in tribute to "Old Man Garrison"—the *Day's* Pulitzer-like founder whose ungrateful daughters are now selling the paper over their mother's objections—and ending with the words "his *Day* is done and gone." The last image of *Deadline, USA* is the lighted sign on top of the newspaper building going dark for good.

What remains is the *Standard,* the paper that has bought the *Day* only to kill it. During the wake, Hutcheson scans the *Standard's* front page, which displays a photograph of Sally's corpse that Hutcheson had refused to print in the *Day.* He says readers no longer are satisfied with just the news: "They want comics, contests, puzzles. . . . And if they accidentally stumble on the first page"—he disgustedly hurls the *Standard* onto the bar—"*news.*" Perhaps after the *Day's* demise there still will be a paper that fearlessly prints the truth about the Rienzis of the world, and perhaps the *Standard* will be it; a brief scene shows the *Standard's* publisher brandishing a copy of the *Day* and ordering his staff to give him the same kind of journalism. It seems unlikely, though, especially with Hutcheson not around.

The *Day's* martyrdom is one element of *Deadline, USA's* appeal for contemporary journalists. As a historian puts it, movies can "feed our nostalgia for an idealized past," and Brooks's film is beloved by those who see it as representing a better age when newspapers reigned supreme and were unafraid to fight.[49] However, *Deadline, USA* represented nostalgia even when it was released, and it was conscious of its own mythmaking. It celebrated the likes of Pulitzer, the *World,* and the immigrants such as Brooks's parents who read such papers. It mythologized journalistic professionalism while depicting freedom of speech and the press that no person or party could muzzle, a powerful symbol during the Cold War (if ironic in the context of the blacklist).

The movie also drew on Bogart's mythic presence. Particularly in confronting Rienzi and his goons, Bogart seems very much himself, living up to his outlaw hero persona. But he is no outlaw in the film. As an executive working within the system to fight corruption and report the truth, he is another official hero. The movie reconciles the outlaw and official types through Bogart, much as *Casablanca* had done a decade earlier by sending off Bogart's cynical loner to fight the Nazis.[50] *Deadline, USA* suggests that a journalist can be a public servant in coat and tie and call a gangster "baby" at the same time, combining the professionalism of journalism's modern age with the insouciance of its remembered past. In all those ways, the movie reinforced not only American mythology but also the press's most cherished self-image.

Yet the filmmakers' decision to kill the paper at the end—made in the interests of tough realism and a boffo finish—also exposed cracks in those myths, or what Robert Ray calls the "discrepancy between intent and effect" in many postwar films.[51] Hutcheson's defiant speech to Rienzi ("People like you have tried it before!") uncannily echoes Walter in *The Front Page* when he lectures the mayor about the power of the press: "Bigger men than you have found out what it is!" Walter and Hildy are saved only by a providential pardon, and in *Deadline, USA* Hutcheson's speech sounds even more like whistling in the dark. At the end of the film, he has a death threat hanging over his head. More tellingly and less romantically, his beloved paper has been done in by the same American values and institutions of free enterprise that the movie ostensibly lionizes (again ironic considering Zanuck's concerns about substantiating "Communistic propaganda").

In that, the film prophesied reality. The *World* in 1931 had been merged into the *World-Telegram*, which in turn merged into the *World-Telegram and the Sun*. That paper and several other New York dailies then ceased publication in the 1960s. Many more of the 1,772 papers whose mastheads *Park Row* had proudly displayed died in the following years, including the *Philadelphia Bulletin*, which had taught Richard Brooks's parents how to read English. As for all those who lost their jobs—who like James Barrett before them had discovered "that it was possible for men and women to cry over the death of a newspaper"[52]—Hutcheson's words to Rienzi could have just as well applied: That's the press, baby, and there's nothing you can do about it.

❦

Those who love *Deadline, USA* probably would see that alternative reading of Hutcheson's speech as far too cynical. "What majestic lines they are, so full of an eternal, beaming truth about this business I am in and would trade for no other," one newspaper journalist wrote fifty years after the movie first appeared. The stories that popular culture tells about journalism are "not wholly guaranteed for accuracy," he acknowledged. "But must myths be guaranteed for anything except to stir us?"[53]

Movies of the noir era reproduced stirring myths about journalism and its relationship to American democracy. The warring impulses within a mogul such as Joseph Pulitzer—both to educate and titillate, uplift the masses and destroy the competition—were resolved in journalism's "Great Emancipator" whose vision was sustained by professionals such as Ed Hutcheson and the staff of the *Day*.[54] The death of such newspapers, rather than being a lesson in the potential incompatibility of freedom of expression and the unfettered marketplace, became one of upholding professional responsibility to one's readers and thumbing one's nose at the bad guys.[55]

Such stories were shaped by politics, including pressure from professional journalism associations and the threat of blacklisting. They also were shaped by Richard Brooks's and Samuel Fuller's rose-colored memories of their journalistic youth, not unlike those of Hecht and MacArthur in *The Front Page*.

However, they also did what myths always have done: use "archetypical figures and forms to offer exemplary models for human life," offering journalists a glimpse of what they once may have been (or wished they had been) and what they might be again.[56] Even movies such as *Ace in the Hole* that many in the press disliked offered exemplary models for how journalists and others should *not* behave, stressing their lessons by punishing their villains or having them recant.

The films were for the most part inherently conservative, reflecting the perceived need during the Cold War for "a firm consensus on U.S. values: the precise meanings of American institutions and their unique superiority to other national traditions, the precise genius of the American character and its unique invulnerability to fascism, the precise classlessness of the American economy and its unique ability to provide luxury for ordinary folk." Those who violated that consensus were made into scapegoats; those who upheld it were venerated in their roles as "defenders and protectors of the status quo."[57]

The status quo embraced the official, respectable journalist and shunned the outlaw journalist to a degree not seen in screwball. It also was much more leery of tough, sardonic women. They were either villains or seductresses such as Lorraine in *Ace* and the rival editor in *Park Row*, or helpmates such as McNeal's wife in *Call Northside 777*.[58] In *Deadline, USA*, Hutcheson's ex-wife had quit journalism, whereas the reporter in the wake scene was left with little money, no family, and no job. The fashion editor in *Gentleman's Agreement* happily exclaimed, "I never let *any* man alone!" but was left alone herself.

Movies in coming years continued to expound on journalism's relationship to freedom and democracy and the role of women in the media. By the 1970s, they presented a tale of media corruption and female heartlessness against which *Ace in the Hole* paled. At the same time, they told a story of journalistic triumph against overwhelming odds that dwarfed anything Hollywood had been able to make up so far.

NOTES

1. James Harvey, *Romantic Comedy* (New York: Knopf, 1987), p. 669. For discussions of film noir and its place in cinema history and American culture, see Alain Silver and Elizabeth Ward, eds., *Film Noir,* 3rd ed. (Woodstock, N.Y.: Overlook, 1992); Foster Hirsch, *The Dark Side of the Screen* (New York: Da Capo, 1981); Lary May, *The Big Tomorrow* (Chicago: University of Chicago Press, 2000), pp. 215–56; Thomas Schatz, *Hollywood Genres* (New York: McGraw-Hill, 1981), pp. 111–49.

2. Stephen Vaughn and Bruce Evensen, "Democracy's Guardians: Hollywood's Portrait of Reporters, 1930–1945," *Journalism Quarterly* 68 (1991): 829–38.

3. Peter Kurth, *American Cassandra: The Life of Dorothy Thompson* (Boston: Little, Brown, 1990), p. 400. For more on Sheean, see Vincent Sheean, *Personal History* (Boston: Houghton Mifflin, 1969; originally published 1935); Paul L. Montgomery, "Vincent Sheean, Journalist, Dies at 75," *New York Times,* March 17, 1975, p. 32.

4. Ben Hecht banged out the "hang onto your lights" speech in one day for Hitchcock, whose film premiered almost two weeks before the London Blitz began in earnest. See Donald Spoto, *The Dark Side of Genius: The Life of Alfred Hitchcock* (Boston: Little, Brown, 1983), pp. 221–35; Clayton R. Koppes and Gregory D. Black, *Hollywood Goes to War* (New York: Free Press, 1987), pp. 26–27.

5. Pauline Kael, "Raising Kane," in *The Citizen Kane Book,* by Pauline Kael, Herman J. Mankiewicz, and Orson Welles (New York: Limelight, 1984), p. 27.

6. Vaughn and Evensen, "Democracy's Guardians"; James Tobin, *Ernie Pyle's War* (New York: Free Press, 1997), pp. 119–23; Bernard F. Dick, *The Star-Spangled Screen* (Lexington: University Press of Kentucky, 1985), pp. 226–28. Lester Cole also wrote *Blood on the Sun* (1945), with James Cagney as a journalist tracking the rise of fascism and militarism in prewar Japan.

7. Jeanine Basinger, *The World War II Combat Film* (New York: Columbia University Press, 1986), pp. 73–75.

8. Tobin, *Ernie Pyle's War,* p. 219.

9. Dick, *The Star-Spangled Screen,* p. 227.

10. For more on the blacklist and on *Roman Holiday,* see Otto Friedrich, *City of Nets* (Berkeley: University of California Press, 1997; originally published 1986); Jan Herman, *A Talent for Trouble* (New York: G.P. Putnam's Sons, 1995), pp. 341–57.

11. Robert Sklar, *Movie-Made America,* rev. ed. (New York: Vintage, 1994), pp. 269–85.

12. See for example Schatz, *Hollywood Genres,* pp. 113–16; Hirsch, *The Dark Side of the Screen,* pp. 53–67.

13. Ed Sikov, *On Sunset Boulevard* (New York: Hyperion, 1998).

14. Jack Fincher, "Dreams of Riches Led Floyd Collins to a Nightmarish End," *Smithsonian,* May 1990, pp. 137–50; Stan Chambers, *News at Ten* (Santa Barbara, Calif.: Capra, 1994), pp. 52–66.

15. May, *The Big Tomorrow*, p. 242.

16. Kevin Lally, *Wilder Times* (New York: Henry Holt, 1996), p. 215.

17. Reviewers' comments come from the *Ace in the Hole* Production/Clippings File, Margaret Herrick Library, Academy of Motion Picture Arts and Sciences (AMPAS), Beverly Hills, Calif.

18. *The Big Carnival* pressbook, AMPAS.

19. Lally, *Wilder Times*, p. 215; Silver and Ward, *Film Noir*, p. 24.

20. Jack Lule, *Daily News, Eternal Stories: The Mythological Role of Journalism* (New York: Guilford, 2001), pp. 62–63. See also Pamela J. Shoemaker and Stephen D. Reese, *Mediating the Message: Theories of Influences on Mass Media Content*, 2nd ed. (White Plains, N.Y.: Longman, 1996), pp. 46–48, 224–28.

21. Ed Sikov, *Screwball* (New York: Crown, 1989), p. 158.

22. Kate Buford, *Burt Lancaster: An American Life* (New York: Knopf, 2000), p. 177. Information on *Sweet Smell of Success* comes from Neal Gabler, *Winchell* (New York: Vintage, 1994), pp. 500–503; Ernest Lehman, "Introduction," in *Sweet Smell of Success*, by Clifford Odets and Ernest Lehman (London: Faber and Faber, 1998), pp. vii–viii; Buford, *Burt Lancaster*, pp. 177–84.

23. Hirsch, *The Dark Side of the Screen*, pp. 65–67; Sklar, *Movie-Made America*, pp. 269–85; Robert B. Ray, *A Certain Tendency of the Hollywood Cinema, 1930–1980* (Princeton, N.J.: Princeton University Press, 1985), pp. 129–52.

24. Frank Krutnik, *In a Lonely Street: Film Noir, Genre, Masculinity* (London: Routledge, 1991), p. 208.

25. George F. Custen, *Twentieth Century's Fox: Darryl F. Zanuck and the Culture of Hollywood* (New York: Basic, 1997); Laura Z. Hobson, *Laura Z: A Life* (New York: Arbor House, 1983). Additional information on *Gentleman's Agreement* comes from Hobson.

26. Friedrich, *City of Nets*, p. 364.

27. John T. McPhaul, *Deadlines and Monkeyshines* (Englewood Cliffs, N.J.: Prentice Hall, 1962), pp. 191–204; "Joe Majczek's Story," *Life*, March 1, 1948, pp. 57–59; Donald Dewey, *James Stewart* (Atlanta, Ga.: Turner, 1996), pp. 273–77.

28. *Call Northside 777* Production/Clippings File, AMPAS.

29. Hirsch, *The Dark Side of the Screen*, p. 67.

30. Krutnik, *In a Lonely Street*, p. 204.

31. Script drafts of the film are in the Twentieth Century Fox Collection, Arts Library Special Collections, University of California at Los Angeles (UCLA); see also Rudy Behlmer, ed., *Memo from Darryl F. Zanuck* (New York: Grove, 1993), pp. 121–24. Quentin Reynolds soon became embroiled in a highly publicized libel suit against columnist Westbrook Pegler, and he never wrote for the movies again.

32. Dewey, *James Stewart*, p. 276.

33. Krutnik, *In a Lonely Street*, p. 205.

34. J. P. Telotte, *Voices in the Dark: The Narrative Patterns of Film Noir* (Urbana: University of Illinois Press, 1989), p. 135; Kevin G. Barnhurst and John Nerone, *The Form of News: A History* (New York: Guilford, 2001), pp. 111–39; Hirsch, *The Dark Side of the Screen*, pp. 172–73.

35. Ray, *A Certain Tendency of the Hollywood Cinema*, p. 158.

36. James W. Carey, "Some Personal Notes on US Journalism Education," *Journalism: Theory, Practice, and Criticism* 1:1 (2000): 16.

37. Ben Hecht and Charles MacArthur, *The Front Page* (New York: Covici-Friede, 1928), p. 31.

38. W. A. Swanberg, *Pulitzer* (New York: Charles Scribner's Sons, 1967), p. 411; James W. Barrett, *The World, the Flesh, and Messrs. Pulitzer* (New York: Vanguard, 1931), p. 8; Richard Norton Smith, "Containing Multitudes," *Columbia Journalism Review*, November–December, 2001, p. 150.

39. Barrett, *The World, the Flesh, and Messrs. Pulitzer*, p. 8.

40. Nicholas Garnham, *Samuel Fuller* (New York: Viking, 1971), pp. 14–15.

41. Ibid., p. 19.

42. Lee Server, *Sam Fuller: Life Is a Battleground* (Jefferson, N.C.: McFarland, 1994), p. 31.

43. Biographical information on Brooks comes from Charles Champlin, "A Veteran of Tough Times and Tough Films," *Los Angeles Times*, October 23, 1990, p. F1.

44. Barrett, *The World, the Flesh, and Messrs. Pulitzer*, p. 16.

45. *Deadline, USA* Production/Clippings File, AMPAS.

46. Richard Schickel, *Matinee Idylls* (Chicago: Ivan R. Dee, 1999), pp. 212, 224.

47. Custen, *Twentieth Century's Fox*, pp. 312–17; A. M. Sperber and Eric Lax, *Bogart* (New York: William Morrow, 1997), pp. 448–49.

48. See the entries for those films in Silver and Ward, *Film Noir*.

49. Robert Brent Toplin, *History by Hollywood: The Use and Abuse of the American Past* (Urbana: University of Illinois Press, 1996), p. 12. For discussions of how *Deadline, USA* still can inspire contemporary journalists, see Pete Hamill, *News Is a Verb* (New York: Library of Contemporary Thought, 1998), p. 90; Christopher Hanson, "Where Have All the Heroes Gone?" *Columbia Journalism Review*, March–April, 1996, pp. 45–48; Judith Servin and William Servin, eds., *Muckraking: The Journalism That Changed America* (New York: New Press, 2002), pp. 387–88; Schickel, *Matinee Idylls*, pp. 211–12.

50. Ray, *A Certain Tendency of the Hollywood Cinema*, pp. 89–112.

51. Ibid., pp. 153–74.

52. Barrett, *The World, the Flesh, and Messrs. Pulitzer*, p. 5.

53. Don Freeman, "Presses, Ink, Personalities (Fedora Optional): Read All about It," *San Diego Union-Tribune*, November 15, 2002, p. E7.

54. The romantic comedy *Teacher's Pet* (1958) similarly resolves tensions between journalism's outlaw side and its idealistic official side as tabloid editor Clark Gable (who calls journalism a "rough, tough, fighting, clawing *business*") falls for journalism teacher Doris Day (who insists the press must report the "why" behind the news). Their subsequent union is described as "the wedding of the old pros and the eggheads."

55. For a discussion of *Deadline, USA* as a journalism ethics case study that also asks whether government should regulate media mergers more strictly, see Howard Good and Michael J. Dillon, *Media Ethics Goes to the Movies* (Westport, Conn.: Praeger, 2002), pp. 21–37.

56. Lule, *Daily News, Eternal Stories,* p. 15; Michael Schudson, *Watergate in American Memory* (New York: Basic Books, 1992).

57. Barnhurst and Nerone, *The Form of News,* p. 208; Hirsch, *The Dark Side of the Screen,* p. 67.

58. Some critics have suggested that noir's femme fatales actually subvert patriarchal values. See for example Ann Kaplan, ed., *Women in Film Noir* (London: British Film Institute, 1980).

News and Conspiracy

The 1970s were a time of remarkable inventiveness and artistic achievement in Hollywood. Directors including Robert Altman, Roman Polanski, Francis Ford Coppola, Steven Spielberg, George Lucas, and Martin Scorsese came to the fore. Film historian Robert Sklar says movies such as *The Godfather, Chinatown, Nashville,* and *Taxi Driver* "marked a period not only of cinematic innovation but of a critical and analytical approach to national institutions rarely seen in mainstream American filmmaking."[1] That reflected the collapse of the traditional Hollywood studio system and the Production Code, both of which had sharply constrained overt politicizing (as had the blacklist, which finally had loosened its grip in the 1960s). It also reflected a broader cultural distrust of national institutions in light of Vietnam, Watergate, and stagflation.

Such conditions helped give rise to the "conspiracy film," which in Fredric Jameson's words explores an age "whose abominations are heightened by their concealment and their bureaucratic impersonality."[2] Conspiracy films shared with noir a theme of alienation and individuals confronting evil forces. Now those forces were rooted in the impersonal bureaucracies of big government and big business, and the shadowy figures working inside them were engaged in conspiracies to cover up dark and terrible truths.[3]

The conspiracy film reflected the angst of the times and also reflected a long tradition of paranoid thought in American culture.[4] One scholar notes that in democratic societies "the necessary balancing act between individual interests and the common good provokes suspicions."[5] In turn, conspiracy stories express fears of an oppressive social order constraining personal freedom. As Timothy Melley writes, they tell how "the 'postindustrial' economy has made Americans more generic and less autonomous than their rugged forebears and about how social structures—especially government and corporate bureaucracies, control technologies, and 'the media'—have become autonomous agents in their own right."[6]

Hence conspiracy movies made the media a focal point, with journalists facing long odds in exposing and resisting official evil. In *All the President's*

Men, the newspaper and the men who work for it represent a shining beacon of truth against the menacing corruption of the nation's capital. In *Network,* the television network and the rest of corporate America constitute an all-encompassing monstrosity that is systematically destroying independent thought and the conscientious professional journalist. Gender also plays a key role: *All the President's Men* is a man's world not only in terms of those who work for Nixon but those who investigate him, with the paper overseen by a rugged old-school newsman. In *Network,* a rugged old-school newsman is ensnared by a rapacious woman who represents the "media" as opposed to journalism and who is central to the conspiracy itself.

The two movies also differ in their relation to history. *All the President's Men* claims documentary-like fidelity in painstakingly recreating the press's exposure of the Watergate scandal. However, the movie "leaves the impression that two *Washington Post* reporters, Bob Woodward and Carl Bernstein, almost single-handedly brought down the Nixon administration."[7] In contrast, *Network* positions itself as satiric prognosticator via its "Mad Prophet of the Airwaves" warning of TV's corruption of the human spirit. Like their cinematic predecessors, though, both movies reproduce individualist mythology with the journalist at its heart, and both are tinged with nostalgia.

ROOTS OF THE JOURNALISM CONSPIRACY FILM

The 1970s film renaissance followed a fallow period during which Robert Sklar says "fewer and fewer pictures were being made, and fewer still made money," so that "studios became interested only in the motion-picture equivalent of a home run," the big box office hit.[8] The result included frothy farces such as *Sex and the Single Girl* (1964), exceedingly loosely based on the Helen Gurley Brown book of the same name. Natalie Wood plays "Dr. Helen Brown," a sex therapist apparently determined to avoid sex at all costs. Tony Curtis is sleazy magazine editor Bob Weston, who tries to discredit the doctor by seducing her. Predictably they fall in love. "I don't want to be a single girl," says Dr. Brown while rocking a stuffed animal like a baby. "I want *Bob Weston.*" When he resists, she wins him by craftily batting her eyes and working up a healthy set of tears.[9]

The film did good business, but it and other mainstream movies did little to address the wrenching social conflicts of the 1960s. Samuel Fuller's *Shock Corridor* (1963) was decidedly nonmainstream. On the surface, its plot was conventional enough: A reporter urged on by his gung-ho editor goes undercover to investigate a murder, much to his girlfriend's consternation. But the reporter is a little crazy to begin with and obsessed with journalistic glory at any price. It does not bode well that he poses as an inmate in an insane asylum. There he is attacked by nymphomaniacs to the strains of "My Bonnie Lies Over the Ocean," and he starts believing that his girlfriend—who works as a stripper—is actually his sister. His price for getting the story is complete catatonia, leading the asylum head to remark sadly, "What a tragedy. An insane mute will win the Pulitzer Prize."

Fuller later said he wanted to portray America as a madhouse on the verge of self-destruction. So the reporter character confronts inmates who represent victims of war, racism, and the arms race: a Korean War veteran who defected to the Communists and now thinks he is an 1860s Confederate soldier, a young African American man who tried to enroll in an all-white Southern university and now spews the racist invective of the Ku Klux Klan, and a nuclear physicist who "got fed up with man taking a daily hammer-and-sickle pill of venom" and now behaves like a small child. Each of the inmates has moments of lucidity during which he expresses his plight, and together they provide a striking critique of 1963 America. *Shock Corridor* was released shortly after Martin Luther King's "I Have a Dream" speech and just before the Birmingham church bombing; President Kennedy's assassination was only a few months away. But the movie was marketed as an exploitation vehicle ("Shocking world of psychos and sex-maddened women exposed!"), and it soon disappeared.[10]

Black Like Me (1964) also vanished quickly from theaters. An adaptation of John Howard Griffin's account of posing as an African American in the Deep South, the movie was created by Carl and Gerda Lerner (the latter of whom became a pioneering women's history scholar). Their movie starred James Whitmore as "John Finley Horton," who darkens his skin for a magazine series. But like Samuel Fuller, they had to contend with a low budget, and Whitmore's countenance in the film was so bizarre that a reviewer wrote "one almost expects him to burst into 'Mammy' a la Jolson."[11]

Although both *Shock Corridor* and *Black Like Me* did poorly at the box office, they signaled a nascent distrust of the media. Fuller's earlier movie *Park Row* had portrayed nineteenth-century journalists as "guardians of the truth." In contrast, *Shock Corridor* showed them as "part of the great conspiracy, part of the totalitarianism of lies" that the modern mass media propagated.[12] *Black Like Me* went beyond the similarly themed *Gentleman's Agreement* in hinting that the journalist's quest to bridge the racial divide might be hopeless and even exploitive. It showed a young African American militant berating Whitmore's character for "sneaking into here all painted up," adding that the reporter's articles "won't make any difference—they're just *words*." Even *Sex and the Single Girl* connected indirectly to that sense of distrust. It was scripted by Joseph Heller, who was looking to earn quick cash while *Catch-22* found its audience. If his screenplay self-consciously looked to the past (Heller called it "a parody of every movie Doris Day ever made"[13]), his novel introduced a catchphrase for a more complicated and less trusting time: "Just because you're paranoid doesn't mean they're not out to get you."

The paranoia manifested itself full flower in Haskell Wexler's *Medium Cool* (1969). Wexler was an Oscar-winning cinematographer who had shot *In the Heat of the Night,* featuring Sidney Poitier as an African American police detective investigating a murder in the South. Although the movie won the best picture Oscar for 1967, Wexler was dissatisfied with it: "I resent films that talk about subjects that I'm interested in and pretend to be on the good side but are superficial."[14] He wanted to write and direct his own film that would combine fiction with documentary techniques.

In particular, Wexler was intrigued by cinema verité, which assumed that standard journalistic and cinematic methods inevitably distorted the truth. Rather than interviewing sources, gathering facts, and writing accounts that asserted themselves as objective renderings of reality, cinema verité sought to provide a more transparent view of the world simply by bearing witness.[15] An example was D. A. Pennebaker's *Don't Look Back* (1967), showing Bob Dylan touring England and putting down interviewers. "If I want to find out anything, I'm not gonna read *Time* magazine," Dylan sneers at a reporter from that very magazine. "I'm not gonna read *Newsweek.* I'm not gonna read any of these *magazines!* I mean, 'cause they've just got too much to lose by printing the *truth.*" It was not just the cinematic technique of such films that appealed to Wexler but also their attitude, which again reflected distrust of the media and the rest of the establishment. "I have very strong opinions about us and the world," he said at the time, adding, "I don't know how in hell to put them all in one basket."[16]

Medium Cool became that basket, an amalgamation of Wexler's views on the war on poverty, Vietnam, the antiwar movement, the black power movement, sex, violence, voyeurism, and the corporate media. The film centers around a Chicago TV news camera operator (Robert Forster). He becomes involved with a young Appalachian woman who has moved to the city and is raising her son alone. The boy runs off when he sees the man kissing his mother, and she searches for him amid the clashes between police and protesters at the 1968 Democratic national convention. She enlists the camera operator's help in the search, but their car crashes, killing her and critically injuring him.

That is the plot, such as it is. The film is a heady and sometimes confusing mix of documentary and dramatic invention, exactly what Wexler had said he sought to do. In addition to cinema verité, it drew on French new wave films and the sociological journalism of Studs Terkel. Wexler's camera captured graphic images of the convention turmoil alongside those of National Guard training exercises and the Poor People's campaign that Martin Luther King was to have led before his assassination. At times, the documentary footage—such as that of guards pretending to be protesters and jokingly singing "We Shall Overcome"—seemed less realistic than the fictional footage of the mother sharing a meal with her son and the boy playing cards with his friends. One of the movie's most dramatic moments showed a tear gas canister exploding while someone was heard warning, "Look out, Haskell, it's *real!*" Although the footage was real, the warning was scripted and dubbed in after the fact, further blurring the line between truth and fiction.[17]

What Wexler evoked most strikingly was the era's anger and violence and the media's complicity in it all. A black power activist directly addresses the camera: "You are the exploiters. You're the ones who distort and ridicule and emasculate us." The camera operator and his sound technician film a moaning woman sprawled in a smashed-up car; only afterward does the camera operator say: "Better call an ambulance." He is fired after discovering that his TV station has given his film of draft card burners to the FBI; he searches futilely in the station's long, windowless corridors for someone in authority to confront. He is the victim of sinister, faceless forces just as the draftees are, and in the end he suffers the same fate as the woman in the smashed-up car: As he lies in his own wrecked auto while protesters are heard chanting "the whole world is watching," a boy leans out of a rusty old station wagon to snap a photo.

Medium Cool has been called "the summation of an era, for it records the process of political enlightenment that was the sixties."[18] The footage of bloodied antiwar protesters at the Democratic convention (ironically accompanied by the Democrats' anthem "Happy Days Are Here Again") implicitly questioned the American presence in Vietnam, the political establishment's collusion in the war, and the media's contentment with merely recording the mayhem.

Like *Shock Corridor* and *Black Like Me, Medium Cool* was a commercial failure. There was government and studio pressure to shelve the film; when it finally was released, it was saddled with an X rating. That was at least partly because of a bedroom scene with full frontal nudity, but Wexler claimed it was primarily because of the film's political content.[19] Regardless, the controversy reflected what Todd Gitlin called the "apocalyptic, polarized political mood" of the era, sustained through the mass media that presented an "image of violence outside reason or context." Gitlin says the resulting atmosphere helped contribute to the bloody confrontations in Chicago, which left the Democrats in disarray and helped elect Richard Nixon. It also gave the incoming administration a pretext "to justify repression—including repression of the press itself for amplifying the bad news—and its own paranoia."[20]

The ultimate result of that paranoia was Watergate, and Watergate was forever enshrined in the public imagination by a movie that bore some commonalities with *Medium Cool.* Again individuals confronted sinister forces in the political economic sector; again those forces were essentially faceless (with the lone whistleblower known only as "Deep Throat" and seen only in shadow); again the story played out against actual historical events. However, *Medium Cool* flirted with the avant-garde in suggesting that truth, especially as transmitted by the mass media, was an iffy proposition. *All the President's Men* was far more traditional not only in its storytelling technique but in implying that "official" figures working for the establishment media could discover the truth and stop institutional abuses.

ALL THE PRESIDENT'S MEN

The film's protagonists were a pair of reporters who had vastly different backgrounds and experiences with the 1960s' upheavals. Carl Bernstein was the son of Jewish union activists who belonged to the Communist party. A Washington, D.C., native, he started as a copyboy at the *Washington Star* at age sixteen. He moved to Greenwich Village in 1965 and busily began building a reputation for womanizing that later came back to haunt him. At the same time, he developed his journalistic skills at the *Elizabeth Daily Journal* across the Hudson, writing a lengthy account of the New York City blackout that climaxed with a bus ride to New Jersey: "Then Boom! Brighter than a thousand suns! A billion-zillion-trillion candlepower. Dazzling, blazing, burning, positively blazing! Magnificent, splendiferous, overpowering, glittering, gleaming, flashing, brilliant! . . . Weehawken, the City of Light!" It was, his biographer writes, "a discount version of Jack Kerouac crossed with Tom Wolfe," but it won Bernstein an award and helped him land at the *Washington Post* the following year.[21]

By that time, Bob Woodward was serving in the U.S. Navy. If Bernstein by upbringing and temperament was sympathetic to the counterculture and demonstrated an outlaw ethos (he tried unsuccessfully to be hired as a rock critic at *Rolling Stone*), Woodward was the opposite. He was born to a Protestant Republican family in Illinois and attended Yale, where he scolded his girlfriend for saying nice things about the Students for a Democratic Society and was called a crypto-fascist by one of his professors. His naval duty aboard the U.S.S. *Wright* dealt with top-secret military communications at the height of the Vietnam era, although Woodward became disaffected with the war and avoided being sent to Vietnam. Later he was stationed at the Pentagon and may have briefed officials at the White House. He developed sources that held him in good stead when he entered journalism and joined the *Post* in 1971.

"Howard, they're *hungry*. You remember when you were hungry?" So metro editor Harry Rosenfeld says to managing editor Howard Simons in *All the President's Men* (1976), talking about Woodward and Bernstein. The popular image from the movie remains: Two young, unattached reporters (Woodward was divorced, Bernstein was separated), eager to make their reputations at a paper not certain whether it should fully trust them, reconciled their differences under the guidance of editor Ben Bradlee to uncover the biggest political scandal in U.S. history and bring down a president. It has been called "the central myth of American journalism." Yet it is also controversial, with one historian branding the film "a milestone in the process of exalting the press while demonizing government."[22]

To interpret the movie, one must take into account the actual events connected to the *Washington Post*'s coverage of Watergate, how Woodward and Bernstein related those events in their book of *All the President's Men*, how a director brought a paranoid sensibility to translating the book into film, and how the film both reproduced and eschewed the conventions of the journalism movie genre in such a way as to celebrate the press in a distinctly noncelebratory age.

First, the events: Early the morning of June 17, 1972, police arrested burglars at the Watergate headquarters of the Democratic National Committee. Woodward and police reporter Al Lewis covered the burglars' arraignment later that day for the *Post*. One burglar revealed he had worked for the CIA. The next morning, police reporter Gene Bachinski was allowed to see items taken from the arrestees' pockets; they included a notebook linking the burglars to the White House. Over the next few months, the *Post* continued to investigate the story, with Woodward and Bernstein taking the lead. By late October, they had reported that the break-in was part of a widespread campaign of political sabotage linked to President Nixon's chief of staff, H. R. Haldeman. The Haldeman story embarrassed the paper, if only temporarily; the reporters misunderstood what one of their sources had told a grand jury and reported his testimony incorrectly. They soon established that their story was essentially accurate: The Watergate scandal extended to the president's closest aide.[23]

Nevertheless, less than two weeks after the Haldeman article appeared, Nixon was reelected in one of the biggest landslides in U.S. history. His political troubles did not begin in earnest until the following year, when the Senate Watergate hearings were broadcast nationwide and public opinion shifted against him. Even then, Nixon stayed on until August 1974—after the book of *All the President's Men* had been published—when the "smoking gun" tape proving his complicity in the cover-up was made public. In short, critics charge, Woodward and Bernstein can hardly be given credit for bringing down the president. They also assert that government officials and not the press exposed Watergate; Woodward and Bernstein relied on those officials to leak them information from investigations that had begun soon after the burglary.[24]

In addition, critics have taken exception to aspects of Woodward's and Bernstein's book. None was the subject of more speculation, even three decades later, than Deep Throat, the mysterious Nixon administration source whom Woodward said he met in a deserted parking garage. The reporters' biographer, Adrian Havill, went so far as to visit the apartment building from which Woodward had supposedly posted signals that he wanted to talk to Deep Throat. Havill concluded that it would have been extremely difficult for a person in the courtyard below to see such signals.[25]

Although Havill suggested that Deep Throat was an invention, in 2003 an investigative reporting class at the University of Illinois asserted that Deep Throat was deputy White House counsel Fred Fielding. Carl Bernstein claimed that the class's investigation violated journalistic principles by seeking to uncover a secret source. Instructor Bill Gaines responded that when a journalist genuinely wants to protect someone, "he or she does not give clues as to who the source is and give the source a name, make a movie character out of the source, say when they met and how they met and what the signal was and what the source said." Gaines added that the class assumed that everything Woodward and Bernstein wrote about Deep Throat was true given that they presented their book as an autobiographical work of nonfiction: "If we're wrong, it's because they've given us wrong information."[26]

If Woodward and Bernstein had exaggerated or made up Deep Throat (and Woodward continually denied that they had done so), they might have been trying to deflect attention from their real sources. Conversely, they simply may have wanted to tell as good a story as possible, especially when Hollywood came calling. Robert Redford had become interested in Woodward and Bernstein during the 1972 campaign while he was promoting his film *The Candidate*— not just in their aggressiveness in pursuing Watergate while the rest of the press largely ignored the story, but in their contrasting personalities. He contacted them the following spring about a possible movie. By then, the reporters had a deal to write a book that was to focus on the Nixon administration's illegal activities dating back to 1970. Redford encouraged them to concentrate instead on themselves and the Watergate break-in; that would make a better movie, and he was offering $450,000 for the rights. At the same time, the reporters' editor at Simon and Schuster urged them to "build up the Deep Throat character and make him interesting." That was the genesis, Adrian Havill argues, of the meetings with Deep Throat in the deserted parking garage and his warnings that the reporters' lives were in danger.[27]

The movie, starring Redford as Woodward and Dustin Hoffman as Bernstein, accentuated even more the journalists' role in Watergate and the cloak-and-dagger aspects of the story. Under director Alan J. Pakula, the film adopted a noir-like look and feel, portrayed the reporters as serious but small and anonymous figures, and depicted the paper and its editor as fearless foes of corruption.

All the President's Men was the third of what has been called Pakula's "paranoia trilogy," following *Klute* (1971) and *The Parallax View* (1974).[28] The latter starred Warren Beatty as a scruffy, vaguely countercultural reporter who goes undercover to investigate a conspiracy behind a string of political assassinations. In the end, he too is killed, and an investigative board (obviously modeled on the Warren Commission) rules that the reporter actually was the assassin and acted alone. Pakula asserted that the film "represents my view of what's happening in the world . . . the individual [being] destroyed in a secret maze by forces of which he has no knowledge."[29] Tellingly, those forces reached to the highest echelons of official America.

The director brought the same conspiracy-mindedness to his Watergate film. He began by stressing the tough realism that had characterized such "documentary noirs" as *Call Northside 777,* with their air of "reportorial accuracy."[30] The filmmakers reproduced the *Post's* newsroom on a movie soundstage, using mirrors to add depth. They copied the reporters' desk decorations, arranged 1972 calendars, phone books, and newspapers around the set, and even flew in trash from the Washington newsroom. Special wastebaskets were set aside for the crew to dispose of its cigarettes so as not to interfere with the prop ashtrays on the set. The tedium of investigative reporting was shown through the reporters' constant phone calls and note taking, which Pakula filmed in long takes and tight closeups. The filmmakers also shot on location at the Watergate and in the Library of Congress, spending $90,000 for the overhead shot of Woodward and Bernstein sifting through library slips to try to link the White House to a smear campaign against Ted Kennedy.[31]

Pakula then overlaid the documentary details with an air of foreboding. He was assisted mightily by cinematographer Gordon Willis, who had filmed both *Klute* and *The Parallax View* and whom screenwriter William Goldman called "the hero" of *All the President's Men.* Willis's approach to the movie, as an observer described it, was "fairly harsh both in lighting and in color because this enhances the aura of eeriness and fear."[32] Whereas the *Post* newsroom was shown in brilliant white light, the rest of Washington was often shrouded in darkness. The noirish tone was especially pronounced in Woodward's nocturnal meetings with Deep Throat, the last of which ended with the reporter running from a phantom pursuer to the ominous strains of David Shire's music.

The movie's depiction of Woodward, Bernstein, and the *Post* was significantly different from what first had been written. Screenwriter William Goldman had won an Oscar for *Butch Cassidy and the Sundance Kid,* and he appeared to draw on both that movie and *The Front Page* in his initial drafts of *All the President's Men.* The result was less noir than screwball. "When Woodward talks to Bernstein," Goldman wrote, "or either of them to Rosenfeld or Simons or Bradlee—it must be fast and clipped and constantly overlapping—

these people are always at war with the clock and the success of their lives depends on getting more words in quicker than the next guy." Also in the journalism movie tradition, Woodward had a girlfriend who complained about him being more concerned about his job than her. Comic scenes showed Bernstein having his bike stolen ("Nazi bastards!" he screamed after the thieves) and Bradlee, Simons, and Rosenfeld playing with a sponge rubber basketball while discussing a key Watergate story ("You think they play basketball at the *New York Times?*" Rosenfeld asked).[33]

The *Post,* which was not sure it even wanted its name associated with the film, was not amused; neither were Woodward and Bernstein. To Goldman's shock, Bernstein and his wife-to-be, Nora Ephron, wrote their own draft. "While Bernstein was depicted as a great lover, swinging from one girl's bed to the next," one observer said of the draft, "Woodward was painted as a vapid, colorless Elmer Fud[d], worshiping at the shrine of Bernstein's brilliance." "Carl, Errol Flynn is dead," Robert Redford said after reading it.[34] (Woodward's reaction went unrecorded.)

Eventually Pakula called in another writer, and the final screenplay took shape with input from both reporters. As for Goldman, he later said if he had had it all to do over again, "I wouldn't have come near *All the President's Men.*" However, the screenplay did win him his second Oscar, and his story structure contributed greatly to the film's lionization of the press. Goldman eliminated the second half of Woodward's and Bernstein's book and ended with the reporters' temporary setback with their Haldeman article; he reasoned that the audience could fill in the rest of the story for themselves, including the Senate hearings and most of the government figures who helped bring down the president. At first, the screenwriter struggled to fit in all of Nixon's cronies who had figured in Watergate. Finally he realized that they did not matter, for the movie at heart was a David and Goliath story.[35]

In this case, "David" was the two reporters, and the movie did all it could to depict the odds against them. It eliminated most of the comedy of the original script drafts with only an occasional barb traded by the reporters ("is there any place you *don't* smoke?" Woodward asks Bernstein in an elevator). It also discarded love interests for both men. That was unusual for stars such as Redford and Hoffman, for whom a script typically provided more humor, sex, and personality, but it highlighted the reporters' single-minded devotion to getting the story. In the film, they have no apparent lives outside their work. Woodward falls asleep in his clothes surrounded by newspapers and appears to subsist on a bachelor's diet of Ritz crackers. When Bernstein flirts with a young woman (something the actual man was all too likely to do), it is only to get information to further the story. At times the reporters are merely specks against the Washington landscape, as in the scenes at the Library of Congress and the reporters driving through nighttime streets while going through end-less lists of people who will not talk to them.

Just as David felled Goliath with his slingshot, the journalists in the movie topple—or seem to topple—the Nixon administration. "I was fascinated by the idea of words as weapons," said director Pakula. "Also the notion of an enormous power being brought down by tiny little things." Therefore, the soundtrack turns up the reporters' pencils scratching on their pads, "like rats furrowing." The opening of the film, a giant close-up of "June 1, 1972" being typed, blends the sounds of the keys striking the paper with those of gun shots and whip lashes. At the close, the cannons being fired to celebrate Nixon's reinauguration are gradually drowned out by a teletype rattling off stories of his downfall.[36]

The movie thus graphically underscores the power of the press much as the climax of *Deadline, USA* had. The paper also has a tough but principled editor similar to Bogart's in the earlier film. Jason Robards's Ben Bradlee is the movie's showiest role, and the other *Post* editors' contributions are downplayed (so much so that Bradlee's real-life relationship with Howard Simons, whom the film depicts unflatteringly, was damaged almost beyond repair).[37] Feet propped on a newsroom desk, Bradlee coolly squelches one of the reporters' early Watergate stories for not having enough facts. He later enjoys two bravura moments when he reviews a story tying John Mitchell to Watergate and growls "*Run* that baby" (much as Bogart had growled, "That's the *press,* baby!") and when he delivers his final speech to the two reporters who have just blundered on the Haldeman story: "Nothing's riding on this except the First Amendment to the Constitution, freedom of the press and maybe the future of the country. Not that any of that matters. But if you guys fuck up again, I'm gonna get mad."

Of course, they do not err again; although the denouement occurs off screen, the paper is triumphant. Not surprisingly, most of the press loved it. "This is a movie journalists can see without either cringing or hooting," Nat Hentoff wrote. "In some places the gritty familiarity is so compelling that a watching reporter may get hit with the nagging feeling that he's missing a deadline while sitting there."

But Hentoff also anticipated many of the criticisms that *All the President's Men* engendered in the years to come. The movie showed Woodward and Bernstein misleading sources and trying to obtain secret grand jury testimony and phone records, and it strongly implied that the ends justified the means. Hentoff mused that the film's idealization of reporters who "cast hard, merciless light" on society could lead journalists to see "themselves being without shadows"—that is, as professional exposers of public transgressions rather

Feet on desk, Ben Bradlee (Jason Robards) nixes an early Watergate story while Woodward (Robert Redford) and Bernstein (Dustin Hoffman) look on glumly in *All the President's Men*. (Courtesy of the Academy of Motion Picture Arts and Sciences)

than as flawed fellow humans, casting judgment on others while remaining above judgment themselves.[38]

That pointed to key differences between *All the President's Men* and the screwball and noir-era journalism films. Screwball had tended to portray the press as less than the ultimate arbiter of truth and justice. *Deadline, USA* and *Call Northside 777* had idealized journalism, but the first movie had killed off its paper and the second had dramatized journalism's role in a case with little impact outside Chicago. Both also showed the journalists experiencing temporary doubt and disillusionment through their encounters with their love interests. *All the President's Men* dispensed with the familiar journalism movie contrast between the protagonists' professional and domestic lives to focus solely on the reporters pursuing the story, driven by their ambition to make their names at the paper. In the process, the film showed "two young men precipitat[ing] the greatest constitutional crisis since the Civil War."[39]

It thus exalted professional expertise and authority—and, some would argue, encouraged arrogance as well. James Carey has asserted that journalists' claim to professional status debases civic life because it implies that they alone may decide what the public should know and think about. In his words, "Professionals are privileged to live in a morally less ambiguous universe than the rest of us." In fact, the book of *All the President's Men* has been analyzed as a "romance narrative," with the reporter heroes pursuing their lonely quest for truth and the narrative glossing over "the ambiguities of everyday life, where everything is a mixture of good and bad, and where it is difficult to take sides or believe that people are consistent patterns of virtue or vice."[40]

So it is with the movie. The press is unambiguously on the side of virtue; the Nixon administration—with the furtive, conflicted exception of Deep Throat—is unambiguously on the side of vice. Those looking for "a more searching study of American compromise" or even for a more "searching inquiry into the secret state or the clandestine dimensions of the U.S. government" will be disappointed. Instead, writes one critic, *All the President's Men* was a snappy thriller that permanently "enshrined the fallacy of indefatigable news hounds" exposing Watergate. It "proved that the sense of fiction was so rampant in America that you could go from fact to legend in three years without passing understanding."[41]

Woodward and Bernstein were increasingly criticized for helping foster that legend. "When journalists are doing their jobs, according to journalists' own professed ideals of objectivity, they are on the sidelines, the transcribers, perhaps the watchdogs, but not the central actors, of society's dramas," writes Michael Schudson. In contrast, the *Post* reporters made themselves the protagonists of their account of investigating Watergate, not unlike Bernstein's first-person account of the 1965 blackout and not unlike the era's "New Journalists," who were "always implicitly writing about [their own] experience of reporting."[42]

Woodward and Bernstein also made themselves rich and famous, offending those who felt they were contributing to the "celebrification" of journalism. When their book *The Final Days*, on Nixon's resignation, appeared just as the movie of *All the President's Men* was released, some lambasted it for its gossipy style, reconstructed dialogue, and extensive use of unnamed sources. "What they have done is institutionalize Deep Throat," said one critic. The implication was that the Watergate heroes represented a disquieting drift from journalism's traditional moorings. In any case, they were not simply "indefatigable news hounds" who reported "just the facts," the way *All the President's Men* had portrayed them.[43]

In the following years, filmmakers took their own shots at the two reporters. Bernstein's womanizing caught up with him when his ex-wife, Nora Ephron, published *Heartburn,* a thinly veiled exposé of their relationship that later became a movie. Woodward's controversial biography of John Belushi, *Wired,* was turned into a critically reviled film in 1989. It depicted Woodward as somehow being able to converse with the late comedian and witness key events in his life. When Belushi's girlfriend administers a fatal drug injection to him, she turns to the reporter: "How 'bout you, Woody? Want a hit?" As he lies dying, Belushi calls Woodward a "cold bastard" but then blurts, "I can't breathe. *Breathe* for me, Woodward!" (Oddly, Woodward consulted on the movie and even promoted it at Cannes.)[44]

By the 1990s, Woodward's and Bernstein's role in Watergate itself had become a target. The producers of a BBC television history of the scandal vowed to "de-Redford-ize" the story and hardly mentioned the reporters or the *Post.* Oliver Stone's *Nixon* (1995) also referred to the reporters only in passing, although it borrowed liberally from *The Final Days.* Finally in 1999 came *Dick,* a comedy about two giggling teenage girls who inadvertently uncover Watergate. The film satirized *All the President's Men* in casting comedians Will Ferrell as Woodward and Bruce McCulloch (sporting a spectacular mop of hair) as Bernstein. "People thought that it was more audacious of us to make fun of Woodward and Bernstein than it was to make fun of the president because in some ways they were more sacred figures," said director and co-writer Andrew Fleming.[45]

Fleming's comments are revealing, for although Woodward and Bernstein have been occasional targets of skepticism or derision, they remain securely ensconced in American mythology. *All the President's Men*'s individualist focus is typical both of journalism and Hollywood. Although he praises the film as "one of Hollywood's better examples of cinematic history," Robert Brent Toplin acknowledges that it exemplifies the "'Great Man' theory" that suggests that change results "almost exclusively from the actions of dynamic individuals."[46]

The dynamic individuals in this case are journalists whom *All the President's Men* celebrates as the people's guardians. They combine outlaw and official virtues: loners who stand in resolute opposition to the official power structure and upstanding citizens who fulfill their prescribed social roles.

Again, *Deadline, USA* pointed the way. Bogart's character was a tough-guy type who nevertheless lectured a neophyte on the necessity of professional training for reporters, and Fox studio head Darryl Zanuck declared the movie's point to be that evil would prosper "unless there is somebody or some newspaper to stop" it.[47] However, unlike *Deadline, USA,* in which the newspaper's triumph over evil was its swan song and its hero lost his job, the *Post* in *All the President's Men* emerges stronger than ever and its heroes emerge as celebrities.

Thus does Watergate represent "the central myth" of American journalism. As Michael Schudson writes, the *Post* and its reporters and editors showed undeniable courage and persistence in keeping alive a story that eventually forced a president to resign: "And that kernel of truth sustains the general myth and gives it, for all its 'inaccuracies,' a kind of larger truth. . . . It offers journalism a charter, an inspiration, a reason for being large enough to justify the constitutional protections that journalism enjoys."[48]

But it is even more than that. Alan J. Pakula's *The Parallax View* told of individual powerlessness; *All the President's Men* tells of individuals standing up to institutionalized power. The Watergate scandal undercut American white-collar ideals by showing how "respectable-looking men" who represented "the living pieties of the middle class" in turn "obstructed justice, violated laws, and betrayed the public trust."[49] *All the President's Men* restores white-collar ideals by showing how similarly respectable, middle-class men uphold justice, law, and trust. If American mythology holds that any boy can grow up to be president, the movie suggests that any boy can grow up to topple a corrupt president, especially if he is "hungry" and has an equally hungry partner, an intrepid editor, and a secret source in a parking garage.

NETWORK AND THE TV CONSPIRACY FILM

In its reliance on sacred, archetypal figures and its idealization of the past, myth is inherently nostalgic, and for all its innovations, 1970s cinema often trafficked in nostalgia. One of the decade's most popular films, *American Graffiti* (1973), conjured an era of white bread innocence just before the assassination of President Kennedy. Nostalgia also colored journalism movies such as Billy Wilder's remake of *The Front Page* (1974), which despite its liberal doses of pressroom profanity remained very much a period piece down to its ragtime score. Even a ripped-from-the-headlines thriller such as *All the President's Men* seemed something of a throwback. One reviewer labeled it "an updated version of *Front Page* razzle-dazzle," and another wrote that it recalled "the triumphs of Frank and Joe Hardy in that long-ago series of boys' books."[50]

The comparison was not far-fetched. Like *The Front Page*, *All the President's Men* depicted a male world with women on the periphery (one reason why *Dick*'s depiction of giggling adolescent girls as Watergate's heroes was so subversive). It also was a newspaper world. The *Post*'s newsroom had a television, but it only recorded and transmitted events, whereas the reporters actively shaped and altered them through their investigations. However, the film's newspaper-dominated milieu seemed to some almost as much a throwback as its characters and plot. Fredric Jameson went so far as to say the movie represented "the heroic legendary moment of a vanished medium."[51]

If the newspaper had not vanished, by the 1970s it did appear to have been supplanted by television in the power it wielded and the fear it generated, as *Medium Cool* already had suggested. Thus it was not surprising that TV became the subject of its own conspiracy films. In *The China Syndrome* (1979), a TV reporter (Jane Fonda) tries to uncover falsified records at a nuclear power plant that has suffered a near-meltdown. She has to overcome the obstacles posed by her smarmy, sexist news director. "Let's face it—you didn't get this job because of your investigative abilities," he tells her. She and her politically radical camera operator (Michael Douglas) also confront their TV station's unwillingness to broadcast the film of the plant accident they secretly recorded. "This is all a goddamn coverup," snaps the camera operator. He then steals the film from the station's vault.

Eventually the journalists are able to report the story with the help of a plant engineer (Jack Lemmon) who pays for his whistleblowing with his life. The reporter is able to get one of the engineer's co-workers to admit live on camera that the plant has serious problems. "There's gonna be an investigation this time," he says. "And the *truth* will come out." The reporter then delivers an emotional summation to the TV audience, saying the engineer had evidence that the plant should be shut down: "I'm sorry; I'm not very objective. Let's just hope it doesn't end here."

The China Syndrome's timing was remarkable, opening two weeks before the Three Mile Island accident seemed to confirm the movie's direst warnings about the nuclear power industry. (Said producer and co-star Michael Douglas, "It was the closest thing I ever had to a religious experience."[52]) Its depiction of the television news industry was somewhat more optimistic. Fonda's reporter finally proved herself a capable journalist while implying that when TV suppressed its schlocky ratings mania, it could be a vital means for ensuring that the "truth will come out." In that, the film was akin to a TV version of *All the President's Men*.

Network (1976) told a different story. Rather than the conspiracy being "out there"—a cover-up in the government or corporate world that the journalist tried to uncover—the conspiracy was located inside the media themselves. Rather than indicting television for being merely silly, the movie branded it as capable of murder. And rather than depicting its female protagonist as a conscientious professional, it made her the epitome of cold-blooded viciousness.

Ironically, screenwriter Paddy Chayefsky had first made his reputation with the television drama *Marty,* which was turned into a 1955 movie that won the best picture Oscar. In 1971, he made a comeback of sorts with the bitter satire *The Hospital.* George C. Scott starred as a doctor who is estranged from his wife and facing a midlife crisis that has driven him to the brink of suicide. He is revived by a fling with a much younger woman. The woman's father, a doctor himself, is also a patient in the hospital. He experiences an apocalyptic vision and systematically begins murdering the doctors, interns, and nurses whose bungling led to the death of a fellow patient.

Much as *Shock Corridor* had, Chayefsky's script presented the hospital as a metaphor for "the whole wounded madhouse of our times" while launching numerous broadsides against institutionalized medicine. Still, it celebrated the dedicated professional in a manner similar to *All the President's Men*. As Alan J. Pakula said of his Watergate film, "If it's a detective story, it's a middle-class, establishment one."[53] Its journalist heroes were not radicals, nor did they operate on society's fringes as the protagonists of other detective stories did. Whatever their personal ambition, they were at heart public servants. So it was with Scott's doctor. "I'm middle-class, and among us middle-class, love doesn't triumph over all: responsibility does," he says. In the end, facing a militant takeover of his hospital (not to mention a likely bevy of malpractice suits), he kisses his young lover goodbye and stays on the job, living up to his responsibilities and fighting the good fight.

Network copied many of *The Hospital*'s character types and plot devices: an old pro facing a midlife crisis and taking up with a younger woman, another old pro threatening suicide and experiencing prophetic visions, a modern institution representing society's insanity. However, its depiction of the professional world was much bleaker. In 1974, NBC turned down Chayefsky's TV pilot for a comedy series on the singles scene, the last of a number of his projects that the networks had rejected. He then began conceiving a movie that would satirize television journalism. Chayefsky was motivated by more than personal pique. He asserted that TV news "totally desensitizes [us to] viciousness, brutality, murder, death, so we no longer actively feel the pains of the victim or suffer for their lives or feel their grief. We've lost our sense of shock, our sense of humanity."[54]

That July, TV talk show host Chris Chubbuck interrupted her morning program in Sarasota, Florida, with an announcement: "In keeping with Channel 40's policy of bringing you the latest in blood and guts and in living color, you are going to see another first: attempted suicide." She then reached into a shopping bag, pulled out a gun, and fatally shot herself in the head. It is unclear whether Chayefsky heard of the incident, but it seems likely given that he began writing *Network* that same month. The film focused on anchor Howard Beale, who announces on the air that he will kill himself. Chayefsky asked NBC anchor John Chancellor whether an anchor could go mad on national TV, and Chancellor replied, "Every day."[55]

Network is all about the deliberate cultivation and exploitation of madness. Television is the movie's target, but so is callow, shallow youth and global capitalism. *All the President's Men* idealized heroic journalists and the newspaper as a source of light; *Network* foretells a fallen media world and rages at the dying of the light.

Diana Christensen (Faye Dunaway) is not the film's sole villain, but her age and gender make her the most prominent. The young programming head vows to raise her network's dismal ratings with angry, countercultural shows: "The American people are turning sullen. They've been clobbered on all sides by Vietnam, Watergate, the inflation. . . . The American people want somebody to articulate their rage for them."

Howard Beale is the answer to Christensen's and presumably the American people's dreams. The network news anchor had vowed to commit suicide on live TV. Now he believes he has been ordered to spread God's message. In one of the indelible moments of 1970s cinema, he takes to the airwaves and commands his viewers, "You've got to say, 'I'm a human being, goddamn it! My life has *value!*' . . . I want you to go to the window, open it, stick your head out and yell: 'I'm as *mad as hell,* and I'm not going to *take* this anymore!'" From coast to coast they oblige. "We've struck the mother lode!" exclaims Christensen.

Beale becomes a national star, dubbed "The Mad Prophet of the Airwaves" and surrounded by such sideshows as "Sybil the Soothsayer." It is one of *Network*'s richer ironies that Beale commands a rapt audience, including one in the TV studio, that nonetheless does not absorb what he says. Standing messianically before a stained glass window, he brands TV "the most awesome goddamn force in the whole godless world" and berates his viewers for being its slave: "You even think like the tube! This is mass *madness,* you maniacs! In God's name, you people are the real thing: *We* are the illusion!" He is a truth-teller, but the television apparatus—the stained glass set dressing, the "Mad Prophet" moniker, the studio audience yelling "We're mad as hell!" on cue—makes him just another sideshow. Begging his viewers to turn off their sets even as he speaks, Beale finally faints dead away, and the studio audience (exhorted by the TV crew) leaps to its feet in cheers while the ratings skyrocket.

Beale is one of Paddy Chayefsky's obvious mouthpieces in the film; news chief Max Schumacher (William Holden) is another. For all its fury, *Network* demonstrates nostalgia similar to that of other movies of its time. Both Beale and Schumacher are holdovers from the Edward R. Murrow era with allegiances to the network's patriarch, who has just passed away. Poor ratings are forcing Beale into involuntary retirement and prompt his threat to kill himself on the air ("You ought to get a hell of a rating out of that—fifty share, easy!"). Schumacher similarly is exiled as his unprofitable news division is made to answer to the vile huckster who is the new chair of the board.

In contrast to Beale and Schumacher, Diana Christensen is one of the maniacs who thinks like the tube. But she is young and beautiful, and Schuma-

Howard Beale (Peter Finch) vainly exhorts his audience to turn off their TVs in *Network*. (Courtesy of the Academy of Motion Picture Arts and Sciences)

cher leaves his wife to live with her, if only briefly. "I feel guilty and conscience-stricken and all of those things that you think sentimental but which *my* generation called simple human *decency*," he tells her. When he asks only that she love him, she replies that she does not know how, and he finally quits her with a memorable kiss-off: "You're television incarnate, Diana. . . . War, murder, death: all the same to you as bottles of beer. And the daily business of life is a

corrupt comedy. . . . You're *madness*, Diana . . . and everything you touch dies
with you. But not me. Not as long as I can feel pleasure, and pain—and love."

One old pro escapes just in time, but Beale falls victim to literally murderous corporate infighting. Corporation boss Arthur Jensen (Ned Beatty) preys
on Beale's insanity in demanding that he atone for having "meddled with the
primal forces of nature" by rallying support against a lucrative corporate deal
with the Arabs. "There is no America. There is no democracy," Jensen tells
Beale. "There is only IBM, and ITT, and AT&T." He commands the anchor to
preach the gospel of a utopian world in which "one vast and ecumenical holding company" will render "all anxieties tranquilized, all boredom amused."

Beale helplessly obliges. His angry rants about the impending demise of the
thinking, feeling person turn into forlorn eulogies for what has been irretriev-
ably lost. When viewers leave in droves, Christensen and her cronies have him
murdered on live TV. "This was the story of Howard Beale," says the narrator
at the end, "the first known instance of a man who was killed because he had
lousy ratings."

Professional journalism and all it represented in *All the President's Men*—
truth, virtue, a democratic counterweight to the powers that be—is symboli-
cally exterminated in *Network*. Director Sidney Lumet (who like Chayefsky got
his start in television) used the camera to depict TV's dehumanization and
unreality. "As the picture progressed, camera setups became more rigid, more
formal," he later wrote. "The lighting became more and more artificial." The
climactic scene in which Christensen and her colleagues decide to kill Beale
was designed to look like a commercial: "The camera also had become a victim of television."[56]

Such a vision predictably did not sit well with many who actually worked
in TV. Barbara Walters, who at the time was being criticized for her multi–
million-dollar contract to anchor ABC's nightly news, nonetheless asserted that
the "kind of show-biz approach to the news" that the movie showed could
never happen at the networks.[57]

That was 1976. In the following years, it was frequently observed that much
if not most of what *Network* had satirized had come true.[58] The airwaves were
glutted with violent and voyeuristic reality programming and infotainment,
and giant multinational corporations seemed to control it all. But the movie
was more than a specific and prescient attack on television. Its warnings about
the media's power to exploit and destroy the individual and squelch good journalism were very much in the journalism movie tradition, as were its worries
about women's place in the media.

Concerning Diana Christensen, *Network* is in some ways even reactionary.
Chayefsky's script described her as "thirty-four, tall, willowy, with the best ass
ever seen on a vice-president of programming."[59] She readily acknowledges

that she is a "lousy lay," and when she has sex with Schumacher, she jumps on top and brings herself to premature orgasm while talking nonstop about television (including a show called *The Dykes* focusing on a woman who falls for her husband's mistress). Faye Dunaway, who disliked doing the sex scene, nevertheless said that for "all her inhumanity and ambition, Diana also represented the price being paid by many women who were trying to dig their way into the top professional ranks." Thus she too could be considered a victim alongside Beale and Schumacher.

Even so, she is depicted as chilly, asexual, and on the verge of hysteria. Conspiracy tales are particularly prone to embrace "a masculinist version of liberal individualism," seeing all types of social controls "as *feminizing* forces" that "violate the borders of the autonomous self," a vision similar to the outlaw's fear of women as domesticators. It was not without cause that one feminist critic branded Diana Christensen the "Great American Bitch."[60]

One must view the character in perspective, however. *Network* seems a regression from *His Girl Friday,* in which Hildy achieved harmony between her personal and professional lives. But that was a screwball romantic comedy comfortable with shades of gray. It showed the press committing awful deeds but did not dwell on them or wring its hands about media responsibility and power. Hildy—not to mention Walter—probably saw the world as a "corrupt comedy" just as Diana Christensen did, but in *His Girl Friday* that was a *good* thing, a necessary form of resistance. There never was any serious question about Hildy's humanity or compassion.

In contrast, *Network* is an angry satire, a conspiracy film painted in black and white. Like *All the President's Men,* it shows journalists confronting institutional corruption. Whereas Woodward and Bernstein were young and put their professional responsibilities above all else, Beale and Schumacher are aging and no longer allowed to uphold those responsibilities; they are irrelevant in a bleak new world ruled by ratings and profits. Although *Network*'s depiction of Christensen's character is hardly progressive, the film is not unrelievedly sexist. Its most sympathetic character is Schumacher's wronged wife (Beatrice Straight), another older person representing humane substance, whereas Christensen represents youthful, empty glamour. She is less a living, breathing woman like Hildy than a straw woman made to stand for all of television's and the corporate world's ills.

Having a woman symbolize the media's dehumanizing powers was nothing new. The most obvious precedent was Frank Capra's *Meet John Doe.* A female journalist—working for a newspaper, of course—begins that movie by exploiting the vulnerable male hero for headlines and money. There is no longer a place for honest, civic-minded journalism: The *Standard,* with its credo "a free press means a free people," has given way to the *New Standard,* "a streamlined paper for a streamlined era." The hero is made the tool of a conspiracy as wide-ranging and evil as anything in *Network*. (Indeed, in both pictures the conspiracy develops around a threatened suicide and new media bosses determined to boost circulation or ratings.) The female journalist finally abandons the media world to preserve her humanity and that of the man she has grown to love. Similarly, Max Schumacher sees that he can save himself only by leaving Diana, whom he calls "television incarnate" and who cannot love anyone. *Network* differs from Capra in that it refuses to have its female protagonist convert to the side of good or allow its media-manufactured celebrity to triumph on his own terms. Otherwise, the movies' themes are much the same.

Network also echoes earlier films in its elegiac tone and its concerns about the audience and the truth. The death of the network patriarch recalls the absent patriarchs in Capra, *Gentleman's Agreement,* and *Deadline, USA.* The manipulation of a spellbound and sheeplike public and the pandering to prurient interests is a theme dating back to *Five Star Final* and running through Capra, *Ace in the Hole,* and *Deadline, USA,* in which readers defected from the *Day*'s sober substance to the sleazy shallowness of the *Standard.* And Howard Beale's words—"Television is not the truth! Television is a goddamned amusement park!"—sound much like Hildy's putdown of the journalist in *The Front Page* as a "cross between a bootlegger and a whore" who spends life "peeking through keyholes" so that "a million hired girls and motormen's wives'll know what's going on."

That is not to detract from *Network*'s potent, prophetic attack on TV. It is to locate the film on a continuum and within a genre that consistently has addressed the purported power of the media in relation to the individual. Newer media that are unapologetically popular arouse particularly acute hopes and fears.[61] In the 1920s and 1930s, the new tabloid newspapers sparked anxieties that were reflected on stage and screen. Starting in the 1950s, television did the same. Elia Kazan's *A Face in the Crowd* (1957) starred Andy Griffith as a small-town con man whom TV turns into a national demagogue.

By the 1970s, such anxieties were even more pronounced. So whereas *All the President's Men* portrayed the older medium of the newspaper as journalistic haven and public savior, *Network* portrayed television as journalistic purgatory and public deluder. (Beale lambastes his TV audience for not reading newspapers or books.) Similarly, the Watergate film exalted intelligent ambition and the masculine professional world whereas the Chayefsky film lamented a world in which the ascendancy of the coldly ambitious woman seemed to have frozen out the old male pros.

Despite their differences, both films spoke to the mood of a time in which malfeasance in high places was routine and expected. Paddy Chayefsky expected nothing less. "His cynicism was partly a pose," Sidney Lumet said of Chayefsky, "but a healthy dose of paranoia was also in his character."[62]

❦

All the President's Men and *Network* demonstrated an enduring belief in the value of individual autonomy and a populist mistrust of social controls that threatened that autonomy. They were liberal-minded critiques of institutional power as the oppressor of personal freedom, with the first showing free and responsible journalists serving democracy and the second showing the "media" squelching the journalist and democracy. The films appeared when Hollywood was receptive to such critiques and conspiracy theories were gaining wider circulation.

But conspiracy theories have their limitations; in one observer's words, they "rarely enable effective political engagement."[63] Watergate could be seen as proof that the government system of checks and balances really did work or, conversely, that fundamental overhaul was needed. Neither viewpoint appeared in *All the President's Men,* which focused almost entirely on two intrepid newspaper reporters and their editor. *Network* was more pointed in its jeremiad about TV and corporatization but offered no answer other than simply to turn off the set and walk out, as Max Schumacher did. Conspiracy films presented individual responses to social problems and deflected attention from structural causes of those problems or systemic solutions to them. In that, they reflected traditional Hollywood mythology while presenting a more conventional view of truth and reality than pictures such as *Medium Cool* had. Their limited liberal vision, Michael Ryan and Douglas Kellner have argued, was inadequate to counter the conservative tide that washed over American politics and culture in the 1980s.[64]

In the coming years, movies continued to elaborate on the themes of *All the President's Men* and *Network.* Like the Watergate film, some focused on questions of professional as well as personal responsibility; like the Chayefsky film, others focused on humanity and reality in a TV-saturated world. All confronted the same myths that their predecessors had, and in many ways they ended up embracing the very things they seemed on the surface to attack.

NOTES

1. Robert Sklar, *Movie-Made America*, rev. ed. (New York: Vintage, 1994), p. 322.

2. Fredric Jameson, *The Geopolitical Aesthetic* (Bloomington: Indiana University Press, 1992), p. 3.

3. See Norman K. Denzin, *The Cinematic Society* (London: Sage, 1995), pp. 162–89; Michael Ryan and Douglas Kellner, *Camera Politica* (Bloomington: Indiana Universi-

ty Press, 1988), pp. 95–105; Ray Pratt, *Projecting Paranoia: Conspiratorial Visions in American Film* (Lawrence: University Press of Kansas, 2001); Jameson, *The Geopolitical Aesthetic.*

4. Richard Hofstadter, *The Paranoid Style of American Politics and Other Essays* (New York: Vintage, 1967); Robert Alan Goldberg, *Enemies Within: The Culture of Conspiracy in Modern America* (New Haven, Conn.: Yale University Press, 2001).

5. Jeffrey C. Goldfarb, *The Cynical Society* (Chicago: University of Chicago Press, 1991), p. 18.

6. Timothy Melley, *Empire of Conspiracy: The Culture of Paranoia in Postwar America* (Ithaca, N.Y.: Cornell University Press, 2000), p. 12.

7. Robert Brent Toplin, *History by Hollywood* (Urbana: University of Illinois Press, 1996), p. 20.

8. Sklar, *Movie-Made America,* p. 289.

9. *Down with Love* (2003), starring Ewan McGregor as a womanizing journalist and Renée Zellweger as an advice book author, was an homage to *Sex and the Single Girl* and similar romantic comedies of the early 1960s.

10. Lee Server, *Sam Fuller: Film Is a Battleground* (Jefferson, N.C.: McFarland, 1994); *Shock Corridor* Production/Clippings File and Pressbook, Margaret Herrick Library, Academy of Motion Picture Arts and Sciences (AMPAS), Beverly Hills, Calif.

11. "Cliché Odyssey," *Newsweek,* May 25, 1964, p. 110.

12. Nicholas Garnham, *Samuel Fuller* (New York: Viking, 1971), p. 152.

13. "Catch $95," *Newsweek,* March 9, 1964, p. 83.

14. Ernest Callenbach and Albert Johnson, "The Danger Is Seduction: An Interview with Haskell Wexler," *Film Quarterly* 21 (Spring 1968): 6.

15. William Rothman, *Documentary Film Classics* (New York: Cambridge University Press, 1997).

16. Callenbach and Johnson, "The Danger Is Seduction," p. 12.

17. Haskell Wexler commentary, *Medium Cool* DVD, Paramount Home Video, 2001.

18. Ryan and Kellner, *Camera Politica,* p. 35.

19. Dennis Schaefer and Larry Sabato, *Masters of Light* (Berkeley: University of California Press, 1984), pp. 259–61.

20. Todd Gitlin, *The Whole World Is Watching* (Berkeley: University of California Press, 1980), pp. 187, 201, 202.

21. Adrian Havill, *Deep Truth* (New York: Birch Lane Press, 1993), pp. 37–39. Biographical information on Woodward and Bernstein comes from Havill.

22. Michael Schudson, *Watergate in American Memory* (New York: Basic Books, 1992), p. 126; William E. Leuchtenburg, "*All the President's Men,*" in *Past Imperfect: History According to the Movies,* ed. Mark C. Carnes (New York: Henry Holt, 1995), p. 291.

23. Carl Bernstein and Bob Woodward, *All the President's Men* (New York: Warner Books, 1976).

24. Gladys Engel Lang and Kurt Lang, *The Battle for Public Opinion* (New York: Columbia University Press, 1983); Edward Jay Epstein, "Did the Press Uncover Watergate?" *Commentary,* July 1974, pp. 21–24.

25. Havill, *Deep Truth,* pp. 77–89.

26. Gaines's comments and other details regarding the class's investigation are on-line at <http://deepthroatuncovered.com>.

27. Havill, *Deep Truth,* pp. 80, 88.

28. Richard T. Jameson, "The Pakula Parallax," *Film Comment,* September–October 1976, p. 8.

29. Quoted in Pratt, *Projecting Paranoia,* p. 130.

30. Foster Hirsch, *The Dark Side of the Screen* (New York: Da Capo, 1981), p. 67.

31. Jack Hirshberg, *A Portrait of All the President's Men* (New York: Warner Books, 1976), pp. 109–14, 135–45; "*All the President's Men:* Production Design Sound Filmstrip," produced by Barla, Orloff and Associates, Los Angeles, Calif., 1976.

32. William Goldman, *Adventures in the Screen Trade* (New York: Warner Books, 1983), p. 235; Hirshberg, *A Portrait of All the President's Men,* p. 127.

33. Script drafts of *All the President's Men* are in the Rare Book and Special Collections Library, University of Illinois at Urbana-Champaign.

34. Hirshberg, *A Portrait of All the President's Men,* p. 93.

35. Goldman, *Adventures in the Screen Trade,* pp. 232–44; William Goldman, *Five Screenplays* (New York: Applause Books, 1997), p. 223.

36. "Alan J. Pakula: Leaving Room for Life," *Films Illustrated,* June 1976, p. 374.

37. See Ben Bradlee, *A Good Life* (New York: Simon and Schuster, 1995), p. 403. The movie left out one key figure entirely: city editor Barry Sussman, who had worked most closely with the reporters on Watergate.

38. Nat Hentoff, "Woodstein in the Movies," *Columbia Journalism Review,* May–June 1976, pp. 46–47. See also Howard Good and Michael J. Dillon, *Media Ethics Goes to the Movies* (Westport, Conn.: Praeger, 2002), pp. 39–61.

39. Promotional blurb from back cover of Woodward and Bernstein, *All the President's Men.*

40. James W. Carey, "A Plea for the University Tradition," *Journalism Quarterly* 55 (1978): 850; Mark Hunter, "Dante's Watergate: *All the President's Men* as a Romance Narrative," *American Journalism* 14 (1997): 303–16; Northrop Frye, *The Secular Sculpture* (Cambridge, Mass.: Harvard University Press, 1976), p. 50.

41. Pratt, *Projecting Paranoia,* p. 132; David Thomson, *A Biographical Dictionary of Film,* 3rd ed. (New York: Knopf, 1996), pp. 293–94, 571–72.

42. Schudson, *Watergate in American Memory,* p. 113; Michael Schudson, *Discovering the News: A Social History of American Newspapers* (New York: Basic, 1978), p. 187.

43. Schudson, *Watergate in American Memory,* p. 112–17; Havill, *Deep Truth,* p. 111; David L. Eason, "On Journalistic Authority: The Janet Cooke Scandal," in *Media, Myths, and Narratives,* ed. James W. Carey (Newbury Park, Calif: Sage, 1988), pp. 205–27.

44. Havill, *Deep Truth,* pp. 196–99.

45. Martin F. Nolan, "Rewinding the Tapes: A Riveting 'Watergate,'" *Boston Globe,* August 5, 1994, Living sec., p. 43; Richard Reeves, "Nixon Revisited by Way of the Creative Camera," *New York Times,* December 17, 1995, sec. 2, p. 1; Andrew Fleming commentary, *Dick* DVD, Columbia Pictures, 1999.

46. Toplin, *History by Hollywood*, pp. 20, 201. See also W. Lance Bennett, *News: The Politics of Illusion*, 3rd ed. (White Plains, N.Y.: Longman, 1996), pp. 37–76.

47. Zanuck's comments on the script drafts of *Deadline, USA* are in the Twentieth Century Fox Collection, Arts Library Special Collections, University of California at Los Angeles (UCLA).

48. Schudson, *Watergate in American Memory*, p. 124. See also Bonnie Brennen, "Sweat Not Melodrama: Reading the Structure of Feeling in *All the President's Men*," *Journalism: Theory, Practice, Criticism* 4:1 (2003): 113–31.

49. Burton J. Bledstein, *The Culture of Professionalism: The Middle Class and the Development of Higher Education in America* (New York: W.W. Norton, 1976), pp. 2–3.

50. Robert Hatch, review of *All the President's Men*, *Nation*, April 24, 1976, p. 506; Vincent Canby, review of *All the President's Men*, *New York Times*, April 8, 1976, p. 42.

51. Jameson, *The Geopolitical Aesthetic*, p. 77.

52. Aaron Latham, "Hollywood vs. Harrisburg," *Esquire*, May 22, 1979, p. 86.

53. Quoted in Pratt, *Projecting Paranoia*, p. 132.

54. Shaun Considine, *Mad as Hell: The Life and Work of Paddy Chayefsky* (New York: Random House, 1994), pp. 305–6. Biographical information on Chayefsky comes from Considine.

55. "Talk Show Hostess Dies after Shooting Self on TV," *New York Times*, July 16, 1974, p. 23; Considine, *Mad as Hell*, p. 306.

56. Sidney Lumet, *Making Movies* (New York: Knopf, 1995), p. 85.

57. Considine, *Mad as Hell*, p. 329.

58. See for example David Bianculli, "Prophetic 'Network' Tuned In to Our Times—20 Years Ago," *Sacramento Bee*, January 21, 1996, p. EN2; Bill Keveney, "Psychic 'Network,'" *Hartford Courant*, March 3, 1996, p. G1; Tim Goodman, "'Network' Revisited," *Chicago Tribune*, December 18, 1996, Tempo sec., p. 3.

59. Considine, *Mad as Hell*, p. 315.

60. Faye Dunaway and Betsy Sharkey, *Looking for Gatsby* (New York: Simon and Schuster, 1995), pp. 294, 298, 312; Melley, *Empire of Conspiracy*, pp. 32, 36; Robert B. Ray, *A Certain Tendency of the Hollywood Cinema, 1930–1980* (Princeton, N.J.: Princeton University Press, 1985), pp. 60–61.

61. Daniel J. Czitrom, *Media and the American Mind: From Morse to McLuhan* (Chapel Hill: University of North Carolina Press, 1982).

62. Lumet, *Making Movies*, p. 42.

63. Mark Fenster, *Conspiracy Theories: Secrecy and Power in American Culture* (Minneapolis: University of Minnesota Press, 1999), p. xvi.

64. Ryan and Kellner, *Camera Politica*, pp. 95–105. See also Fenster, *Conspiracy Theories*; Melley, *Empire of Conspiracy*.

7

Myth and Antimyth in Contemporary Film

The decades after Watergate were trying for American journalism. The rapid growth of the Internet and cable and satellite television reduced the audiences for older media. By the end of the century, little more than half of U.S. households bought a daily newspaper, and the major TV networks' share of the audience had similarly shrunk to 55 percent.[1] Venerable newspapers passed from the scene. The major television networks came under new corporate ownership that imposed budget cuts and layoffs on the news divisions while demanding that they pay more attention to the bottom line.

Desperate to hold the readers and viewers they still had, many news outlets resorted to an old strategy: going downmarket. Tabloid-like stories such as Amy Fisher, O.J. Simpson, and Monica Lewinsky dominated public attention. On top of that, ethical embarrassments affected the nation's most respected news organizations, from 1981, when the *Washington Post* returned a Pulitzer Prize for Janet Cooke's fabricated story about a child heroin addict, to 2003, when the *New York Times* admitted that reporter Jayson Blair had similarly made up stories.[2]

Some argued that the press had grown too big for its britches. Renata Adler wrote that journalists had come to see themselves as "a class apart, by turns lofty, combative, sullen, lame, condescending, speciously pedantic, but above all, socially and, as it were, Constitutionally arrogant." Janet Malcolm was even more scathing: "Every journalist who is not too stupid or too full of himself to notice what is going on knows that what he does is morally indefensible. He is a kind of confidence man, preying on people's vanity, ignorance, or loneliness, gaining their trust and betraying them without remorse."[3]

Journalists themselves lamented the erosion of traditional values. Some traced it to the growing use of composite and anonymous sources that investigative reporting and "New Journalism" of the 1960s and 1970s had made fashionable. The co-author of the greatest investigative story ever told, Carl Bernstein, attacked the media for helping propagate an "Idiot Culture" and "a ravenous celebrity-and-sensationalism-and-scandal machine that is consuming decent journalists."[4]

To a degree, Bernstein's and other journalists' criticisms reflected a modernist sensibility grappling with a postmodern age. Investigative journalism as practiced by Woodward and Bernstein promoted a scientific, impartial model of newsgathering that sought verifiable truth in the public interest. "In our postmodern world," one critic noted by way of contrast, "'knowingness' is the new religion, and the very notion of accuracy—in the sense of getting things right—seems rather quaint."[5] Family-owned newspapers such as the *Washington Post* appeared anachronistic in an era of "late capitalism" marked by conglomeration, globalization, and commodification of every sphere of life. By 2000, the U.S. media were dominated by six corporations for which cyberspace, cinema, television, and journalism were merely different avenues toward profit. Hence developed the "ravenous" media machine of which Bernstein spoke, devoted not to lofty-minded conceptions of public interest but to whatever the market would bear. The quest for truth was supplanted by pervasive irony and cynicism.[6]

The result, according to Michael Schudson, was the opposite of *All the President's Men:* a vision of "Watergate-in-journalism" that excoriated the press for imperiously putting itself above the public and exploiting the innocent.[7] The press was viewed as both official villain (an arrogant "class apart") and outlaw villain (the journalist as a sleazy "confidence man"). Closely related was the notion that the media, both print and television, had become exactly what *Network* had prophesied: the tool of "one vast and ecumenical holding company" rendering "all anxieties tranquilized, all boredom amused."

Critics argued that movies of the post-Watergate era reflected that shift. "What we are seeing in recent productions is the demise of a myth that has been a mainstay of American film—the Truth-Seeking Reporter who will stop at nothing to keep the public informed," wrote one. In its place, wrote another, was the depiction of journalists as the new "bad guys in films about the white-collar world."[8]

However, this chapter suggests that contemporary films' depictions of journalism are more complex than that. Although some movies are in many ways highly critical of the existing press, they still reproduce the same mythology that films of earlier eras expressed. For example, in *Absence of Malice* and *The Killing Fields,* journalists' professional ambition causes them to lose sight of their responsibility to their fellow human beings; they then learn their lessons and repent. In *Salvador* and *The Insider,* journalists (one nominally an outlaw hero and the other nominally an official hero) struggle to report the truth in the face of institutional evil. In *The Paper* and *True Crime,* journalists pay nostalgic homage to a simpler time when the tabloid newspaper and outlaw-like journalist reigned supreme.

Other movies are more skeptical toward the idea of an objective news media separating truth from fiction and serving the public. Those films express more of an "antimyth" vision of the press: a postmodern "Watergate-in-journalism," "all boredom amused" vision. For example, in *Under Fire* and *Street Smart,* journalists openly lie to serve political or personal ends. In *Broadcast News* and *To Die For,* women are seduced by television's empty-headed glamour. Nevertheless, Hollywood never stops reaffirming the old myths: In *Up Close and Personal,* a woman lies to gain entrée into the glamorous TV world and is transformed into a principled newswoman in love with a principled newsman.

In short, although contemporary movies raise pointed questions about professional responsibility and culpability, they also reinforce journalism's just place in society. Although they focus on the slippery nature of truth and changes for the worse in a TV-saturated world, they also show how exciting that world can be.

MYTH IN FILM

Absence of Malice *and* The Killing Fields

Absence of Malice (1981) may seem an odd choice to begin a discussion of how contemporary movies reproduce myths valorizing journalism's place in American society. Michael Schudson has said the movie perfectly encapsulates the anti-press sentiments of the post-Watergate era.[9] In actuality, the movie is similar to a film noir such as *Ace in the Hole* in presenting a morality tale that focuses on a wayward journalist discovering the errors of her ways.

The movie was written by Kurt Luedtke, formerly executive editor of the *Detroit Free Press.* Sally Field plays Megan Carter, a Miami newspaper reporter who pursues liquor wholesaler Michael Gallagher (Paul Newman). Gallagher is honest, but he has a racketeer uncle who is being investigated in connection with a union leader's disappearance. To try to pry information from Gallagher, the chief federal investigator manipulates Carter into writing that Gallagher himself is a suspect. Disastrous consequences ensue. Gallagher's Catholic schoolteacher friend provides an alibi for him, but when Carter writes that the teacher had an abortion, she kills herself. Gallagher then launches an elaborate revenge scheme against everyone concerned, including Carter (even though they have been having an affair). In the end, the federal investigator is fired, the district attorney resigns, and Carter and her paper are humiliated.

The movie seems almost diametrically opposed to *All the President's Men.* Instead of unmasking institutional abuses, the newspaper becomes a tool of them; instead of saving the Republic, it destroys a pathetically vulnerable woman. Screenwriter Luedtke said the film did not "show a number of the very good, very healthy things that the press does every day," adding that it was not meant to indict journalism as a whole: "I hope nobody takes it that way."[10]

Nevertheless, that was precisely how many journalists took it, particularly because it appeared close on the heels of Janet Cooke and other press ignominies. "What the movie does, is to give the public a distorted view of newspapers and reporters—at a time when the business can least afford it," said one. Another declared that the journalists in the film were "as grotesquely distorted as if seen in a funhouse mirror," adding that their conduct was "astonishing not [just] for its unethicality but for its stupidity."[11]

But one said he saw more truth in the movie than most of his peers were willing to acknowledge. Nat Hentoff—who had warned that *All the President's Men* could lead to reporters seeing themselves as having no shadows—wrote four consecutive *Village Voice* columns defending *Absence of Malice*. "Cops and journalists are more edgily defensive in reaction to criticism than any other groups of professionals," he said. He added that all of the abuses in the movie happened regularly in the real-life press: "Indeed, in some respects, *Absence of Malice* is kinder than it could have been—or than it would have been had I written the screenplay."[12]

To an extent, both critics and defenders of the film were correct. Its characters commit such a string of professional faux pas that the movie almost seems designed as a how-*not*-to lesson for journalism schools.[13] At the same time, the movie is kinder toward the press than some of its critics may have realized.

When measured against journalistic ethics codes, *Absence of Malice*'s characters perform abysmally. For example, the Society of Professional Journalists declares that acting independently and being accountable are fundamental principles.[14] The editor in *Absence of Malice* is a rumpled, mealy-mouthed sort who never questions why the federal investigator is so eager to plant information in his paper. "If we try to figure out why people leak stories, we'll publish monthly," he says. For his part, Gallagher recognizes the paper's dependence on such leaks and hearsay. "You don't write the truth," he tells Carter. "You write what people say, what you overhear. You *eavesdrop!*" He eventually is able to exploit that proclivity in bringing down the federal investigator and embarrassing the journalists. Even then, the paper refuses to acknowledge responsibility—"We're not going to retract anything," says the editor—and that clearly is depicted as a bad thing.

Also bad is the paper's inability to live up to other principles that the Society of Professional Journalists says should guide press conduct: reporting truth while minimizing harm. After the teacher kills herself, the editor tells Carter that he does not know how to print truth without hurting people. In reality, the "truth" of what Carter reports is "irrelevant," according to the newspaper's oily attorney: "We have no knowledge the story is false, therefore we're absent malice. We've been both reasonable and prudent, therefore we're not negligent. We may say whatever we like about Mr. Gallagher; he is powerless to do us harm. Democracy is served."

Such codified, legalized language is a far cry from Ben Bradlee telling Woodward and Bernstein that if they err again the future of the country might be at risk. It also turns the principle of minimizing harm on its head, protecting the profession and the institution at the expense of the individual. In *Absence of Malice*, the cool, professional detachment that had held Woodward and Bernstein in such good stead is depicted as inhuman. Carter pays the price when an enraged Gallagher hurls her to the ground and rips her blouse. "Couldn't you see what it meant to her?" he demands to know, referring to the fatal story Carter wrote about his friend's abortion. "Couldn't you stop scribbling for a second, and just put down your goddamn ballpoint pen, and just *see* her?"

At heart, *Absence of Malice* is a story of Paul Newman getting even with everyone who has wronged him and his friends. He is a classic outlaw hero: "the traditional loner, fearless and honest, and beyond every institution in moral acumen," according to Andrew Sarris.[15] Significantly, that includes not just the press but also the judicial system. His relationship with Carter recalls that between Max Schumacher and Diana Christensen in *Network*, an older man becoming involved with a younger woman who he hopes will treat him as a human being rather than a means toward an end. Inevitably he is disappointed. "I'm a reporter. What'd you *expect?*" Carter tells Gallagher. She is the cynical journalist who says things usually are what they seem—rotten—and who suffers for it instead of being rewarded as she would have been in a screwball film. Gallagher first assaults her and then uses his charms to place her at his beck and call before finally setting her up to be disgraced. (It is not without reason that the movie, like *Network*, has been branded as sexist.[16]) She is left alone and apparently jobless.

In such ways, *Absence of Malice* does undercut the myth of the heroic reporter and paper while promoting an image of an arrogant, destructive press. But, as Kurt Luedtke said, it is not meant to indict journalism as a whole. Carter pays attention to its how-not-to lesson. Toward movie's end, she refuses to name a source even though it means she could go to jail: "It's really very simple: I can hurt someone or not hurt someone." Later, she is questioned by another reporter whom the paper has assigned to put the best spin on her relationship with Gallagher. "Just say we were involved," Carter tells the reporter. "That's true, isn't it?" the reporter replies. "No," says Carter after a pause, "but it's *accurate.*"

The difference between reporting accurately and reporting truthfully is a theme as old as the journalism movie genre itself. In *Citizen Kane*, most of what

Michael Gallagher (Paul Newman) demands to know where Megan Carter (Sally Field) is getting her information in *Absence of Malice*. (Courtesy of the Academy of Motion Picture Arts and Sciences)

the reporter Thompson gathered about Kane seemed superficially accurate, but Thompson recognized that it did not add up to a true picture of the man; the movie implies that it is impossible ever to discover the "truth" about anyone. In contrast, *Absence of Malice* endorses the notion that the truth is out there. All of Carter's presuppositions about Gallagher's alleged misdeeds are conclusively proven false, even though she has accurately reported what she has been told. And even though she says she and Gallagher were "involved"—accurate in that they had a fling (another ethical lapse on her part)—they never were *truly* involved because she was unable to engage him as a man as opposed to a source.

Absence of Malice's final scenes are bittersweet but also implicitly optimistic, which finally makes the movie more like *All the President's Men* than *Network:* It underscores the individual's power to make a difference. Gallagher's single-handed score-settling with the powers that be is the most obvious example, but there also is a gruffly plainspoken and honest justice department official (Wilford Brimley) who ties up the loose plot ends and helps punish his wayward colleagues.

If Brimley's character represents hope for good government, there is also hope for good journalism. "I know you think what I do for a living is nothing," Carter tells Gallagher. "But it isn't really nothing: I just did it badly." "You probably *are* a hell of a reporter," he says. "Not yet," she replies. The implication is that having learned from her mistakes and forsaken her cynicism, one day—assuming anyone ever hires her again—she will practice her profession correctly. For all its apparent skepticism toward journalism ethics, *Absence of Malice* extols the same values of individual autonomy that most media ethics codes do.[17] It suggests that journalism done badly can wound and kill, but when journalists and others take responsibility for their actions and make the right choices, institutional abuses can be prevented and stopped.

The Killing Fields (1984) is similarly optimistic. It tells of *New York Times* reporter Sydney Schanberg and his assistant, Dith Pran, in the years surrounding the 1975 Khmer Rouge takeover of Cambodia. Schanberg was a driven and volatile reporter who went so far as to kick Pran, yet they were close friends. Both stayed in Phnom Penh after the Khmer Rouge occupied the city (Pran had put his wife and children on a helicopter evacuating American personnel). Schanberg and other Western reporters were detained and nearly executed until Pran persuaded soldiers to release them. The journalists then took refuge in the French embassy and faked a passport in a futile attempt to save Pran from Khmer Rouge seizure. Schanberg recalled his emotions at that moment: "He saved my life and now I cannot protect him. I hate myself."[18] The correspondent returned to America, where he won a Pulitzer Prize, but he could not forget Pran or stop searching for him. Finally in 1979, he received word that after enduring four years of forced labor, starvation, and torture, Pran had escaped to Thailand, where the two men were reunited.

Producer David Puttnam saw the story as an ideal movie subject. He assigned it to British writer Bruce Robinson, who overcame his initial dislike of Schanberg to write a script that showed both the reporter's flaws and his conscience. Schanberg and other reporters who had covered Cambodia were consulted on the screenplay. Roland Joffé was signed to direct after he read the script and told Puttnam that he saw it not as a war film but as "a love story set in a war."[19]

Joffé's conceptualization could not have appealed more to Puttnam, who had grown up in Britain with a Norman Rockwell–like image of America nourished by the movies of Hollywood's golden age. He had little use for many of the highly praised U.S. films of the 1970s: "In looking at the nihilistic output of that decade, I can't imagine how anyone could perceive the United States as anything other than a completely insane self-destructive society."[20] So *The Killing Fields* would not be a conspiracy film; Puttnam toned down what he perceived as the anti-Americanism of the first screenplay drafts. Rather than dwelling on the failings of U.S. journalism or foreign policy in the Vietnam era, it would tell of mutual respect and need between two journalists.

The story echoed that of *The Year of Living Dangerously* (1983), in which a journalist's attempts to break a story of an impending Communist incursion in Indonesia drive a rift between him and his native assistant. The assistant scolds the reporter for "making a fetish of your career and making all relationships temporary lest they disturb that career. Why can't you give yourself? Why can't you learn to love?" After the assistant martyrs himself to protest social conditions, the reporter abandons the story and leaves Indonesia on a plane with his lover. When real-life journalists expressed astonishment at the reporter's actions in the movie, director Peter Weir responded that "the only way he can ever continue to be a good journalist and a complete human being is to take that plane."[21] The assistant's self-sacrifice helps shame the reporter into stopping his betrayal of those who love him as a man and not as a reporter. The moral is that to be a truly good journalist, one must first be a complete human being.

So it is in *The Killing Fields*. As the Khmer Rouge closes in, Schanberg (Sam Waterson) berates Pran (Haing S. Ngor) for being unable to arrange a prompt wire transmission back to New York.[22] Then he brusquely asks Pran whether he wants to be evacuated along with his family. "I'm [a] reporter too, Sydney," Pran tearfully replies. He wants to stay as much from his sense of personal obligation to his friend as from his professional obligation to see the story through. However, Schanberg does not fully realize that until later in the embassy, after the ruse to try to smuggle out Pran has failed and the fate that awaits him has become apparent. "For Christ's sake, Sydney, why didn't you get him out when you had the chance?" one of the journalists says, adding, "Funny sense of priorities!" Pran intercedes on his friend's behalf: "I know his heart. I love him like my brother. And I do anything for him. *Anything!*"

After Pran disappears into a living hell, Schanberg descends into one of his own back in the relative comfort of New York. He obsessively scans videotape of the carnage in Cambodia and America's complicity in it to the strains of Puccini's "Nessun Dorma." When he wins a major award for his Cambodian reporting, he is confronted by Al Rockoff (a real photojournalist played by John Malkovich). "You know what bothers me?" says Rockoff. "You let Pran stay in Cambodia because you wanted to win that fucking award and you knew that you needed him to do it!"

Rockoff and Schanberg neatly represent the outlaw-official dialectic. Director Roland Joffé described their relationship as "the journalist as renegade, the journalist as outsider, the journalist who in his anger comments on the fakeries, the falsities of society; and the journalist as kind of philosopher [and] Greek citizen who works to make society better."[23] The "renegade" Rockoff disappears from the film after helping make the "Greek citizen" Schanberg realize that professional ambition and detachment can extract a human cost and that he bears personal responsibility for Pran's plight.

The Killing Fields also briefly addresses U.S. responsibility for Cambodia: "Maybe what we underestimated was the kind of insanity that seven billion dollars worth of bombing could produce," Schanberg tells an interviewer. But in accordance with Puttnam's and Joffé's design, the picture is concerned less with global politics and assigning blame than it is with individual reconciliation and perseverance. It devotes most of its second half to Pran's successful struggle for freedom. When finally they are reunited, Schanberg asks Pran: "Forgive me?" "Nothing to forgive, Sydney," he tearfully replies. As they embrace, the song "Imagine" swells on the soundtrack. That struck some critics as mawkish if not downright offensive, with one saying it "effectively trivializes Pran, Schanberg, Cambodia, and John Lennon all at once."[24]

But the song's utopian vision of the world living as one fits the context of a male love story with an international backdrop. Schanberg and Pran are no longer a journalist and his assistant on deadline; that impersonal relationship has deepened into an enduring bond of brotherly love cutting across racial and national lines. The real-life Schanberg had expressed a desire that the film not be about "some macho American journalist,"[25] and he got his wish: His screen counterpart forsakes his story-at-all-costs mindset and receives forgiveness for his professional excesses without having to surrender his job (a closing title notes that he and Pran still work for the *New York Times*). As in *The Year of Living Dangerously,* the implication is that now he will be a better man and journalist.

Salvador *and* The Insider

If Schanberg represents official journalism, Richard Boyle in Oliver Stone's *Salvador* (1986) is the prototypical outlaw: a cynical, gonzo reporter. As played by James Woods, Boyle begins the movie wildly down on his luck. His landlord has evicted him, his wife and child have left him, and his career has ground to a halt because of his drunken misdeeds. He drags his best friend with him to El Salvador with promises of great sex and drugs, only to be plunged into a brutal civil war.

Like *The Killing Fields, Salvador* is part autobiography; the real Richard Boyle co-wrote the movie with Stone. (Boyle originally was to play himself, but Stone said a screen test did not work: "He'd been drinking a bit and he'd be green one minute and blue the next and red and orange the next."[26]) Stone was attracted to Boyle's "reckless" and "devil-may-care" attitude and his disrespect toward official codes of law and morality: "It's the Boyles of the world that fuck up the systems, that make for change."[27]

Before he can change things, though, Boyle first must abandon his devil-may-care stance, at least toward the war he is covering. The reporter becomes radicalized and harangues the American military advisors he encounters: "I don't want to see another Vietnam. I don't want to see America get another bad rap. . . . I believe in America. I believe that we stand for something. For a constitution. For human rights—not just for a few people, but for everybody on this *planet!*" In return, Boyle sees U.S.-supplied planes strafe and kill his idealistic photojournalist friend. He barely escapes the country with his Salvadoran girlfriend, but immigration officials haul her and her child away as Boyle cries her name in anguish.

Although Salvadoran government thugs commit the movie's worst atrocities, they are abetted by the American government—not just the preppy military advisors representing the yuppie scum that Boyle loathes but the immigration officers as well. Boyle's friend's death results from his attempt to document America's secret role in the Salvadoran war. Boyle loses the woman he loves to a heartless bureaucracy that will return her to the hell she has just escaped.

Thus *Salvador*'s title is ironic. Although Stone said Boyle was the sort who could disrupt the system, the forces confronting the journalist are too vast and evil for him to change or save anything on his own. The movie (which Stone candidly called "agitprop") is much like a conspiracy film, as one might expect from the man who went on to direct *JFK*.[28] Unlike *The Killing Fields, Salvador* is sharply critical of American institutions, including the mainstream media: Boyle's fellow reporters do nothing to question U.S. military propaganda.

Still, the movie implies that if change ever is to occur, it must begin with one brave person willing to question official lies. In *Salvador*, that person is a renegade journalist (just as in *JFK* it is a renegade attorney, Jim Garrison). The film reproduces the familiar figure of the cynical reporter-turned-idealist, willing to risk all to tell the truth with the hope that somehow it will make a difference.

Boyle is a consummate outsider. *The Insider* (1999), as the title implies, tells of those within the system who fight institutional abuses. The picture is based on Jeffrey Wigand, a tobacco company executive whom Brown & Williamson fired in 1993.[29] Wigand signed a confidentiality agreement to get his severance benefits. He met *60 Minutes* producer Lowell Bergman the following year when CBS hired Wigand as a consultant for a story about fire-safe cigarettes. Wigand told Bergman that Brown & Williamson had boosted nicotine's potency in cigarettes even as tobacco company executives testified before Congress that nicotine was not addictive. Over the next several months, Bergman tried to persuade a reluctant Wigand to tell his story on *60 Minutes*. "You can have documents; you can have experts," Bergman later said. "But the *insider* is what makes television. The face, the person saying: this is what happened."[30]

In 1995, Wigand—whose marriage was disintegrating under the strain—finally consented to an interview with Mike Wallace. The timing was not propitious. That same month, ABC News apologized to two tobacco companies for reporting that they had spiked the nicotine levels of cigarettes. The apology was issued soon after Disney acquired ABC. At the same time, CBS announced that it was being bought by Westinghouse. Lowell Bergman was summoned to CBS corporate headquarters and told that Brown & Williamson could file a multi–billion-dollar lawsuit against the network for inducing Wigand to breach his confidentiality agreement. CBS decreed that the *60 Minutes* interview could air only in a severely truncated form that did not reveal Wigand's identity. The *Wall Street Journal* scooped *60 Minutes* by publishing Wigand's revelations, although it did not name him in the story. After that, and after a *New York Times* editorial chided CBS for its actions, *60 Minutes* finally aired the Wigand interview in its original form.

The Wigand controversy nearly tore *60 Minutes* apart. Many staffers were upset that executive producer Don Hewitt consented to squelch the interview at first. In a 1998 TV documentary, Hewitt was alternately contrite and defensive: "It was not my proudest moment. . . . I wish that I had conducted myself as well as Mike [Wallace] had during that time, and Lowell Bergman, who was wonderful on this subject. I was more prone to give in than they were. But it was *not my decision* whether to give in or not."

Mike Wallace was vocal enough about CBS's actions that he angered other *60 Minutes* correspondents who wanted to move on from the controversy. Wallace said he thought seriously about quitting but decided against it: "If I'm outside, that piece would *never* have gotten on the air. *Period.*" Wallace also said he tried to enlist Hewitt's support: "Don didn't want to hear it. . . . He was on the company side, and Lowell Bergman and I and a couple of others here were not." Wallace and Bergman had had a long, close relationship that some compared to that between a father and son, and in 1998 Wallace still spoke of him as an ally.

That changed the following year with *The Insider*'s release. Marie Brenner had written a *Vanity Fair* article on the Wigand controversy. She originally intended to focus strictly on the tobacco whistleblower, but after talking to Bergman, she decided that "the story was a double narrative"—not just about Wigand's agonizing struggle over going public with what he knew but also Bergman's struggle to get the interview on the air.[31] In turn, film director Michael Mann amplified the double narrative in telling of *two* company insiders, Wigand and Bergman. Both begin as official, professional types. Corporate malfeasance thrusts them outside and transforms them into outlaw

Al Pacino as intrepid *60 Minutes* producer Lowell Bergman in *The Insider.* (Courtesy of the Academy of Motion Picture Arts and Sciences)

heroes. They successfully fight to tell the truth in the face of villainous corporate bosses and those—including Don Hewitt and Mike Wallace—who kowtow to them.

The Insider recalls noir and conspiracy films when Wigand finds a bullet in his mailbox and confronts a menacing stranger at night on a deserted golf driving range. But in making Bergman the moral compass of the story, it stands firmly in the line of movies celebrating the professional journalist. Al Pacino depicts Bergman as a paragon of principle who sticks by Wigand (Russell Crowe) through every travail. "I'm just a commodity to you, aren't I?" Wigand asks him. "To a network, probably we're all commodities," Bergman replies. "To me, you're not a commodity. What you are is important." When Wigand retorts that Bergman is only putting up words, the journalist fires back that while the tobacco executive has been out playing golf, "I've been out in the world giving my word, and backing it up with action!"

Bergman eventually convinces Wigand to take action himself. The former tobacco executive consents to the *60 Minutes* interview and testifies against big tobacco in a Mississippi courtroom despite the threats against him. Then CBS asserts that the more Wigand reveals, the more legal and financial danger the network faces. Bergman realizes that what he offhandedly told Wigand is true: Both of them are commodities that have grown too risky for their corporations to tolerate. Their proud professionalism, normally an official virtue, means nothing to their employers; it matters only to them. "I'm runnin' out of heroes, man. Guys like you are in short supply," Bergman tells a desolate Wigand. "Yeah, guys like you too," Wigand replies.

So Bergman turns his back on official rules and legal and corporate posturing to take matters into his own hands, a classically outlaw thing to do. He helps orchestrate the *Wall Street Journal*'s coverage of Wigand, secretly meeting the *Journal*'s reporter in scenes recalling those between Woodward and Deep Throat in *All the President's Men*. Then he leaks details of CBS's treachery to the *New York Times*. Under normal circumstances, such actions would be grave professional sins, and they infuriate Don Hewitt (Philip Baker Hall), who calls Bergman an "anarchist."

Still, they have the desired effect. *60 Minutes* finally airs the Wigand interview. Mike Wallace implores Bergman to let bygones be bygones, but Bergman does not listen: "What do I tell a source on the next tough story? 'Hang in with us; you'll be fine—maybe'? No. What got broken here doesn't go back together again." Then, in a visual parallel to Wigand's earlier exit from the tobacco company, Bergman turns away from the speechless Wallace and strides out alone into the sunlight.

Don Hewitt's rage at Bergman on screen paled next to his rage in actuality. In his autobiography, Hewitt wrote that when a journalist "conspires with a screenwriter to concoct a movie about himself that portrays him by name doing things he never did and saying things he never said, and is so comfortable with the fraudulent portrayal that he lends himself to 'hyping' the movie, that is not someone I would want within a hundred miles of my newsroom or a thousand miles of a journalism school."[32]

Mike Wallace's reaction was no less heated. He sardonically suggested that the movie's title should be "On the Seventh Day Bergman Rested." Especially rankling was its portrayal of him as what he called a "soulless and cowardly laggard."[33] In fact, Christopher Plummer's performance makes Wallace rather more sympathetic. He is pompous and temperamental but also deeply conflicted. When Bergman pointedly asks him why he did not show more courage on the Wigand story, Wallace responds, "I'm talking about when you're nearer the end of your life than the beginning. . . . I did Irangate, and the Ayatollah, and Malcolm X, Martin Luther King, Saddam, Sadat, etc. . . . But history only remembers most what you did last. And should that be fronting a segment that allowed a tobacco giant to crash this network—does it give someone at my time of life pause? Yeah."

Wallace's "nearer the end of your life than the beginning" line echoes one uttered by Max Schumacher in *Network,* but unlike Schumacher—and unlike Wigand and Bergman—Wallace is unable to break free of corporate America's web. That makes him a tragic figure in the movie's eyes. It does not matter whether in reality Wallace's decision to remain inside CBS finally helped get the Wigand story on the air or whether Bergman himself stayed on the network's payroll for more than two years after the controversy. (For his part, Bergman compared *The Insider* to "a historical novel," which recalled some of the criticisms leveled at Woodward and Bernstein and *All the President's Men.*[34]) In granting Wigand and Bergman their escape, the movie reproduces traditional individualist mythology. The fear of being reduced to a commodity is not solely a postmodern concern; at heart, it is the fear of personal autonomy being constrained or lost. *The Insider* celebrates two men who forsake their insider status to walk alone into the sunlight, breaking free of society's strictures to serve the causes of freedom and truth. In that, Lowell Bergman is not far removed from Richard Boyle in *Salvador.*

The Paper *and* True Crime

By the 1990s, it seemed as though the story of a newspaper reporter getting a big scoop and reporting it to the world—a popular movie theme from *The Front Page* through *All the President's Men*—no longer could be told straight. Of course, *The Front Page* had not told that story completely straight either, but by now its conventions were so shopworn that they seemed difficult to take seriously. Pictures such as *I Love Trouble* (1994) pandered to nostalgia. A knockoff of the battle-of-the-sexes movies of Hollywood's golden age, the film starred Julia Roberts and Nick Nolte as rival Chicago newspaper columnists who gradually fell in love while trading repartee that made no one forget Tracy and Hepburn. ("Where did you say you were from—*Bitch*ville?" he asks her. In return, she tells him she has named her dog after him: "Little Dick.")

On the surface, *The Paper* (1994) seems an equally cynical exercise. The movie tells of a day in the life of a New York City tabloid called the *Sun* with the motto "It Shines for All" and a building near fabled Park Row. The paper's star columnist carries a revolver that he fires to get attention in the newsroom. The male metro editor and the female managing editor have a bloody knockdown brawl in the pressroom. The managing editor is accidentally shot with the columnist's gun and is carted off to the hospital just as the metro editor's pregnant wife (who has been pleading with him to quit the tabloid) ends up in the hospital herself. There is a prissy, hypochondriac reporter and a crusty editor-in-chief. There is raucously profane newsroom banter. There is a gangland murder case, a nocturnal visit to a police station to crack open the case, and even a call to "stop the presses!" to replate for the scoop. Naturally, there is also a happy ending.

If *The Paper* is more heartfelt than *I Love Trouble,* it is largely because the director seemed to take the material seriously. Ron Howard had first gained fame as a child TV sitcom star and then as a director of such viewer-friendly films as *Parenthood.* "I think about the audience," he said in discussing how he selected his projects. "I think about whether I would enjoy seeing such a movie and whether I think audiences would, because I'm one of those guys who aims to please."[35]

The Paper was very much in that crowd-pleasing vein, but it also sought to provide a more serious message. Screenwriters David and Stephen Koepp (the latter a *Time* magazine editor) focused on the contemporary travails of the New York tabloid newspaper world in which the *Post* and the *Daily News* seemed perpetually on the verge of extinction. At the same time, they explored the changes in that world. "In the old days, guys would get drunk a lot, but these days, family life is a factor," said Stephen Koepp. "Now people don't go to bars. They go home and spend time with spouses who also work. They want to have a life." (Both brothers had themselves recently fathered children.)[36]

So *The Paper* is as much about the family lives, or lack thereof, of its central characters as it is about their work. The metro editor, Henry Hackett (Michael Keaton), is increasingly pressured by his wife, Martha (Marisa Tomei), to leave the *Sun* for a position at the rival *Sentinel,* a "respectable" paper that bears an uncanny resemblance to the *New York Times.* The new job presumably would grant Henry more time to spend with his wife and their soon-to-be-newborn, but Martha—who only recently left her *Sun* reporting job to have the baby— is leery of motherhood preventing her from resuming her career. Editor-in-chief Bernie White (Robert Duvall) has two ex-wives, an estranged daughter, and "a prostate the size of a bagel," and managing editor Alicia Clark (Glenn Close) has both a husband and a lover, neither of whom she seems especially enamored with. As for the columnist McDougal (Randy Quaid), he sleeps on a couch in the office, apparently having no other home.

Although the conflict between home and work appeared as early as *The Front Page, The Paper* has no Walter Burns to scorn notions of conventional marital bliss; it seems to find such notions appealing. It would be criticized for being "a kinder, gentler newspaper movie, domesticated, detoxed and defanged," and for trying to adapt the "outsize and magical" formula of classic journalism movies "to fit nice, family-minded professionals."[37] But that was to be expected from the director of *Parenthood* and from screenwriters who themselves were family-minded professionals. The choices with which they confronted their characters, including the women, were ones that such professionals actually faced: attempting to increase productivity with a reduced staff, sacrificing one's career to raise children, and forfeiting a well-loved job for a higher-paying one to provide for a growing family.

The Paper gives its characters earnestly serious journalistic dilemmas to accompany their earnestly serious personal ones. Two African American youths have been falsely accused of the gangland murder. Henry and McDougal shake the truth out of the police and return to the *Sun* with their scoop. But they have missed their deadline and find that Alicia has ordered the publication of a story trumpeting the youths' arrest with a one-word headline, "GOTCHA!" She tells them the paper can print the correct story tomorrow. After she and Henry brawl, McDougal reprimands her over drinks in a bar: "We run maimings on the front page because we've got good art. . . . But at least it's the *truth*. And as far as I can remember, we never, ever, *ever* knowingly got a story wrong—until tonight."

Everything works out. Alicia has an epiphany underscored by the jukebox strains of "A Change Is Gonna Come." She orders Henry's story published, even though an angry city official gunning for McDougal accidentally shoots her in the leg. Martha, despite a medical crisis, delivers a healthy baby. Henry realizes he has put his work ahead of his wife and crawls fully clothed into her hospital bed to sleep beside her. Even Bernie enjoys a small triumph as he spies on his daughter and discovers that she reads his paper. "Your whole world can change in twenty-four hours," says a voice on the radio at the final fade-out, and it apparently has for the better for all concerned.

Thus *The Paper* seems aimed at pleasing journalists along with everyone else. Its characters struggle with real-life concerns and finally choose the correct path. It is a movie that seeks to have it both ways, to be immersed in the excitement of big-city journalism while also being ensconced in the respectability and security of marriage and family, reconciling outlaw virtues with official ones. *Salvador* attacked yuppiedom; *The Paper* celebrates it.

No one would confuse Clint Eastwood with Ron Howard. Yet *True Crime* (1999), directed by Eastwood and starring him as well, treats many of the same themes as Howard's film. Steve Everett is an alcoholic, womanizing reporter who has landed at the *Oakland Tribune* after losing his previous newspaper job for cavorting with the owner's daughter. (Now he is sleeping with the city editor's wife.) When Everett gets a hunch that a prisoner who is scheduled to be executed the next day is innocent, he interviews the condemned man in prison. "You don't know me," he tells the prisoner, who has just expressed his devout religious faith:

> I'm just a guy out there with a screw loose. Frankly, I don't give a rat's ass about Jesus Christ. I don't care about justice in this world or the next. I don't even care what's right or wrong—never have. But you know what this is? . . . That's my

nose. To tell you the pitiful truth, that's all I have in life. And when my nose tells me something stinks, I gotta have faith in it, just like you have your faith in Jesus. When my nose is working well, I know there's truth out there somewhere. But if it isn't working well, then they might as well drive me off a cliff, cause I'm nothin'. Well, lately I haven't been a hundred percent sure my nose has really been working that great. So I've gotta ask ya: Did you kill that woman or not?

He did not, and Everett saves the man's life at the last possible moment by delivering the facts about the real killer to the governor's mansion after a wild car chase as unashamedly corny as anything in *The Paper*. The reporter wins a lucrative book deal and a Pulitzer Prize nomination.

However, he loses his wife and child. A trip with his little girl to the zoo ends disastrously when he accidentally injures her while rushing to pursue another interview. Then his wife learns of his latest adulterous betrayal. "You and your famous nose for a story," she tells him tearfully. "You think you can just sniff your way along, you know? From one hunch to another. One girl to another; one drink to another when you're drinking. But I'm not one of your stories." She orders him out of the house. At movie's close, he has just bought a Christmas gift for his daughter, from whom he is now separated. "Santa Claus rides alone," he growls before dropping his cigarette and loping off into the night.

Steve Everett could be Hildy after leaving Peggy on the train in *The Front Page*, or Chuck Tatum if he had survived *Ace in the Hole*, or Richard Boyle had he never gone to Central America. Indeed, as played by Clint Eastwood, Everett could be Dirty Harry's reporter cousin (his "Did you kill that woman?" speech sounds a lot like Harry's famous "Do you feel lucky?" speech). He is the latest in a line of deeply flawed journalists who are unwilling or unable to play by others' rules. They inevitably botch such nice, family-minded activities as taking a child to the zoo. *Any* sort of niceties or codes of correct personal and professional conduct are beyond their grasp. In Everett's case, he has nothing but his nose for a story. That dooms him to solitude, but it also bestows on him a certain grace.

True Crime represents the flipside of *The Paper*. Howard's film showed professional, official types coping in an anachronistic tabloid world. Eastwood's film shows an outlaw type coping as an anachronism in a professional, official world. The first film ended with the official journalist in bed with his wife and newborn; the second ends with the outlaw journalist going off alone (à la the Western gunslingers of yore) without his wife and daughter. However, both films show their protagonists doing the right thing: Henry fighting to free two youths and uphold the principle that the press must be right not just "tomorrow" but every day and Everett fighting to save a man from execution and serve the cause of truth. In the end, as in so many of the movies of the past that inspired *The Paper* and *True Crime,* the journalists emerge as heroes—imperfect ones to be sure, but heroes nonetheless.

ANTIMYTH IN FILM

Under Fire *and* Street Smart

Journalism mythology holds that truth can be separated from fiction and that reporting the truth serves the interests of democracy. That was a central thesis of both *The Paper* and *True Crime* as well as the other movies just discussed. But some films question the myth of the heroic truth-telling journalist while suggesting that the line between truth and fiction is necessarily blurred.

Under Fire (1983) is another in the cycle of 1980s foreign correspondent films. Like *Salvador,* it tells of a gonzo journalist covering a civil war in Central America and confronting U.S. malfeasance while gradually converting from cynicism to idealism. Unlike in *Salvador, The Killing Fields,* or *The Year of Living Dangerously,* the journalist becomes a hero by telling a lie.

Nick Nolte plays photojournalist Russell Price. He traipses between war zones with little concern for the people or politics involved: "I don't take sides; I take pictures." Price lands in Nicaragua during the 1979 civil war with fellow reporter Claire Stryder (Joanna Cassidy). "You're gonna love this war, Russell," she tells him. "There's good guys, bad guys, and cheap shrimp." Their cavalier attitude evaporates when Sandinista rebels take them to a secluded site to see their leader, "Rafael." He turns out to be dead, but the rebels ask Price to take a photograph making him seem still alive to rally support for their cause. Price is stunned: "I'm a journalist!" "This has nothing to do with journalism," a rebel replies. When Price still hesitates, Stryder tells him that although he may have won a lot of prizes, "you've never won a war."

Price does take the photo, and the Sandinistas are reinvigorated in their battle against U.S.-backed troops. Then Price's journalist friend Alex Grazier (Gene Hackman), the odd man out in a love triangle involving Price and Stryder, is gunned down in cold blood by Somoza government soldiers. Price photographs the killing, and it decisively shifts public opinion against Somoza.[38] The rebels emerge victorious. "You think we fell in love with too much?" Stryder asks Price. "I'd do it again!" he says.

The makers of *Under Fire* said they were inspired by Phillip Knightley's history of war correspondents, *The First Casualty.* Knightley took his title from Hiram Johnson's 1917 declaration that "the first casualty when war comes is truth" and wrote a stinging account of how easily journalists could be manipulated and co-opted in wartime.[39]

From that perspective, the movie can seem an ironic critique of journalists such as Price and Stryder. At the start, they and their colleagues are detached and opportunistic. Rather than question government propaganda, they celebrate their scoops and play trivia games. Photos Price takes of the rebels inadvertently lead to their slaughter. When the images of Grazier's murder are broadcast worldwide, a Nicaraguan woman acidly observes that up until now the U.S. news media have ignored the deaths of 50,000 of her compatriots: "Maybe we should have killed an American journalist fifty years ago." An American mercenary (Ed Harris) pops up occasionally to commit awful deeds, and Price seems little better than he; in effect, both are hired guns. "You get paid by the hour or by the body?" Price asks him. "I get paid the same way you do!" the mercenary retorts.

Nevertheless, Price's fabricated photo of Rafael contributes mightily to the Sandinista victory, and far from condemning him for his action, the movie congratulates him. The filmmakers said they wanted to show how "once in a while one has a chance to do something that will change history rather than just record it." In the same vein, critic Pauline Kael praised the film for depicting an "automaton" journalist who in faking the picture is "humanized [by] letting himself be governed by his own core of generosity."[40] *Under Fire* suggests that the "truthful" recording of events—assuming such a thing is even possible in wartime—cannot effect meaningful change by itself; it may even be inhumane. The rebels teach Price and Stryder that some things are more important than journalism's claims to be able to render reality objectively and that a falsehood can serve the greater good.

Street Smart (1987) similarly shows a journalist telling a lie, although this time the act is distinctly unheroic and in the end helps no one. The movie bears similarities to *Perfect* (1985) and *The Mean Season* (1985), which depict reporters too smart or dumb for their own good being goaded by editors who are even worse. The reporters exploit subjects for sex or fame (in *Perfect* it is a comely aerobics instructor; in *The Mean Season* it is a psychotic serial killer) only to see the subjects turn the tables on them (the aerobics instructor calls the reporter a "sphincter muscle"; the serial killer kidnaps the journalist's girlfriend). Both *Perfect* and *The Mean Season* have conventionally happy endings, however: One reporter goes to jail for refusing to reveal a confidential source and then is reunited with the aerobics instructor; the other reporter personally dispatches the serial killer and departs with his girlfriend to edit a small-town newspaper.

Street Smart is more subversive. It stars Christopher Reeve as Jonathan Fisher, a writer for a New York magazine. His career is in trouble, and in desperation he pitches a story about a pimp. When he cannot get one to talk to him, he makes up the story instead and parlays it into a TV news job. Unfortunately for Fisher, the fictional pimp bears an uncanny resemblance to the real-life

Fast Black (Morgan Freeman), who is wanted for murder. The district attorney subpoenas the reporter's nonexistent notes, and Fisher goes to jail. In the meantime, he has become involved with a prostitute named Punchy (Kathy Baker), who seduces him with alarming ease even though he already is living with another woman. He also has been targeted by Fast Black, who sees him as an ideal alibi exonerating him of the murder charge. Mayhem ensues: Fisher's girlfriend leaves him and is attacked by one of Fast Black's henchmen, Punchy talks to the district attorney and is killed by Fast Black in retaliation, and Fisher—after getting out of jail—sets up Fast Black to be killed himself while Fisher reports the event for TV.

Screenwriter David Freeman based the script on his experiences at *New York* magazine, where in 1969 he himself had fabricated a story about a pimp. "I was trying to write fiction in the form of journalism," he later recalled. "It was also the time before fact-checking, at least at *New York* magazine. And I got away with murder." He used his gift for fiction in starting a lucrative script-doctoring career in Hollywood. The Janet Cooke scandal prompted him to reexamine his past, which resulted in *Street Smart.*

Even then, Freeman expressed no particular regret for his journalistic sins. (He said of his *New York* editors that their "claims that they didn't know always reminded me of the moment in *Casablanca* where Claude Rains says, 'I'm shocked, shocked to hear there's gambling here.'")[41] However, his script for *Street Smart* painted a singularly unflattering portrait of his cinematic counterpart. As Christopher Reeve later wrote, the film shows that "the smarmy young writer and the treacherous pimp are much alike but that the pimp is actually more honest."[42] On the surface, Fisher seems an upstanding official type not unlike Gregory Peck's journalist in *Gentleman's Agreement:* handsome, educated, polite. In fact, he is "a weak Harvard boy, a fool, a dilettante—and a lousy reporter as well" who "gets a prostitute killed and his girlfriend knifed."[43] *Street Smart* thus undercuts myths idealizing not only journalism but also white-collar, upwardly mobile professionalism. Like *Perfect* and *The Mean Season,* the movie pulls back somewhat at the end; the newly "street smart" Fisher helps finish off the bad guy while expressing some remorse for his prior misdeeds. Still it seems likely that the reporter soon will return to jail: On top of everything else, he has committed perjury.

Broadcast News *and* To Die For

There are parallels to Christopher Reeve's shallow but attractive TV reporter in *Broadcast News* (1987). The film was written, directed, and produced by James L. Brooks, who had worked as a CBS news copyboy in the early 1960s. He co-created the hit television series *The Mary Tyler Moore Show,* starring Moore as a TV news producer. Then he moved into film with *Terms of Endear-*

ment (1983), which won Brooks Oscars for best picture, direction, and screen-play. For his follow-up, he conceived a movie that he said would deal with "fundamental changes" in contemporary romance and the workplace. "I had no idea what broadcast news was anymore because it had changed so much and was changing quicker than anything else I was aware of," he said. "And that made me want to do it against this background."[44]

Brooks paid particular attention to his female protagonist: "I knew that I didn't want to do a picture that could be in any way a feminist picture. . . . There was great effort given to presenting what I hoped was a new kind of heroine." He began observing the three major networks' newsrooms, where women confronted the same dilemmas that Adela Rogers St. Johns and others had in an earlier era. "After facing incredible competition to get into their positions and after working hard to get promoted," a 1988 study of women in TV news reported, "they find themselves having to make difficult choices between their careers and personal lives."[45]

In the movie, those choices are thrust onto Jane (Holly Hunter), a talented producer on the rise in a Washington network news bureau. Her personal life leaves much to be desired; she schedules regular intervals when she can have a good cry. Jane is best friends with Aaron (Albert Brooks), a gifted but neb-bishy reporter who secretly loves her. At the same time, she is powerfully attracted to pretty-boy journalist Tom (William Hurt), who came to the network from local TV sports and freely admits he knows nothing about news. When Jane reveals her feelings for Tom to Aaron, he tells her that Tom represents everything she loathes and then reveals his own love for her. Complicating the romantic triangle is a network cutback that terminates several employees but results in promotions for Jane and Tom. They make plans for a romantic get-away, but Aaron—who has quit his job—tips off Jane that Tom faked part of a story. She ends up without either man.

Brooks drew on several models for Jane, including CBS news producer Su-san Zirinsky. Another inspiration may have been correspondent Lesley Stahl, who was distressed when Brooks shared scuttlebutt he had heard from being around CBS. "I think you should know that your bosses consider your stiff, look-into-the camera style as 'yesterday,'" Stahl remembered him telling her. "I'd hate to see you left in the dust."[46]

"Yesterday" being "left in the dust" is a major theme of *Broadcast News,* which explores the wrenching cutbacks and changes that were befalling the network news divisions. Aaron represents the past, when presumably image and ratings were irrelevant; Tom represents the ghastly future. Aaron compares him to the devil, telling Jane that Satan will not appear in scary garb: "He will be attractive; he'll be nice and helpful; he'll get a job where he influences a great God-fearing nation; he'll never do an evil thing. . . . He'll just bit by little bit

Connected "far apart and electronically": Jane (Holly Hunter), Tom (William Hurt, top right), and Aaron (Albert Brooks) in *Broadcast News*. (Courtesy of the Academy of Motion Picture Arts and Sciences)

lower our standards where they're important. Just a tiny little bit, just coast along—flash over substance!" Tom, meanwhile, makes no apology. When a livid Jane accuses him of crossing the line, he responds, "They keep *moving* the little sucker, don't they?"

If Jane finds Tom revolting, she also lusts after him, and their never-quite-consummated relationship also is key to the film. While Aaron watches at home on his TV, Jane guides Tom through a live news special by speaking into a microphone connected to his earpiece. The camera shows her finger squeakily rubbing against the button that lets her communicate with him. "This is where you get into work as sex," James Brooks said. "We worked forever on the sound of just her finger on that button. This is the way these two people made their connection—far apart and electronically." The scene immediately following makes the same point as an exultant Tom rushes to Jane. "There was like a *rhythm* we got into," he tells her. "It was like—*great sex!*" But that is as close to actual sex as they get. Jane and Aaron fare no better; when he declares that he loves her, she reacts as though she has been slapped.

"What the picture was about was three people who had missed their last chance at real intimacy in their lives," said Brooks.[47] Presenting only the simulation of intimacy was a particularly postmodern conceit, and it suggested that television isolated and dehumanized people and failed to distinguish truth from illusion, much as *Network* had charged. That is underscored by *Broadcast News*'s ending, or at least its "first" ending. Each of the three protagonists is left alone: Aaron, disillusioned by Jane's attraction to Tom and the humiliations the network has inflicted on him, quits; Jane, appalled at Tom's ethical lapses, refuses to accompany him on their planned vacation; Tom, who pointedly tells Jane that he was promoted for doing the very things she is excoriating him for, boards the plane by himself.

Then comes the movie's "second" ending, which flashes forward seven years. Aaron has found not only professional happiness—in local TV news, no less—but also personal happiness with a wife and children. Tom is about to become the new network anchor and is engaged to a blonde journalist who early in the movie had been heard disparaging Jane's looks. Jane has agreed to move to New York to be Tom's managing editor. She also reveals that "there's a guy" who is teaching her how to water ski and who "says he'll fly up a lot" to visit her in her new job.

Jane is another long-suffering professional insider whose uncommon intelligence only causes her grief. "It must be nice to always believe you know better: to always think you're the smartest person in the room," the news president tells her. "No, it's *awful*," she sadly replies. Some critics recognized what Brooks openly acknowledged, that *Broadcast News* was not a feminist picture, and scolded the director for not allowing Jane true sexual intimacy.[48] The flash-forward ending, which granted the two male protagonists romantic fulfillment while giving Jane only a tenuous shot at it (will the "guy" really "fly up a lot"?) seemed to reinforce such arguments.

Regardless, many women who worked in network TV journalism loved *Broadcast News*.[49] Its depiction of a woman having to make a greater sacrifice for her career than her male colleagues was hardly unrealistic. Moreover, it appeared to present what Todd Gitlin called "a media pro's version of herself and her troubles," adding, "If only cutthroat capitalists would keep out of the pros' way, the film seems to be saying, the pros would be free to tell it the way it is."[50] That was a message similar to that of *Deadline, USA* and *The Insider*, to name just two.

Yet the flash-forward ending undermines that message. Jane, who previously had stood on professional principle in refusing to accompany Tom to the tropics, now consents to be his editor. *Broadcast News* punches holes in screwball's mythic view of American romance in which smart and funny folk find their perfect mates and rise above their slower peers. Although none of the protagonists end up with one another, the film does end with a wedding of sorts: the marriage between flash and substance, with flash holding the upper hand. It does not matter that Tom is slow. He simulates authority through his looks and charm. That makes him attractive not just to women and TV audiences but even to Aaron, who dearly longs to be as charming and smooth (although his attempt to anchor the news dissolves in a river of sweat).

Whereas Tom is the supremely confident anchor representing TV's excitement, Jane is the supremely competent editor who will make all the excitement possible. It is not surprising that at least one female high school student enrolled in a television class because "I watched *Broadcast News* and wanted to do what she did."[51] The irony is that Jane finally does what Aaron had feared all along: She makes her pact with the devil.

Alongside *Broadcast News*'s comparatively subtle critique of television were movies depicting the seductive effects of TV and celebrity on impressionable young women. In *Hero* (1992), Geena Davis plays a tough TV journalist who still is taken in rather easily by a handsome young man falsely claiming to have rescued her and dozens of others from a burning plane. In *Mad City* (1997), Mia Kirshner quickly graduates from newsroom intern to full-fledged correspondent in scarlet suit and lipstick, eagerly telling a dazed bombing survivor not to wipe the blood off his face: "It looks *good!*"

In *To Die For* (1995), the quest for TV stardom leads to murder. The film was inspired by twenty-two-year-old Pamela Smart, who aspired to be the next Barbara Walters but settled for being media services director for a New Hampshire school district. One week shy of her first wedding anniversary, her husband Gregg was shot to death in their condominium. It developed that Pamela had been carrying on with a fifteen-year-old named Billy whom she had met at school. She told Billy that they could continue their affair only if her husband were killed, and he and another boy did the deed. Pamela raised suspicions when she called a local TV station on the day of Gregg's wake and asked to be interviewed, telling the reporter, "I'm always so fascinated by the murder stories you cover." The media avidly covered Pamela's murder trial, which ended with a guilty verdict and a sentence of life without parole.[52]

Among those mesmerized by the case was Joyce Maynard. She had garnered notoriety for her youthful affair with a much-older J. D. Salinger and then for her nationally syndicated newspaper column discussing her domestic life and strife. Although some found the column insufferably narcissistic, others loved it. "It's my favorite soap opera: 'Joyce's Life,'" said one fan. "She's the literary equivalent of 'The Truman Show' or Princess Diana." (Revealingly, *The Truman Show* was a 1998 movie about a man who discovers his entire life is a TV show.) Maynard may have identified with Pamela Smart's craving for attention. In introducing her novel *To Die For,* she acknowledged that although the Smart case had suggested the outline, "all the characters in this and every other novel I'm ever likely to write represent elements of my own self."[53]

To Die For focused on self-obsession in a mass-mediated world. *Hero*'s producer, Laura Ziskin, also produced the movie version of Maynard's novel. To her, it was a "cautionary tale" about television, which she described as "the most powerful institution in the history of civilization." Screenwriter Buck Henry similarly asserted that TV "captures the imagination more than anything else in people's lives. The country is somehow held together by celebrities. . . . It's this jungle of junk." Gus Van Sant directed, and Nicole Kidman played the Suzanne Stone role.[54]

Suzanne lives in aptly named Little Hope, New Hampshire, with her amiable lunk of a husband, Larry (Matt Dillon). She has a pastel wardrobe, a junior college degree in electronic journalism, and an insatiable hunger to be on the air. "You're not anybody in America unless you're on TV," she says. "On TV is where we learn about who we really are. Because what's the point of doing anything worthwhile if nobody's watching? And if people are watching, it makes you a better person." When Suzanne decides that Larry stands in the way of her career, she arranges for his demise. She has been taping a documentary on a sad-sack group of local teens including Jimmy (Joaquin Phoenix), whom she lures into an affair and persuades to murder Larry. When it appears as though she will get away with it, Larry's parents call on the local Mafia to eliminate her.

To Die For skewers celebrification-via-television as Buck Henry's screenplay shows the characters "all entertaining on different media."[55] Larry's and Suzanne's parents appear side-by-side on a talk show as a TV crew and an unseen reporter (evoking *Citizen Kane*) interview the film's other principals. Suzanne delivers her inane monologues directly to the camera while making a video she hopes will promote her TV career. At movie's end, Jimmy's friend Lydia reveals that she has been booked to appear on *Oprah*. "It's really something when you think that *I'm* the one who's gonna be famous," she says. "Suzanne would *die* if she knew."

To Die For's ironic jibes at TV paralleled those in films such as Oliver Stone's *Natural Born Killers* (1994) and *Wag the Dog* (1998). In Stone's film, a Bonnie-and-Clyde–like couple achieves fame via a wave of murderous slaughter broadcast on tabloid TV; in *Wag the Dog*, a media spin doctor and Hollywood producer conspire to save a philandering president's political career via a made-for-TV war. The films anticipated reality. *Wag the Dog* was released right before the Monica Lewinsky scandal befell President Clinton, and *To Die For* opened just as the televised circus of the O.J. Simpson murder trial ended with a not guilty verdict. "There are times when we get exactly the satire we deserve," wrote Janet Maslin of *To Die For*, "and this is one of them."[56]

However, the film's condemnation of a gullible, sensation-hungry culture was nothing new. *Chicago* provided an especially instructive comparison. The 1926 Broadway play—and the 2002 Oscar-winning movie musical—similarly

Suzanne Stone (Nicole Kidman) murders her way to media celebrity in *To Die For*. (Courtesy of the Academy of Motion Picture Arts and Sciences)

were inspired by real-life women who had achieved fame via murder and the media, but *Chicago* played it for gleeful farce and rewarded the protagonist for her crime. In *To Die For*, Suzanne is a malevolent cartoon who, like Diana Christensen in *Network*, is made to stand for all that is stupid and exploitive about television. This time, though, there is no Max Schumacher–like old pro to serve as a voice of conscience. There is only a smarmy and sleazy network executive (George Segal) who mouths platitudes about the television journalist "bringing the world into our homes and our homes into the world" while leering at Suzanne and feeling her up under the table. *To Die For* represents Paddy Chayefsky's worst fears come true.

MYTH REAFFIRMED

Up Close and Personal

Of course, Hollywood does not make a habit of delivering bad news. It tells upbeat stories because audiences pay to see them. *Up Close and Personal* (1996) reaffirms the same myths of journalism and romance that *Broadcast News* and

To Die For implicitly questioned. That was particularly striking given the movie's source material and its authors.

The inspiration was Jessica Savitch, who rose from local TV news as a young woman to become an NBC News anchor. Although she was one of the nation's most trusted TV news personalities, many at NBC scorned her. The network dumped her from a Senate beat for which she had been ill-prepared, and she became increasingly addicted to cocaine. The second of two marriages ended when her husband hanged himself with her dog's leash. Soon after a well-publicized incident in which she appeared to be intoxicated and nearly incoherent on the air, she died in 1983 when her companion drove his car into a canal.[57]

Although Savitch was hardly the homicidal ninny that Suzanne Stone was in *To Die For,* in many ways she seemed a real-life Suzanne, a woman with unbridled ambition who saw television as her path to fame and eventually was destroyed. (She was exactly the kind of woman Suzanne and Pamela Smart would have been fascinated by and tried to emulate.) Savitch's tumultuous romantic life made her story even more lurid. Apart from her two marriages, she had a long-standing relationship with TV journalist Ron Kershaw, who beat her and fell prey to addiction himself.

If Hollywood had really wanted to update *His Girl Friday* for the TV age, it could have skipped the remake it actually produced (1988's *Switching Channels,* a romantic comedy handicapped by the fact that stars Kathleen Turner and Burt Reynolds loathed each other).[58] Instead it could have made a drug-, sex-, and violence-laced melodrama via a straightforward telling of Savitch's and Kershaw's relationship. A made-for-TV movie, *Almost Golden: The Jessica Savitch Story* (1995), showed Kershaw hitting Savitch but soft-pedaled the abuse and other unpleasant biographical details in turning her life into sob story.

That was nothing compared with what appeared in cinemas the following year. Disney, of all companies, had bought the rights to the Savitch story and contracted Joan Didion and John Gregory Dunne to write the script.[59] Didion was known for the New Journalism classics *Slouching towards Bethlehem* and *The White Album,* whereas Dunne had written an acerbic insider's account of Hollywood, *The Studio.* Despite that, the two moved easily into screenwriting. Money was a major attraction, but they also enjoyed the challenge and collaboration.[60]

It took Didion and Dunne eight years to write *Up Close and Personal.* Disney was leery of presenting the depressing details of Savitch's and Kershaw's lives. The screenwriters and director Jon Avnet finally united behind producer Scott Rudin's conception of the film: "It's about two movie stars."[61]

Up Close and Personal became an adult soaper centered around the personas of Robert Redford and Michelle Pfeiffer. It drew less on the Jessica Sav-itch story than on *A Star Is Born,* the most recent version of which had been scripted by Didion and Dunne. Redford played Warren Justice, a one-time network correspondent whose career was declining not because of addiction but because he was unwilling to compromise his principles. Pfeiffer was Sal-lyanne Atwater, an ambitious working-class woman who was as much con-cerned with providing for her sister as with achieving fame.

Warren hires Sallyanne at a Miami TV station even though he knows she faked her audition tape. "I figure if you're hungry enough to fake it, you might be hungry enough to do it," he tells her—a moment that unlike in *Street Smart* is presented completely without irony. Gradually Warren molds her into a polished professional, changing her name to Tally (she has a lisp). The two marry, and she becomes a network news star while he loses his job. "Wasn't the whole idea for us to be together?" Tally implores when Warren leaves her to pursue a story in Panama. "It was," he says. "But it can't be me putting wine on ice while you wrap up the evening news—and it can't be you turning down a story because you don't want to leave me at loose ends!"

Tragedy ensues: Warren is killed after getting a big scoop for Tally's network, IBS. In the climax, Tally forsakes a canned speech extolling the network's de-termination to win the ratings race to speak extemporaneously about her late beloved's Panama story: "He had a hunch, and he went out alone, and he did all the legwork. And at the end of the day, he got it. . . . I thought if I ever stood up at something like this, it would be about glory, or showing people. It's dif-ferent; I know that now. I'm only here for one reason: to tell the story. My husband told me that, not so long ago."

It was reminiscent of the "This is Mrs. Norman Maine" speech in *A Star Is Born,* and to reinforce the message Disney commissioned a ballad for Celine Dion featuring the refrain "I'm everything I am / Because you loved me." It was too much for some, including female TV journalists, who panned the movie.[62]

However, Warren's farewell to Tally is much like Sam's final speech to Tess in *Woman of the Year:* an argument that they must be equals for their relation-ship to work. The film presents a mythic vision of romance based on reciproc-ity. She is the callow neophyte whom he teaches to be a conscientious jour-nalist; he is the jaded veteran who rediscovers his idealism through her. Warren's death in the line of duty recalls not so much *A Star Is Born* as it does *Love Is a Many-Splendored Thing* (1955), in which a foreign correspondent is killed just when it seems he and his lover will live happily ever after.

Such star-crossed endings are clichéd, as John Gregory Dunne cheerfully acknowledged. He said both negative and positive reviews of *Up Close and Personal* correctly branded it as "schmaltzy, shallow, and predictable." However, the positive reviews went on to praise it as a throwback to the star-driven Hollywood romances of the golden age.[63] Dunne and Didion were hardly given to naive sentimentality (Didion had lost a job at *Vogue* for panning *The Sound of Music*). They were pragmatists thoroughly conversant in Hollywood formula, as reflected in Tally's closing lines. Although she says glory is unimportant, TV news has bestowed on her the fame she had always wanted. That she is played by Michelle Pfeiffer and romanced by Robert Redford makes her rise to the top even more glamorous. The movie aims a few barbs at television news but ultimately makes it seem not just romantic but heroic.

The film's old-fashioned message was ironic not only in comparison with the Savitch-Kershaw story that inspired it but also in the context of the 1990s corporate synergy that produced it. Dunne penned a memoir of the making of the film called *Monster*, the title alluding to Disney's ferocious devotion to protecting its financial interests. *Up Close and Personal* fed the monster without apology. It grossed more than $100 million in its first few months of release. Possibly it is not surprising that the film eschewed a more direct critique of TV news; Disney had bought ABC and its news division not long before the movie's release (and not long before ABC News apologized to the tobacco companies for its coverage of them).

However, the movie served corporate interests the most in that, quite simply, it sold. Disney used all its business and marketing savvy in leaving nothing to chance: directing Didion and Dunne to soften the story, casting Redford and Pfeiffer, and getting Dion to sing the soundtrack ballad. The end result peddled myths that proved as lucrative as ever: If you work hard enough, you can make it to the top and find your one true love all at once.

❦

A recurring theme in movies of the post-Watergate era was reconciling one's professional and personal identities. To paraphrase Paul Newman in *Absence of Malice*, it was about putting down one's pen and finally seeing one's subject as a living, feeling person; serving the interests of humanity instead of pandering to vulgar sensationalism with headlines such as "GOTCHA!"; recognizing one's obligations to one's loved ones; and reintegrating oneself into the community. Again, that theme dated to *The Front Page,* in which Peggy had told Hildy that leaving the newspaper to marry her was his chance "to have a home and be a human being." Now, though, the criticisms of the press at times seemed more pointed and the calls for reintegration more direct.

Perhaps such a shift was to be expected. The movies' rueful evocation of an earlier age when a reporter could shout "Stop the presses!" without being hooted at—either by the characters on screen or the moviegoers in the theaters—recalled Fredric Jameson's characterization of *All the President's Men* as "the heroic legendary moment of a vanished medium."[64] The Watergate myth of investigative journalists systematically exposing official wrongdoing to promote social reform had apparently given way to a more derisive view of public institutions that extended to the news media.[65]

Still, movies resolutely maintained the view that the press could serve a vital social function. Journalists who at first might have seen themselves as a class apart could learn to live up to their personal and professional duties. Even when they remained outside the boundaries of polite society, they could do good deeds. More often than not, the films were earnest rather than cynical, implying that cynicism only isolated one from the rest of humankind.

In short—and contrary to what many critics asserted—Hollywood still promoted the myth of the journalist as hero in either official or outlaw garb. In reconciling journalists' professional and personal roles, the movies performed the mythic function of suturing cultural contradictions. They showed the press learning not to be too big for its britches or too threatening toward the innocent individual while maintaining its role as the public's truth-teller and watchdog.

To be sure, some pictures presented a more caustic view while still addressing the same conflicts that journalism movies always had. If prior films had targeted journalists' propensity to treat the people they covered as means to further personal ambition instead of means unto themselves, so did *To Die For,* in which Suzanne ruthlessly exploited the teens she was profiling in her video documentary. If in the past movies had shown reporters finding it difficult to achieve a meaningful rapprochement between home and work, *Broadcast News* suggested that it had become well nigh impossible in the postmodern world in which people could make contact only electronically and at a distance. If truth had sometimes been a slippery commodity in journalism films, *Under Fire* and *Street Smart* subverted the notion that journalists had unique power or responsibility to report the truth.

The same myths reasserted themselves, though: *The Insider*'s Lowell Bergman placing his loyalty to his source above his selfish career interests, *Salvador*'s Richard Boyle abandoning his cynicism to declare his allegiance to American democratic ideals, *Absence of Malice*'s Megan Carter pledging to live up to the standards of her profession, *The Killing Fields*'s Sydney Schanberg declaring devotion both to Dith Pran and to reporting the facts about Cambodia, *Up Close and Personal*'s Warren and Tally smooching to the strains of Celine Dion, *The Paper*'s and *True Crime*'s journalists freeing the innocent. Yes, the movies said, big corporations ran the media and controlled much of our lives; yes, TV could be idiotic; yes, our culture was being cheapened and coarsened; yes, the tenets of liberal individualism were increasingly under siege. Still there were heroism and romance as individuals made the right choices, changed things for the better, and fell in love, and still the excitement of American mass-mediated culture provided fodder for popular storytelling. One suspects that Ben Hecht would not have felt out of place.

NOTES

1. Ben H. Bagdikian, *The Media Monopoly,* 6th ed. (Boston: Beacon, 2000), pp. xxxi–xxxiii.

2. For more on the Cooke and Blair scandals and other press embarrassments, see Mike Sager, "Janet's World," *Gentlemen's Quarterly,* June 1996, pp. 200–211; Adrian Havill, *Deep Truth* (New York: Birch Lane Press, 1996), pp. 136–50; Ben Bradlee, *A Good Life* (New York: Simon and Schuster, 1995), pp. 435–52; Tim Rutten, "Ripples of Blair Affair Widely Felt," *Los Angeles Times,* May 21, 2003, pp. E1, E12.

3. Renata Adler, *Reckless Disregard* (New York: Vintage, 1988), p. 133; Janet Malcolm, *The Journalist and the Murderer* (New York: Knopf, 1990), p. 3.

4. David L. Eason, "On Journalistic Authority: The Janet Cooke Scandal," in *Media, Myths, and Narratives,* ed. James W. Carey (Newbury Park, Calif.: Sage, 1988), pp. 205–27; George Garneau, "Trash Journalism," *Editor & Publisher,* October 29, 1994, pp. 8, 11.

5. Quoted in Rutten, "Ripples of Blair Affair Widely Felt," p. E12.

6. Fredric Jameson, *Postmodernism: Or, the Cultural Logic of Late Capitalism* (Durham, N.C.: Duke University Press, 1991); Michael R. Real, *Exploring Media Culture* (Thousand Oaks, Calif.: Sage, 1996), pp. 237–66; Bagdikian, *The Media Monopoly,* pp. viii–xlvii; James S. Ettema and Theodore L. Glasser, "The Irony in—and of—Journalism: A Case Study in the Moral Language of Liberal Democracy," *Journal of Communication* 44:2 (1994): 5–28; Todd Gitlin, "Bites and Blips: Chunk News, Savvy Talk and the Bifurcation of American Politics," in *Communication and Citizenship: Journalism and the Public Sphere,* ed. Peter Dahlgren and Colin Sparks (London: Routledge, 1991), pp. 119–36.

7. Michael Schudson, *Watergate in American Memory* (New York: Basic, 1992), p. 109.

8. Christopher Hanson, "Where Have All the Heroes Gone?" *Columbia Journalism Review,* March–April 1996, p. 48; James Fallows, *Breaking the News* (New York: Vintage, 1997), p. 44.

9. Schudson, *Watergate in American Memory,* p. 120.

10. Jonathan Friendly, "A Movie on the Press Stirs a Debate," *New York Times,* November 15, 1981, sec. 2, p. 26.

11. John Consoli, "'Absence of Malice': A Flawed Indictment," *Editor & Publisher,* November 28, 1981, p. 7; Lucinda Franks, "Hollywood Update," *Columbia Journalism Review,* November–December 1981, p. 62.

12. Nat Hentoff, "If You Can't Take the Heat—Become a Journalist," *Village Voice,* December 9–15, 1981, p. 8.

13. *Absence of Malice* has been featured in at least one journalism ethics textbook. See Philip Patterson and Lee Wilkins, *Media Ethics: Issues & Cases* (Boston: McGraw-Hill, 1998).

14. For a discussion of these and other principles, see Jay Black, Bob Steele, and Ralph Barney, *Doing Ethics in Journalism*, 3rd ed. (Boston: Allyn and Bacon, 1999).

15. Andrew Sarris, review of *Absence of Malice*, *Village Voice*, January 6–12, 1982, p. 43.

16. See for example Howard Good, *Girl Reporter: Gender, Journalism, and the Movies* (Lanham, Md.: Scarecrow, 1998), pp. 118–22.

17. See Clifford G. Christians, John P. Ferré, and P. Mark Fackler, *Good News: Social Ethics and the Press* (New York: Oxford University Press, 1993), pp. 18–48.

18. Sydney Schanberg, "The Death and Life of Dith Pran," *New York Times Magazine*, January 20, 1980, p. 22. See also Joyce Waddler, "Odyssey out of 'The Killing Fields,'" *Washington Post*, February 4, 1985, p. B1.

19. Andrew Yule, *David Puttman: The Story So Far* (London: Sphere, 1989), pp. 219–25; Elizabeth Becker, "The War, as It Was," *Washington Post*, January 13, 1985, p. L1; Roland Joffé, Director's Commentary, *The Killing Fields* DVD, Warner Brothers, 2001.

20. Yule, *David Puttnam*, p. 248.

21. Sue Mathews, *35 mm Dreams* (Ringwood, Victoria, Australia: Penguin, 1984), p. 106.

22. Haing S. Ngor was a Cambodian refugee who like Pran had lost most of his family to the Khmer Rouge. He won an Oscar for his performance.

23. Joffé, *The Killing Fields* DVD.

24. J. Hoberman, review of *The Killing Fields*, *Village Voice*, November 13, 1984, p. 57.

25. Naomi Glauberman, "Ripped from the Headlines," *American Film*, March 1984, p. 53.

26. James Riordan, *Stone* (New York: Hyperion, 1995), pp. 154–55.

27. Oliver Stone, Director's Commentary, *Salvador* DVD, MGM Home Entertainment, 2001.

28. Ibid. One historian says Stone actually soft-pedaled some of the harshest details of Salvadoran oppression and American complicity in it. See Walter LaFeber, "Salvador," in *Oliver Stone's USA: Film, History, and Controversy*, ed. Robert Brent Toplin (Lawrence: University Press of Kansas, 2000), pp. 93–109.

29. Information on the making of *The Insider* comes from D. M. Osborne, "Real to Reel," *Brill's Content*, July–August 1999, pp. 74–79; Richard Lacayo, "Truth & Consequences," *Time*, November 1, 1999, pp. 92–98.

30. *90 Minutes on 60 Minutes*, television documentary written and directed by Susan Steinberg. Originally aired on PBS's *American Masters*, May 13, 1998. The quotes that follow from Don Hewitt and Mike Wallace come from the same documentary.

31. Marie Brenner, "The Man Who Knew Too Much," *Vanity Fair*, May 1996, pp. 170–81, 206–16; Osborne, "Real to Reel," p. 77.

32. Don Hewitt, *Tell Me a Story* (New York: Public Affairs, 2001), p. 199.

33. "Fox Demands Apology, Threatens to Sue Drudge," *USA Today*, November 17, 1999, p. 3D; Mary Murphy, "Mighty Mike," *TV Guide*, September 18–24, 1999, p. 32.

34. Lacayo, "Truth & Consequences," p. 98.

35. Ron Howard, guest on *Inside the Actors Studio* TV program, May 7, 1999.

36. Maureen Dowd, "'The Paper' Replates 'The Front Page' for the '90s," *New York Times*, March 13, 1994, sec. 2, pp. 15, 19.

37. Ibid., p. 15; Janet Maslin, "A Day with the People Who Make the News," *New York Times,* March 18, 1994, p. C19.

38. That scene was loosely based on the real-life killing of ABC journalist Bill Stewart in Nicaragua, an incident captured on film.

39. Phillip Knightley, *The First Casualty* (New York: Harvest, 1976); Aljean Harmetz, "5 Films with Political Statements Due in Fall," *New York Times,* September 10, 1983, sec. 1, pp. 1, 11.

40. Harmetz, "5 Films," p. 11; Pauline Kael, "Image Makers," *New Yorker,* October 31, 1983, p. 125.

41. David Denby, review of *Street Smart, New York,* March 30, 1987, p. 89; Irene Lacher, "Reinventing Tinseltown," *Los Angeles Times,* August 2, 1991, p. E1.

42. Christopher Reeve, *Still Me* (New York: Random House, 1998), p. 223.

43. Denby, review of *Street Smart,* p. 89.

44. Michael Cieply, "Brooks Takes Another Look at 'Broadcast News,'" *Los Angeles Times,* November 23, 1987, Calendar sec., p. 1; David Ansen, "Zooming In on TV News," *Newsweek,* December 28, 1987, p. 44.

45. *American Cinema: Romantic Comedy,* film documentary, writer-producer-director Molly Ornati, Fox Video, 1995; Marlene Sanders and Marcia Rock, *Waiting for Prime Time* (Urbana: University of Illinois Press, 1988), p. 84.

46. Lesley Stahl, *Reporting Live* (New York: Simon and Schuster, 1999), pp. 203, 247–48, 272–73.

47. *American Cinema: Romantic Comedy.*

48. See for example David Edelstein, review of *Broadcast News, Village Voice,* December 22, 1987, p. 88.

49. Cheryl Gould, "'Lines Straight Out of My Life,'" *Newsweek,* December 28, 1987, p. 50; Linda Ellerbee, "'Broadcast News'—And So It Really Goes," *Los Angeles Times,* January 11, 1988, Calendar sec., pp. 1–2; Stahl, *Reporting Live,* p. 273.

50. Todd Gitlin, "Down the Tubes," in *Seeing through Movies,* ed. Mark Crispin Miller (New York: Pantheon, 1990), pp. 35, 39.

51. Steve Johnson, "High School Class Makes Its Own Broadcast News," *Chicago Tribune,* June 6, 1989, Tempo sec., p. 1.

52. Rosalind Wright, "The Temptress Bride," *Ladies' Home Journal,* July 1991, pp. 93–95, 152–55; James Robert Parish, *Gus Van Sant* (New York: Thunder's Mouth Press, 2001), p. 195. Before the film version of *To Die For,* Helen Hunt starred in a made-for-TV movie about the Pamela Smart case: *Murder in New Hampshire* (1991).

53. Larissa MacFarquhar, "The Cult of Joyce Maynard," *New York Times,* September 6, 1998, sec. 6, p. 32; Joyce Maynard, *To Die For* (New York: Signet, 1993), pp. 365–66.

54. *To Die For* Production/Clippings File, Margaret Herrick Library, Academy of Motion Picture Arts and Sciences (AMPAS), Beverly Hills, Calif.; Bernard Weinraub, "How 'To Die For' Managed to Open at Simpson Finale," *New York Times,* October 10, 1995, p. B1.

55. Parish, *Gus Van Sant,* p. 197.

56. Quoted in Weinraub, "How 'To Die For' Managed to Open at Simpson Finale," p. B1.

57. Biographical information on Savitch comes from Gwenda Blair, *Almost Golden* (New York: Avon, 1989); Alanna Nash, *Golden Girl* (New York: Harper Paperbacks, 1996).

58. For an account of the making of *Switching Channels*, see Reeve, *Still Me*, pp. 228–29.

59. Information on the making of *Up Close and Personal* comes from Benjamin Svetkey, "Not Necessarily the News," *Entertainment Weekly*, March 8, 1996, pp. 20–25; John Gregory Dunne, *Monster* (New York: Random House, 1997).

60. Dan Cryer, "Word by Word," *Newsday*, September 25, 1996, p. B04. See also Sara Davidson, "Back Draft," *Los Angeles Times*, March 7, 1997, p. F1.

61. Dunne, *Monster*, pp. 117, 105.

62. Jane Horwitz, "'Up Close': Nothing but Bad News," *Washington Post*, March 7, 1996, p. C07; Judith Marlane, *Women in Television News Revisited* (Austin: University of Texas Press, 1999), pp. 44–46, 50.

63. Dunne, *Monster*, pp. 201–3.

64. Fredric Jameson, *The Geopolitical Aesthetic* (Bloomington: Indiana University Press, 1992), p. 77.

65. See Ettema and Glasser, "The Irony in—and of—Journalism."

＊ 8

An Unseen Power

In 1999, a small independent film went so far as to resurrect Ben Hecht, or at least a fanciful facsimile of him. *Man of the Century* told of a New York reporter who seemed blissfully oblivious that he was living in the 1990s. Instead he spoke, dressed, and behaved as though he were living in the heyday of big-city jazz journalism. "In today's world of cynicism and despair—of loneliness and rage—there is one man whose virtue and character recall the values of a happier time," announced the movie's trailer. "He's Johnny Twennies, and boy, does he have moxie!" Johnny bangs out stories on a manual typewriter, downs chopped beef with onions and coffee for lunch, stands up to tough guys with lines like "You keep ridin' me like this, you're gonna have to pay the fare," and chivalrously fends off the advances of his frustrated art dealer girlfriend. "Are you gay?" she demands to know. "Of course I'm gay," he sunnily replies. "I'm as gay as a day in May!"

Adam Abraham directed and co-scripted *Man of the Century* with Gibson Frazier, who starred as Johnny. Their movie shared some similarities with *The Hudsucker Proxy* (1994), which also featured an old-fashioned, fast-talking reporter whom Jennifer Jason Leigh played as a cross between Katharine Hepburn and Rosalind Russell. However, Joel and Ethan Coen's film was a quintessentially postmodern pastiche that took its plot and characters from the Capra and screwball films of the 1930s, put them in a fantastically contrived 1950s setting, and overlaid it all with 1990s irony. In contrast, Abraham and Frazier mostly played *Man of the Century* straight. "Unabashedly pure and sweet and genuine, it is a film that makes you want to fall in love," raved one critic. Nevertheless, without the backing of a major studio, the movie quickly vanished from the handful of theaters it played.[1]

Man of the Century could be seen not just as a wistful evocation of happier times but as proof of the futility of trying to recapture them in a sour, postmodern age. The sweet and genuine seemed as out of place as Johnny himself. Hollywood was obsessed with big opening weekends and the adolescent male audience. Traditional reporters and newspapers were supplanted by "con-

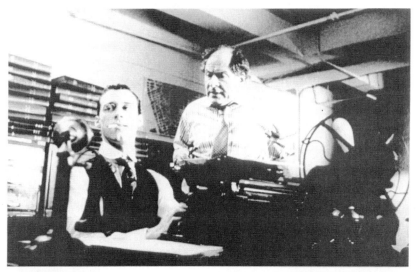

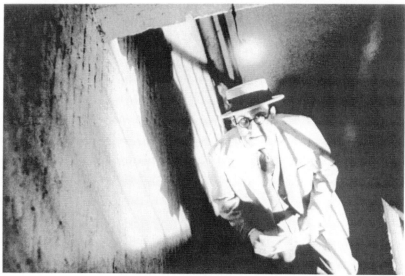

Gibson Frazier as Johnny Twennies in *Man of the Century*. (Courtesy of the Academy of Motion Picture Arts and Sciences)

tent providers" and new computer-driven technology. Standing up to tough-ies was fine if it served a market niche and enhanced the bottom line; if not, the crisis or scandal of the moment could be endlessly rehashed and recycled. Journalism was sick, dying, or dead, and when movies told stories about the press, it was no longer to praise it but to bury it.

As for Walter Burns, the fearsome editor whom Ben Hecht and Charles

MacArthur had created for the stage, his kind was also out of date. Walter's boast about an "unseen power" that watched over the press—"Bigger men than you have found out what it is! Presidents! Yes—and Kings!"—sounded utterly foolish in the context of the contemporary media world.

Or so it may have seemed to some. To pronounce journalism mortally ill or deceased was as much an overstatement as to assert that Hollywood's depiction of the news media over the decades had shifted from being largely positive to entirely negative. Both views were colored by nostalgia for a nonexistent past. Ben Hecht and his peers were a good deal more complicated than Johnny Twennies. The stories they told about the press in their novels, plays, and movie scripts were not always cheerful or free of irony (just as Walter's boast in *The Front Page* was not irony-free). The concerns raised about journalism at the start of a new century were not wholly different from those raised in the Hecht and MacArthur play that launched the journalism film genre. And the myths that the play helped propagate had not lost their currency seventy-five years later.

This concluding chapter uses Walter's "unseen power" speech from *The Front Page* to help think about what journalism movies represent. The chapter reviews the unseen powers behind the films, including one-time journalists. It highlights the often overlooked power the movies exert in depicting tensions inherent in journalism and American culture. The films also invest journalism itself with power: not unlimited, and not always for the good, but power nonetheless to play a vital, essential role in American life.

INFOTAINERS AND MYTHOLOGIZERS

If Ben Hecht ever were afflicted by innocence, it wore off quickly. Not for him was Johnny Twennies's quaint chivalry. He wrote with lip-smacking delight of his nights spent in Chicago's bordellos alongside his journalist cronies. He prided himself on seeing the world for the seedy and corrupt place that it was. And although he wrote that he and his colleagues also prided themselves on caring not a whit for other careers that promised them greater fame and fortune, Hecht pursued every other occupation that his facility with words offered him, from public relations to the theater. When Hecht and MacArthur migrated to New York, they associated with the city's artistic elite such as Jed Harris and George S. Kaufman, who were sophisticates and (in Harris's case) sons-of-bitches to boot. The playwrights concocted *The Front Page* as both a loving tribute to their journalistic past and a renunciation of it but, more importantly, as a calculated attempt to score a Broadway hit, pushing the envelope with coarse language topped by the famous curtain line.

The result was a docudrama for its era. In criticizing *The Insider* more than

Walter (Adolphe Menjou, far right) and Hildy (Pat O'Brien) invoke the "unseen power" watching over the press in *The Front Page*. (Courtesy of the Academy of Motion Picture Arts and Sciences)

seventy years later, Carl Sessions Stepp branded it "the essence of infotainment, blurring all sorts of lines between reality and invention in ways that viewers cannot possibly fathom."[2] The same was true of *The Front Page*. On one hand, it was a ripped-from-the-front-pages exposé of jazz journalism at a time when the Ruth Snyder execution photo was still fresh in public memory, a portrayal of the press provocative enough to stir the wrath of the *New York Times* and others that were trying to raise the standard of the profession. On the other hand, the play was a flat-out farce built on speed and coincidence and taking whatever creative liberties served those ends. Thus did a reviewer observe at the time that "such a night in a press room never was, on sea or land." Although the 1931 film of *The Front Page* is included in a collection of essays on how the movies have depicted history, Arthur Schlesinger Jr. praises it not so much for mirroring historical reality but for "catch[ing] best the legend of Chicago in the Roaring Twenties."[3]

Film and genre are particularly good at cultivating legend and myth, and

169

journalism movies provide unique insight into the profession's mythology. That is due in large part to those who inspired and wrote the films. Time and again current or former journalists have written for the movies: Louis Weitzenkorn, who used *Five Star Final* to atone for his tabloid sins; Herman Mankiewicz, who co-authored *Citizen Kane;* Ernie Pyle, who consulted on what purported to be his true-life story in *The Story of G.I. Joe;* Quentin Reynolds, who dabbled in screenwriting with *Call Northside 777;* Billy Wilder, the one-time tabloid reporter who directed and co-wrote *Ace in the Hole;* Samuel Fuller and Richard Brooks, who created the eulogistic *Park Row* and *Deadline, USA;* Joseph Heller, the former *Time* staffer who banged out *Sex and the Single Girl* while waiting for *Catch-22* to succeed; Haskell Wexler, the documentarian who blended fact and fiction in *Medium Cool;* Woodward and Bernstein, who at the urging of Robert Redford put themselves at the center of *All the President's Men* and may or may not have invented Deep Throat; Kurt Luedtke, who penned a journalistic morality tale in *Absence of Malice;* Sydney Schanberg and Richard Boyle, whose foreign correspondent days became the gist of *The Killing Fields* and *Salvador;* Lowell Bergman, who seemed to be settling a few scores in his contribution to *The Insider;* Stephen Koepp, the *Time* editor who co-wrote *The Paper;* David Freeman, who alluded to his checkered past in *Street Smart;* James Brooks, who returned to his TV copyboy roots in *Broadcast News;* Joyce Maynard, who knowingly wrote of self-obsession and celebrity in *To Die For;* and Joan Didion and John Gregory Dunne, who turned the sad tale of Jessica Savitch into the romantic *Up Close and Personal.*

Like Ben Hecht, most of them demonstrated mixed feelings toward the press. They sought some measure of creative freedom, attention, or cash that journalism could not give them and found that their newsroom skills and experiences translated well into screenwriting. That was especially true when they were prepared to do as they were told, although at times they may have complained about it. John Gregory Dunne's memoir of writing *Up Close and Personal* detailed the frustrations he and Joan Didion experienced, and Ben Hecht recalled in his own memoirs, "I discovered early in my movie work that a movie is never any better than the stupidest man connected with it."[4]

However, journalists typically are used to shaping their news stories to meet editorial demands. Their gripes about stupid movie folk are similar to reporters' gripes about editors, a contentious relationship at the heart of *The Front Page* and countless movies since. Even when they have had more creative control, they still have been ready to write both flattering and unflattering portraits of the press: Hecht, who said no profession "produces as fine a version of the selfless hero as journalism does,"[5] penned the less-than-heroic *Nothing Sacred;* Samuel Fuller created both *Park Row* and *Shock Corridor;* Richard Brooks wrote and directed both *Deadline, USA* and the wretched *Fever Pitch*

(1985), in which a sports reporter researches a gambling story only to turn into a gambling addict himself.

Contributing to the mixed portrayals is that professional press associations have had only limited success in lobbying Hollywood for more positive depictions. Although they did exert some influence especially in the years surrounding World War II, there never has been the full-fledged symbiosis between the profession and the entertainment world that once existed between institutionalized medicine and TV doctor shows.[6] More important have been the movies' producers, directors, and stars. Fox studio chief Darryl Zanuck urged Brooks to come up with *Deadline, USA*'s "hardhitting" title and climax; he also shaped *Gentleman's Agreement* and *Call Northside 777.* Director Alan J. Pakula brought his conspiracy-minded sensibility to Woodward and Bernstein's book of *All the President's Men.* Paul Newman, Robert Redford, and Michelle Pfeiffer turned *Absence of Malice* and *Up Close and Personal* into films that were as much about the stars' personas as they were about journalism.

Most important of all, with the odd exception of low-budget films such as *Shock Corridor* or *Black Like Me,* have been Hollywood's estimations of what would entice moviegoers, from the mass audiences of the golden age to the narrower niches of later years. Those estimations were affected by the zeitgeist of the times in which the films were made—the short-lived postwar optimism of the 1940s, the paranoia of the 1970s, the postmodern disaffection of the 1990s—but more directly by that which people had always paid to see. Surefire storytelling formulas sold, and even harsh satires (e.g., *Network*) and high-minded films (e.g., *The Killing Fields*) drew on them.

The Front Page itself used conventions already established by newspaper novels and plays such as *Chicago* that preceded it on Broadway. Hecht and MacArthur were perfectly willing to subordinate intellectual and artistic aspirations to commercial considerations, and the result was an entertainment from which the new talking pictures could readily borrow. Inevitably, much of what was fresh about the play hardened into cinematic cliché, as was typical of Hollywood. "A movie is basically so trite and glib that the addition of a half dozen miserable inanities does not cripple it," wrote Hecht, who as a top screenwriter should have known.[7]

And yet for all their glibness and inanities, journalism movies have demonstrated staying power, whether appearing in the 1930s or the 1990s, dealing with print or with television, or being romantic comedies, film noirs, conspiracy movies, or some combination thereof. Historian Warren Susman observed that the "tension between the mythic beliefs of a people—their visions, their hopes, their dreams—and the ongoing, dynamic demands of their social life . . . provides many artists with their theme, a theme reflecting a basic conflict within the culture itself."[8] Conflicts between home and work, cynicism and idealism, objectivity and subjectivity, public interest and institutional interest, and public interest and private interest were present in *The Front Page* and have persisted in the films that followed. The movies also have spoken to the broader conflicts between official and outlaw mythologies in American life and characteristically sought to reconcile the opposing sides. In so doing, they have remained true to Hollywood convention and to the ambivalent nostalgia toward the press that their ex-journalist creators brought to them.[9]

Home versus Work

Romantic comedy is about love and marriage, which confirm traditional bonds and integrate individuals into the social and cultural order. In some ways, journalism movies subvert all that. *The Front Page* does not end in marriage; matrimony seems not to compare to the footloose excitement of journalism. The screwball comedy remake *His Girl Friday* concludes with an imminent remarriage, but instead of relegating the woman to traditional subordinate status (never mind that it ends with her chasing after him with the bags), it shows a full-fledged integration of personal and professional lives in a mutually rewarding relationship. The romantic comedies of the 1930s and 1940s show strong women finding romance without sacrificing the best parts of themselves; in the cases of journalists such as Hildy in *His Girl Friday* and Tess in *Woman of the Year,* those best parts include their work. Hildy and Tess affirm their identities by giving up their pretensions to being domestic servants. The very existence of female journalists, often portrayed as equal to or better than their male counterparts, implicitly challenges the notion that women belong in the private home realm and men in the public work realm. When the women give up their work in films such as *Mr. Deeds Goes to Town,* it is a little sad.

Still, it is not atypical. Stereotypes of female journalists have a long tradition in popular culture and have persisted in the movies, in which women always have found "having it all" difficult or impossible.[10] In *Broadcast News,* Jane wins a promotion but fails to find steady romance. In *Absence of Malice,* Megan Carter loses her lover and, it is implied, her job as well. In *Network,* Diana Christensen conspires to assassinate the low-rated anchor after her journalist paramour dumps her; in *To Die For,* Suzanne similarly arranges for her husband's murder when he blocks her ambitions. That movies choose to depict TV's triviality and shallowness through women-turned-psychopaths is disturbing; it forces women to play the mythic role of scapegoats for society's fears and ills.[11] The films' depictions also reflect the fear of women prominent in outlaw mythology and conspiracy tales. Nevertheless, that does not negate that the films do address real dilemmas faced by women in journalism and other professions.

Male on-screen journalists find it somewhat easier to blend their private and professional identities. Yet they also face tough choices such as that at the crux of *The Front Page*. Their long-suffering love interests continually point out that the men's obsession with work and "the story" is endangering their relationships. In *The Year of Living Dangerously,* the journalist abandons the scoop of a lifetime to board a plane with his beloved. In *Network, The Paper,* and *True Crime,* journalists' womanizing endangers or destroys their marriages.

The movies thus suggest that journalism is not for normal people, which is its blessing and its curse. American outlaw mythology prizes romantic individualism: the wanderer, the improviser, the person who can move easily between different realms and strata of society and who is free of traditional social bonds. The journalist can represent all those things. In addition, there is something satisfyingly democratic and egalitarian in screwball comedy about women moving in the same circles as the men and proving themselves their equals or superiors. Film noir also presents women who, although they may be devious and even murderous, are still strong and subversive.[12] Even a far more traditional film such as *Up Close and Personal* shows its principals making each other better and stronger people as well as journalists.

But Americans also are threatened by iconoclasm. Journalists often are depicted as living outside society's norms, having less in common with doctors than with scruffy private eyes and shyster lawyers.[13] If one wants to be respectable, get ahead, climb the social ladder, keep up with the Joneses—that is, live up to official American mythology and middle-class ideals—journalism as seen in the movies often is not the best path.[14] For every depiction of it as a decent, family-oriented profession (as in *Gentleman's Agreement, Call Northside 777,* and *The Paper*), one has depicted it as a dead-end existence that the journalist desperately wants to escape (witness again *The Front Page*). Although professional ambition sometimes is rewarded (*All the President's Men; Up Close and Personal*), clawing to the top on the backs of others is ruthlessly punished (*Ace in the Hole, Sweet Smell of Success, To Die For*).

In the end, though, conflicts between the personal and professional worlds typically are resolved in a manner reinforcing prescribed social roles. The wayward, womanizing journalist in *Ace in the Hole* not only dies for his sins but first makes a point of returning the young man who idolizes him to the side of the truth-telling, happily married editor. The vagabond reporter in *True Crime* ambles off alone after reuniting a wrongly condemned man with his wife and daughter. The women in Capra's films abandon their smart-aleck stances to help serve the noble causes of their loved ones. Otherwise exemplary reporters who overreach are brought back into line as in *The Killing Fields,* and in the process achieve harmony between their private and professional selves.

Cynicism versus Idealism

Cynicism can be seen as good or bad. It is good if it means that one knows the score, is streetwise (a reason why cynicism is a recognized stereotype in the portrayal of the big-city newshound), and is able to stand up to the self-important and power-mad. "In a society deeply suspicious of the discrepancies between public pronouncement and the hidden workings of power, there is something genuinely attractive about the way a cynic expresses a truth," writes William Chaloupka.[15] From that perspective, cynicism promotes an outlaw conceit: There is no one whose pretensions cannot be seen through and who cannot be made fun of. Again, ideals of individualism and egalitarianism are served.

On the other hand, cynicism is bad when it becomes an instrument of pessimism. Americans like to think of themselves as an optimistic people: Things will get better; we can solve our problems and improve ourselves. That is an official conceit, and not to buy into it seems almost unpatriotic.[16]

The contemporary debate over press cynicism and "civic" or "public" journalism throws the cynicism-idealism clash into relief. It has been said that the press focuses too much on sinister motives, caring only about political strategy and trying to seem clever. Television's ascendancy over the printed word has exacerbated that state of affairs. Civic journalism's advocates seek to restore democratic ideals by writing stories around themes of consensus rather than conflict and becoming involved facilitators who promote public discussion rather than detached observers who inhibit it. It has been labeled a neo-Progressive reform effort.[17]

Ben Hecht and his cronies had little use for such reformers in their day, and although today's press cynicism reflects cultural and institutional changes since then, it also represents a continuation of a strand of American thought to which journalists always have had an affinity.[18] The journalist sees the powerful up close with all their warts and is subject to manipulation because he or she is their conduit to the public; it has been so since the first generation of urban reporters.

For its part, popular culture always has portrayed journalistic cynicism as problematic, despite suggestions that it now shows the press to be much more cynical than in earlier years.[19] Turn-of-the-century reporters used cynicism as a way of coping with their jobs. Those who turned their experiences into fiction commonly wrote of burned-out journalists whose idealism had turned sour, a theme alluded to in the stage version of The Front Page in which Hildy tells his colleagues that they will end up as "gray-headed, humpbacked slobs, dodging garnishees when you're ninety."

The movies have carried on that theme, alternating between celebrations and condemnations of the journalist as cynic. They show reporters wising up the naive and putting the sanctimonious in their place (as in *The Front Page* and many others) while also showing reporters being converted to a cause or otherwise having their idealism restored (as in *Mr. Deeds Goes to Town, Meet John Doe, Call Northside 777,* and *Salvador*). When journalists are thus awakened or converted, they are brought back into the fold and reintegrated into society. They do the same for others when they cure those who are overly credulous or pious. The movies seem to use journalists to teach audiences to strive for a healthy balance between cynicism and idealism and between outlaw and official mythologies. Failing to do so can mean dying bitter and alone, like Charles Foster Kane, or constantly being duped, like Bruce in *His Girl Friday.*

Objectivity versus Subjectivity

Films are fuzzy concerning the nature of truth and how journalists should find it (just as lawyer films are fuzzy on how justice should be achieved).[20] The professional model of scientific, impartial newsgathering often does not work well in the movies, where reporting can be a messy and confusing business taking a high personal toll. Some on-screen journalists engage in careful investigation and successfully discover truth, as in *Call Northside 777, True Crime,* and *All the President's Men.* Other times their scoops are the product of dumb luck (*The Front Page*), lies and deceit (*Ace in the Hole, Under Fire, Street Smart*), or unhealthy obsession. For all their pride in knowing the score, they may be taken in by phonies, as in *Nothing Sacred.* Sometimes their quest for truth leads nowhere or even to madness and death, as with the reporter pursuing the story of Rosebud in *Citizen Kane* or the reporter losing his sanity in *Shock Corridor.* Their own zeal or hubris may blind them to the real story and lead to their disgrace, as in *Absence of Malice.* And their continuing propensity to fall in love with their stories mocks their efforts to remain detached.

The conflict between objectivity and subjectivity is closely related to that between cynicism and idealism. When journalists in the movies stand to the side, aloof and sardonic, that resonates with cynical, outlaw mythology. When in the end they declare allegiance to their new true loves or their newly found ideals, outlaw myths are reconciled with official ones.

In addition, despite the obstacles the journalists confront, more often than not the true facts finally emerge. The crooked mayor and sheriff in *The Front Page* are exposed. The outlaw types in *Ace in the Hole* and *Sweet Smell of Success* confess all or are otherwise exposed. The reporter in *Nothing Sacred* learns the young woman is in fact not mortally ill (and he promptly marries her). The reporter in *Shock Corridor* uncovers the killer in the insane asylum. Carter in *Absence of Malice* discovers that Gallagher is innocent and that she still has a lot to learn before she becomes a good journalist. Movies such as *Citi-*

zen Kane, Medium Cool, and *Under Fire* that refuse to draw a clear distinction between fiction and reality are the exception; on the whole, movies reinforce journalists' roles as finders and tellers of truth.

Public Interest versus Institutional Interest

Movies dramatically show the effects of commercial and political pressures on journalism. In *Five Star Final, Nothing Sacred, Meet John Doe,* and *Network,* the drive for circulation and ratings leads to suicide, fraud, and murder. In *The China Syndrome,* corporate interference nearly quashes the story of an unsafe nuclear plant. In *Deadline, USA* and *Park Row,* newspapers face takeover or collapse. In *Broadcast News,* the TV network imposes layoffs; in *The Insider,* it blocks the broadcast of a story that threatens its financial interests. Almost all those movies have journalistic voices of conscience who decry what is happening, yet typically they cannot stop it.

Public Interest versus Private Interest

The notion that journalists prey on and exploit their subjects often is validated by the movies, starting with the reporters hounding Earl Williams and Mollie Malloy in *The Front Page* and continuing through *Five Star Final, Ace in the Hole, Sweet Smell of Success, Network, Absence of Malice,* and *To Die For.* But other movies have shown journalists as heroes who uncover stories that others try to suppress or ignore, who do uphold the public's right to know (as in *Foreign Correspondent, Keeper of the Flame, Gentleman's Agreement, Call Northside 777, Deadline, USA, The China Syndrome, All the President's Men, The Insider, The Paper,* and *True Crime*).

The two sets of conflicts just described express the broader conflict between individual interests and the common good. The movies show journalists walking over and exploiting the little guy to sate the mindless, salacious mass public that has been a source of fear and derision for the past century; conversely, they show journalists sticking up for and saving the neck of that same little guy. The films also depict the press either standing up or caving in to government or big business with the public interest at stake. "Public interest" can refer either to voyeuristic delight at other people's misfortunes and misdeeds or to the citizenry having access to the information and ideas needed to further the democratic experiment.

Again, such conflicting depictions reflect conflicting myths. There is the belief that journalism should play a central role in the political process and that people need journalists' help to govern themselves. That is in keeping with many or most journalists' self-image and with official mythology. It is bound up with other beliefs: that we *can* govern ourselves, that citizens can influence events and policymaking, that technology and the professions better our lives, that the system works, that the truth will emerge.

There is also the belief that journalism's claims to being society's appointed storytellers or arbiters of truth are full of bunk. That belief holds that the media and their vast technological apparatus disempower the citizenry and prop up the powerful at the expense of the powerless. Consistent with outlaw mythology, it views the press as just another impersonal, oppressive institution that restricts individual self-determination and liberty.

Typically, the movies seek to smooth away the differences between those competing beliefs. If Americans look up to professionals but also distrust their authority and their entanglements with dominant interests, films present morality tales showing conscientious journalists confronting rapacious media companies or mendacious public officials. Conversely, movies depict sleazy journalists abusing innocent sources or loved ones. In the first set of portrayals, journalists are heroes who clearly fight the good fight even if they do not always win; in the second, they are villains who almost invariably pay a steep price for their misdeeds. The result is that movies valorize an independent press dedicated to competition and profit (but not to greed or exploitation) at the same time they valorize journalists' professional authority and privilege (but only if they are used wisely and not abused).

In the process, films depict the press as having extraordinary power. They show recurring images of the presses in full roar or the newscaster broadcasting into millions of homes. The consequences are direct and immediate. People throw open their windows and scream into the night (*Network*). A woman hides her neighbors' newspapers and slashes her wrists (*Absence of Malice*). Lives are destroyed (*Five Star Final, Ace in the Hole*); the Republic is saved (*All the President's Men*). Humphrey Bogart in *Deadline, USA* holds the phone toward the running presses and then tells the gangster who is threatening him, "That's the press, baby! The press! And there's nothing you can do about it. Nothing!"

Significantly, there are also limits to journalism's power. Bogart's editor character can do nothing to save his paper. Charles Foster Kane can do nothing to earn the public's love in *Citizen Kane*. Chuck Tatum can do nothing to save the "perfect story" he is trying to pull off in *Ace in the Hole*. Max Schumacher can do nothing to save Howard Beale or Diana Christensen from TV's destructiveness in *Network*. Megan Carter can do nothing to save herself or her paper from humiliation in *Absence of Malice*.

Such tales of impotence reproduce the same myths. Journalists who misuse their power see it vanish. Others represent the sorry consequences of "cutthroat capitalists" failing to "keep out of the pros' way." The latter group often demonstrate the familiar journalism movie theme of nostalgia, responding to "the contradictions of journalistic life" (such as that between public service and private profit) by seeking "a return to an idealized past" when such contradictions presumably were not an issue.[21]

IDEOLOGY AND RITUAL

It is not surprising that the movies focus so heavily on the dilemmas faced by journalist heroes or villains as opposed to a more nuanced examination of journalism as an institution. As historian Robert Rosenstone puts it, "Film insists on history as the story of individuals," the result being that "the personal becomes a way of avoiding the often difficult or insoluble social problems pointed out by the film."[22]

So journalism movies focus on personal relationships between reporters, editors, sources, and love interests. *All the President's Men* is more about two reporters acting as detectives than the complex historical reality of Watergate. *The Killing Fields* and other foreign correspondent films pay less attention to the global politics underlying their respective conflicts than to the trauma their journalist protagonists suffer. When Hollywood depicts the news media committing abuses, it shows the pain inflicted on solitary victims. As popular entertainment, movies naturally are unconcerned with weighty, abstract questions of journalism's role in society. They again seem to have followed the example of Hecht and MacArthur, who wrote in their epilogue to *The Front Page* that "it remains for more stern and uncompromising intellects than ours to write of the true Significance of the Press."[23]

However, the movies have managed to address the press's significance precisely through their generic, formulaic nature that focuses on the personal rather than the political. Their dualistic structure—pitting reporter versus editor, reporter versus source, reporter versus love interest—speaks to journalism's conflicts and contradictions.

In so doing, they do more than simply reflect predominant ideology. They also form the basis of an ideological critique of journalism, consistent with Thomas Zynda's assertion that they "de-sanctify the press, much as the press itself impiously reports on government."[24] In regularly showing journalists and other media types as official and outlaw villains, the movies have suggested that powerful, selfish interests control the media and that reporters are cynics who make a mess of their personal and professional lives even as they wreck the lives of others. The films have undercut some of the more sanctimonious claims journalists have made on behalf of their profession, which makes it hardly surprising that journalists have often complained about them. They threaten journalism's cultural authority by implying that the press is not at the center of the universe—or that if it *is* at the center, it should not be.

That is consistent with the movies' role as purveyors of myth. Scholars note that myths are inherently "polysemic" and "can be read many ways," including ways that are critical of the status quo. In general, though, myth "not only confirms beliefs but also constricts beliefs [and] defends the dominant social consensus."[25] Journalism movies enable criticism of the press but tend to constrain that criticism in favor of stories of powerful news media that either potentially or in actuality serve the public interest. They legitimate the press as an institution, much as the press legitimates other institutions by continually focusing attention on them.[26]

Thus the movies are themselves ideological. They indicate that democracy works thanks to the actions of principled individuals, including journalists themselves. Official journalist heroes may call attention to abuses in the system, but they help stop those abuses and never question the system itself. As James Stewart's reporter says at the end of *Call Northside 777* (a movie depicting egregious official corruption), "It's a big thing when a sovereign state admits an error. . . . There aren't many governments in the world that would do it." Outlaw journalist heroes may thumb their noses at authority, but their romantic individualism deflects attention from institutionalized inequities and inhibits social change.[27]

Such depictions of the press and democracy can be criticized on ideological grounds. They reinforce journalism's appointed role as the people's guardians and society's "mappers," and according to Kevin Barnhurst and John Nerone, that "has always entailed more power for the mapper than for the citizen." Thomas Leonard makes a similar argument concerning journalism movies: "In the dominant entertainment medium of the twentieth century, the American public saw itself as consumers of news who were credulous, impulsive, and dependent."[28] From such a viewpoint, and contrary to what the movies themselves suggest, democracy does not work as well as it should because a robust civic culture does not exist to make it work. In propagating myths exalting journalists at the expense of the citizenry, journalism movies—like modern, professionalized, corporatized journalism itself—do little to redress the situation.

However, if polling data are any indication, the public is hardly uncritical toward the press; they regard it with a mixture of fear and expectation. In one poll, 84 percent of respondents said government should require balanced reporting, 70 percent said government should impose fines for media bias or inaccuracy, and more than half thought journalists should be licensed. At the same time, three-quarters said it was "very important" for the press to "hold public officials accountable," and two-thirds said the press was responsible for "protecting the public from abuses of power."[29]

Movies ritualistically mediate between those conflicting hopes and concerns. *The Front Page* appealed both to popular suspicions of journalism and to popular notions of its power to thwart evil. So it has remained with the films that have followed in its wake. They have shown journalists doggedly and uncompromisingly ferreting out wrongdoing yet making the grossest errors of judgment and tact. They have celebrated the sanctity of home and family while revealing a not-so-secret envy of those who are free of such obligations. They have demonstrated the power of a free and privately owned press in serving as a watchdog but also have shown it dozing on the job and barking up the wrong tree. They have presented portrayals as resplendent as *All the President's Men* and as gloomy as *Network*.

At worst, the movies do what *Network* accused television of doing: They tranquilize our anxieties either by persistently resolving conflicts in the journalist's favor and implying that we need not worry about the state of the press or democracy, or by cynically suggesting that there is little we can do in the face of vast media power. At best, they can help us think critically and conscientiously about the press's role in democratic society and, in the spirit of *All the President's Men,* remind us of what is at stake: not only freedom of the press but also the future of the country.

What is more, they offer grounds for hope. As Richard Slotkin and others have argued, Americans need myths that reject false nostalgia in favor of a "usable national consensus."[30] We abandon myths of a free press and a free citizenry at our peril. Movies offer visions in which the two cannot be separated.

Michael Schudson has offered an analogy that is especially poignant in that it comes from popular culture: "Critics look at the press and see Superman when it's really just Clark Kent."[31] One can argue that the problem with real-life journalism is not that it is too powerful but that it is too mild-mannered. On screen, that is rarely an issue. There journalists do thrilling and wondrous things, and if they do not always coincide with the tidy image that professional associations promote, they seem more likely to stir the imagination and stoke the flames.

That holds true not only for journalists themselves but also for the people sitting and watching in the dark. They should not hope for a superhero to fly down and rescue them from all that ails them. But they can and should expect the press to shed its figurative coat and tie when necessary and report what they need to know, even if—*especially* if—that happens to be politically or economically risky. And they should expect themselves to do their own part in organizing and mobilizing to redress the ills that have been exposed.[32]

When that happens, nobody will need Superman. Journalists and citizens can work together to fight the never-ending battle for truth, justice, and—in the truest and most patriotic sense—the American way.

NOTES

1. Sarah Hepola, "The Kid's Got Moxie!" *Austin Chronicle,* December 3, 1999. Online at <www.auschron.com>. Although the movie barely played theaters, it was later released on DVD.

2. Carl Sessions Stepp, "Film Dour," *American Journalism Review,* January–February 2000, p. 57.

3. Francis R. Bellamy, "The Theatre," *Outlook,* August 29, 1928, p. 705; Arthur Schlesinger Jr., "'The Front Page,'" in *Past Imperfect: History According to the Movies,* ed. Mark C. Carnes (New York: Henry Holt, 1995), p. 203.

4. Ben Hecht, *A Child of the Century* (New York: Simon and Schuster, 1954), p. 475.

5. Ibid., p. 191.

6. Joseph Turow, *Playing Doctor: Television, Storytelling, and Medical Power* (New York: Oxford University Press, 1989).

7. Hecht, *Child of the Century,* p. 476.

8. Warren I. Susman, *Culture as History: The Transformation of American Society in the Twentieth Century* (Washington, D.C.: Smithsonian Institution Press, 2003), p. 11.

9. Pauline Kael, "Raising Kane," in *The Citizen Kane Book,* by Pauline Kael, Herman J. Mankiewicz, and Orson Welles (New York: Limelight, 1984), p. 25.

10. Loren Ghiglione, *The American Journalist: Paradox of the Press* (Washington, D.C.: Library of Congress, 1990), pp. 121–27; Howard Good, *Girl Reporter: Gender, Journalism, and the Movies* (Lanham, Md.: Scarecrow, 1998).

11. Jack Lule, *Daily News, Eternal Stories* (New York: Guilford, 2001), pp. 60–80.

12. James Harvey, *Romantic Comedy* (New York: Alfred A. Knopf, 1987); Ann Kaplan, ed., *Women in Film Noir* (London: British Film Institute, 1980).

13. Peter Roffman and Jim Purdy, *The Hollywood Social Problem Film* (Bloomington: Indiana University Press, 1981), pp. 31–45; Howard Good, *Outcasts: The Image of the Journalist in Contemporary Film* (Metuchen, N.J.: Scarecrow), 1989.

14. Burton J. Bledstein, *The Culture of Professionalism: The Middle Class and the Development of Higher Education in America* (New York: W.W. Norton, 1976).

15. William Chaloupka, *Everybody Knows: Cynicism in America* (Minneapolis: University of Minnesota Press, 1999), p. xv.

16. Matthew C. Ehrlich, "Myth in Charles Kuralt's 'On the Road,'" *Journalism & Mass Communication Quarterly* 79 (Summer 2002): 327–38; Robert B. Ray, *A Certain Tendency of the Hollywood Cinema, 1930–1980* (Princeton, N.J.: Princeton University Press, 1985), p. 158.

17. See Arthur Charity, *Doing Public Journalism* (New York: Guilford, 1995); Jay Rosen, *What Are Journalists For?* (New Haven, Conn.: Yale University Press, 1999); Roderick P. Hart, *Seducing America: How Television Charms the Modern American Voter* (New York: Oxford University Press, 1994); Michael Schudson, "What Public Journal-

ism Knows about Journalism but Doesn't Know about 'Public,'" in *The Idea of Public Journalism*, ed. Theodore L. Glasser (New York: Guilford, 1999), pp. 118–33.

18. Michael Schudson, "Social Origins of Press Cynicism in Portraying Politics," *American Behavioral Scientist* 42:6 (1999): 998–1008.

19. See for example Christopher Hanson, "Where Have All the Heroes Gone?" *Columbia Journalism Review*, March–April 1996, pp. 45–48.

20. See for example John Denvir, ed., *Legal Reelism: Movies as Legal Texts* (Urbana: University of Illinois Press, 1996); Anthony Chase, *Movies on Trial: The Legal System on the Silver Screen* (New York: New Press, 2002).

21. Todd Gitlin, "Down the Tubes," in *Seeing through Movies*, ed. Mark Crispin Miller (New York: Pantheon, 1990), p. 39; David L. Eason, "On Journalistic Authority: The Janet Cooke Scandal," in *Media, Myths, and Narratives*, ed. James W. Carey (Newbury Park, Calif.: Sage, 1988), pp. 222–23.

22. Robert A. Rosenstone, *Visions of the Past: The Challenge of Film to Our Idea of History* (Cambridge, Mass.: Harvard University Press, 1995), p. 57.

23. Ben Hecht and Charles MacArthur, *The Front Page* (New York: Covici-Friede, 1928), p. 192.

24. Thomas H. Zynda, "The Hollywood Version: Movie Versions of the Press," *Journalism History* 6:1 (1979): 32.

25. Michael Schudson, *Watergate in American Memory* (New York: Basic Books, 1992), p. 124; Lule, *Daily News, Eternal Stories*, p. 191.

26. See Gaye Tuchman, *Making News: A Study in the Construction of Reality* (New York: Free Press, 1978).

27. Ray, *A Certain Tendency of the Hollywood Cinema*; Rosenstone, *Visions of the Past*.

28. Kevin G. Barnhurst and John Nerone, *The Form of News: A History* (New York: Guilford, 2001), p. 24; Thomas C. Leonard, *News for All: America's Coming-of-Age with the Press* (New York: Oxford University Press, 1995), p. 210.

29. Jennifer Harper, "Poll Finds Reporters Obnoxious," *Washington Times*, December 18, 1996, p. A4.

30. Richard Slotkin, *Gunfighter Nation: The Myth of the Frontier in Twentieth-Century America* (Norman: University of Oklahoma Press, 1998), p. 653.

31. Michael Schudson, *The Power of News* (Cambridge, Mass.: Harvard University Press, 1995), p. 17.

32. See Judith Servin and William Servin, eds., *Muckraking: The Journalism That Changed America* (New York: New Press, 2002), pp. 387–88.

❦ INDEX

MATTHEW C. EHRLICH is an associate professor of journalism at the University of Illinois at Urbana-Champaign. His articles have appeared in a number of journals, including *Journalism and Communication Monographs, Journalism and Mass Communication Quarterly,* and *Journalism: Theory, Practice, Criticism.*

The History of Communication

The University of Illinois Press
is a founding member of the
Association of American University Presses.

───────────────────────────

University of Illinois Press
1325 South Oak Street
Champaign, IL 61820-6903
www.press.uillinois.edu